Eastern Africa Series

REIMAGINING THE GENDERED NATION

Reimagining the Gendered Nation

Citizenship and Human Rights
in Postcolonial Kenya

CHRISTINA KENNY

JAMES CURREY

James Currey
is an imprint of
Boydell & Brewer Ltd
PO Box 9, Woodbridge, Suffolk IP12 3DF, UK
www.jamescurrey.com

and of

Boydell & Brewer Inc.
668 Mt Hope Avenue, Rochester,
NY 14620-2731 (US)
www.boydellandbrewer.com

© Christina Kenny 2022

The right of Christina Kenny to be identified as
the author of this work has been asserted in accordance with
sections 77 and 78 of the Copyright, Designs and Patents Act 1988

All Rights Reserved. Except as permitted under current legislation
no part of this work may be photocopied, stored in a retrieval system,
published, performed in public, adapted, broadcast, transmitted,
recorded or reproduced in any form or by any means, without the
prior permission of the copyright owner

The publisher has no responsibility for the continued existence or
accuracy of URLs for external or third-party internet websites referred
to in this book, and does not guarantee that any content on such
websites is, or will remain, accurate or appropriate

British Library Cataloguing in Publication Data
A catalogue record for this book is available from the British Library

ISBN 978-1-84701-299-9 (James Currey hardback)

Mary Ellen Kenny
17 February 1920–24 November 2016

[That was] the year the old ones,
the old great ones
[left] us alone on the road.*

*   'September, 1961' by Denise Levertov, from *POEMS 1960–1967*, © 1964 by Denise Levertov (New York: New Directions Publishing, 1983), 81; Reprinted in World excluding British Commonwealth by permission of New Directions Publishing Corp. 'September, 1961' by Denise Levertov, *New Selected Poems* (Bloodaxe Books, 2003); Reproduced in UK and Commonwealth with permission of Bloodaxe Books. www.bloodaxebooks.com.

Contents

List of Illustrations viii

Acknowledgements ix

Note on Ethnic Identities xi

List of Abbreviations xv

Introduction 1

1. The Kenya Colony in British East Africa: A History of Ethno-patriarchy 20

2. Bodies as Battlefields, Bodies as Weapons: The Colonial Regulation of Women's Bodies 40

3. Myths of Sorority: Kenyan Women's Community Organisation 72

4. Everyday Violence: Violence against Women during Elections and Times of Peace 108

5. Gendered Citizenship, Politics and Public Space: Women's Participation in Government 151

Conclusion 180

Appendix: Field Work, Focus Groups and Interviews 191

Bibliography 195

Index 221

Illustrations

Map

1 Map of Kenya 2020, with inset of field work locations   xvii

Figures

1 *MPs Salary Raise*, cartoon by Gado, 3 June 2013   6
2 Rate of female genital cutting among women aged 15–49,
   by ethnic group in Kenya, 2014   50
3 *I didn't slap her and I have evidence to defend my case*,
   cartoon by Gado, 8 September 2013, http://gadocartoons.
   com/?s=I+DIDN%27T+SLAP+HER   171

Full credit details are provided in the captions to the images in the text. The author and publisher are grateful to all the institutions and individuals for permission to reproduce the materials in which they hold copyright. Every effort has been made to trace the copyright holders; apologies are offered for any omission, and the publisher will be pleased to add any necessary acknowledgement in subsequent editions.

Acknowledgements

A project of this magnitude could not have been completed without having been equipped with a spirit of perseverance and stubbornness, which perhaps at other times in my life I understand may have been less appreciated. Nevertheless, I have been thankful for it over the course of this undertaking. I am from long lines of stubbornness and perseverance on both sides of my family, and have been so fortunate to have known three of my grandparents as an adult myself. Three of the four of them post-war migrants, they instilled in their children, my parents Dianna and Patrick, and in turn in my sister Giselle and me, the quiet integrity of work, the centrality of family and of the responsibility of our talents. 'The real heroes', as Hemingway put it, 'are the parents'. I love you all.

Matthew has been here from well before the beginning of this project, and I hope to share many more with him. I promise we can go on holidays in places other than Kenya next time. I'm so glad of the life we've built together, with Robespierre, the cat (and the only living monument to the Revolution).

I gratefully acknowledge field work grants from the Australian Federation of Graduate Women through the Georgina Sweet Fellowship, the Australian National University and the British Institute for East Africa. I also appreciate the unstinting institutional support of the Kenya Human Rights Commission (KHRC) during my time there. The sound advice and patient ears of my KHRC colleagues, particularly George Morara, James Mawira, Esther Waweru, Diana Nyakairu, Benson Chakaya, Carol Warunga, Vincent Musebe, Lillian Kantai and Lyons Njenga, during my time in Kenya was invaluable. I am fortunate to have made such firm friends so far from home. I am also greatly indebted to Alfred Anangwe, an intelligent, tireless and patient researcher in his own right, without whom I think I would still be in the Kenya National Archive looking for documents.

To the people who were unstinting collaborators and generous and thoughtful friends – who organised focus groups, introducing me to their families and communities – and to the women who trusted me with their stories, particularly those who facilitated and translated our meetings in school classrooms, market sheds and rice fields across Kenya – Camilla Mwenda, Joseph Ochieng and Caren Omanga – my deepest thanks and appreciation. All information relayed here about these facilitators, their families and communities has been expressly approved by each of them.

I have been fortunate in my travels to call others comrades, and their constant challenge to seek authentic post- and decolonial methodologies and strategies was one of the most critical elements in the development of my thinking. Roaming around Nairobi with you all, and finding the moon in Roysambu, has been one of my life's treasures. *Nashukuru sana, sana*, Immah, Blessol, Neo, Fadzai, Lee. I constantly think of your commitment and struggle when my own is failing.

Thanks to Ambreena Manji, Gabrielle Lynch and Nic Cheeseman, for your support and encouragement, and generous and engaged reading; and to Sam Balaton-Chrimes for years of chats about Kenya, flatting in Nairobi and your rigorous critique. Thanks also to the team at James Currey for shepherding this project through to publication, in particular, Jaqueline Mitchell's early and consistent support for this work is greatly appreciated.

Finally, my gratitude and appreciation to Richard Eves, whose support and quiet faith in this mammoth undertaking has never wavered (I don't think!) and whose patience and hospitality, along with Roe, have been the difference. Thank you.

The ideas in Chapters 4 and 5 began in a workshop with Sally Engle Merry at the Australian National University, and a workshop on Gender and Transitional Justice at the University of Technology, Sydney, and benefited from those generous discussions. The subsequent papers were published in a special issue of the journal *Intersections: Gender and Sexuality in Asia and the Pacific*, 'Grounding Travelling Concepts: Dialogues with Sally Engle Merry about Gender and Justice', edited by Margaret Jolly and Hilary Charlesworth; and in *Rethinking Gender Justice: Transformative Approaches in Post-Conflict Settings*, edited by Rita Shakel and Lucy Fiske (Palgrave Macmillan, 2019). They are reproduced here with permission.

Note on Ethnic Identities

Although the territories now included within Kenya's national boundaries host over 100 cultural and linguistic communities, a subset of more populous communities, identified, codified and enumerated by the colonial regime, has come to occupy the Kenyan 'ethnic imaginary' as the 42+ tribes.[1] In postcolonial Kenyan politics, this imaginary has driven a 'political tribalism' where 'groups compete for public resources' and where ethnic identity is used 'in political competition with other groups'.[2] The differing sizes, locations and levels of colonial and postcolonial political engagement have meant that the literature dedicated to the different groups is very uneven. Groups whose lands were areas of interest to British settlers came into contact and conflict with British authorities earlier than more remote communities. As a result, they became the subjects of sustained anthropological, missionary and government interest. Therefore, significant attention has been paid to ethnic groups living in and around, what became under the colonial government, Nairobi and Central Province, including the Gĩkũyũ, Meru[3] and Embu, as well as ethnic groups that have sustained larger populations, such as the Luo in Kisumu County in western Kenya, and those whose nomadic lifestyle brought them into contact and conflict with other pastoralist ethnic groups and central colonial governance, such as the Maasai, Samburu, Pokot and Turkana. A number of other larger ethnic groups are perceived to have managed

[1] Samantha Balaton-Chrimes, 'Who Are Kenya's 42(+) Tribes? The Census and the Political Utility of Magical Uncertainty', *Journal of Eastern African Studies*, 15:1 (2021), 43–62.
[2] John Lonsdale, 'Moral Ethnicity and Political Tribalism', Occasional Paper, *Inventions and Boundaries: Historical and Anthropological Approaches to the Study of Ethnicity and Nationalism*, 11 (2014), 131–50, quoted in Balaton-Chrimes 'Who Are Kenya's 42(+) Tribes?' 49.
[3] See, for instance, Lynn Thomas's explanation of her choice of Meru region for her study: 'Meru became the geographical focus of this study because of its extraordinary and largely unexamined history of colonial interventions.' Lynn M. Thomas, *Politics of the Womb: Women, Reproduction and the State in Kenya* (Berkeley: University of California Press, 2003), 9.

some representation in national politics or, at least, some acknowledgement of their concerns, through strategic political alliances.

Much research on the Colony of Kenya, or British East Africa, uses Gĩkũyũ experiences in and around Nairobi and the so-called White Highlands as a proxy for the experiences of African Kenyans in general during this period. As Gĩkũyũ occupied the areas on which the capital city of Nairobi and its surrounding counties now stand, their early and prolonged contact with British interests in East Africa located the Gĩkũyũ tribe at the geographic, political and academic centre of research regarding Kenyan peoples and the effects of colonialism. The colonial government's theft of land, forced labour, onerous taxation and restriction on movement were met with increasingly organised resistance which, in turn, was met with pervasive and unrelenting state violence.

The emphasis on Gĩkũyũ culture and experiences of resistance are derived from a combination of their geographic proximity to British interest in land and natural resources and their early contact with the colonial school system that produced Harry Thuku, Jomo Kenyatta and several other key Kenyan nationalists and anticolonial political organisations. Kenyatta's personal dominance over the development of political discourse, the nascent Kenyan national identity and his grip on postcolonial power resulted in a Gĩkũyũ-centric legacy that other ethnic groups have struggled to counter. It is instructive that one of the most influential ethnographies of Gĩkũyũ people is Kenyatta's own study, *Facing Mount Kenya*, which was heavily inflected with the Gĩkũyũ cultural concerns of the period – including a defence of Gĩkũyũ marriage and cultural structures and an in-depth discussion of female circumcision – his authority here being derived from his aunt, a circumciser in their community.[4]

Finally, as the Mau Mau guerrilla resistance movement which rose against the colonial regime in the 1950s comprised a majority Gĩkũyũ fighting force, the cultural products of the resistance were often Gĩkũyũ-language resistance songs that conflated Gĩkũyũ independence with Kenyan nationalism. Speaking in June 1971, at a rally in Uhuru Park in Nairobi, Jomo Kenyatta explicitly claims Gĩkũyũ privilege under the new regime:

> some want to tell us that Kenya belongs to all the people. Granted, I know that much. But I have a question to ask: when we were shedding blood, some languished in prison and some suffering in the forests, fighting for uhuru [Sw. freedom], where were the bloody others? ... if you want honey, bear the sting of the bee.[5]

[4] Jomo Kenyatta, *Facing Mount Kenya* (New York: Random House, 1962), 125–49.
[5] Daniel Branch, *Kenya: Between Hope and Despair, 1963–2012* (London: Yale University Press, 2011), 102. 'Sw.' indicates a translation from KiSwahili.

This sentiment has translated into a Gĩkũyũ dominance (albeit ambivalent and partial) of the memorialisation of Mau Mau and the achievement of independence. Such dominance has become allied with a postcolonial emphasis on ethnic representation in national politics.

Other resistance movements which proliferated during the colonial period across British East Africa – for example, the Giriama revolt on the coast, and the Somali secessionist war on the north-eastern border between Kenya and Somalia – have not been absorbed into the linear narrative of the independence struggle, particularly where their goals were not explicitly tied to a proto-nationalist agenda promoted by organisations that were run by the emergent African urban elite. Further, these geographic and metaphoric border histories have not been taken up by the Kenyan academy with much interest – existing, as they have done for decades, 'at the periphery of Kenya's imagined geography'.[6] As a result, the experiences of Gĩkũyũ and, to a lesser extent, Meru and Luo women form the basis of historical case studies of women's treatment by colonial and tribal authorities.

In anthropological accounts, discourses of ethnicity and tribe (almost exclusively as understood and recorded by outsiders) become manifest. The complexities of the content and expression of ethnic identity are central to understanding the dynamics of colonial rule, local African resistance and postcolonial politics. In cases where I discuss these histories, I use the designation 'tribe' where it mirrors the language of the day utilised by both colonial administration, and African political leaders I quote here, including Thomas (Tom) Mboya and Jomo Kenyatta. I acknowledge that the terms 'tribe' and 'ethnicity' have attracted a great deal of scholarly attention (although there is not room for an in-depth analysis of these dynamics here).[7] Ethnic identities and affiliations are complex, and boundaries between ethnic groups are porous. Carolyn Shaw describes the tribal organisations in Kenya as 'partial communities' and refutes the rigid boundaries on tribes imposed by the colonial regime.[8]

---

[6] Nanjala Nyabola, 'Kenyan Feminisms in the Digital Age', *Women's Studies Quarterly*, 46:3&4 (2018), 262.

[7] Patrick Harries, 'Exclusion, Classification and Internal Colonialism: The Emergence of Ethnicity among the Tsonga-Speakers of South Africa', in, Leroy Vail (ed.), *The Creation of Tribalism in Southern Africa* (London: James Currey, 1989), pp. 82–118; Terence Ranger, 'Missionaries, Migrants and the Manyika: The Invention of Ethnicity in Zimbabwe', in Vail, *The Creation of Tribalism in Southern Africa*, pp. 118–50; John L. Comaroff and Jean Comaroff, *Ethnicity, Inc.* (Chicago: University of Chicago Press, 2009); P.H. Gulliver, *Tradition and Transition in East Africa* (London: Routledge, 1969); Balaton-Chrimes, 'Who Are Kenya's 42(+) Tribes?'.

[8] Carolyn Martin Shaw, *Colonial Inscriptions – Race, Sex and Class in Kenya* (Minneapolis: University of Minnesota Press, 1995), 6.

In focus groups and interviews I conducted, I took groups as I found them, never foregrounding tribal or ethnic identities in my questions. The groups comprised women invited through facilitators either directly or where the facilitators had contacted someone in the area who then invited local women who might be willing to attend a meeting and share their experiences and thoughts in a focus group. Some of these women met with me as community-based women's groups, or human rights advocacy groups, with a history of working together, while others were not previously affiliated with each other – although, of course, village life means most were at least acquainted with each other before they attended the focus group meeting. Women themselves only occasionally invoked ethnic identities to explain their local custom of marriage or dispute resolution. At times, this may have been because the interviewees were predominantly from one ethnic group, which was more likely to occur in rural areas such as Bar Ober and Ahero where the population is predominantly Luo, although Butere was a mixed group of Luo and Luhya women; and the population of the suburb of Kibera called Kisumu Ndogo (Little Kisumu) also hosted a majority population of Luo people (see Appendix). I engaged with such groups on their own terms as 'partial communities' who, in our conversations, prioritised their gender, class and geographic identities in our discussions, which focused on their knowledge and understanding of human rights ideas and principles; the Kenyan Constitution; women's civil and political rights, and their perceptions and experiences of violence committed by people outside their homes, through either theft or intercommunal violence; gender-based and intimate partner violence; and the effectiveness of the police and other local government offices.

Abbreviations

BBI	Building Bridges Initiative
CAT	Convention against Torture
CIPEV	Commission of Inquiry into Post-Election Violence
CEDAW	Convention on the Elimination of Discrimination Against Women
CRC	Convention on the Rights of the Child
CREAW	Centre for Rights Education and Awareness
EAA	East African Association
ECK	Electoral Commission of Kenya
FGC	female genital cutting
HuRiNet(s)	Human rights network(s) (community groups set up and trained in human rights-based advocacy by the Kenya Human Rights Commission)
IBEAA	Imperial British East Africa Association
IBEAC	Imperial British East African Company
ICCPR	International Covenant on Economic, Social and Cultural Rights
ICERD	International Convention on the Elimination of Racial Discrimination
KADU	Kenya African Democratic Union
KAU	Kenya African Union
KANU	Kenya African National Union
KCA	Kikuyu Central Association
KHRC	Kenya Human Rights Commission (national NGO)

KNCHR	Kenya National Commission on Human Rights (national, independent commission)
LegCo	Legislative Council of Kenya
MYWO	Maendeleo ya Wanawake Organisation
MDG(s)	United Nations Millennium Development Goals
NGO	non-government organisation
ODM	Orange Democratic Movement
OHCHR	Office of the High Commissioner for Human Rights
PNU	Party of National Unity
SGBV	sexual and/or gender-based violence
SOGIE/SC	sexual orientation, gender identity and/or expression and/or sex characteristics
SDG(s)	Sustainable Development Goal(s)
UNICEF	United Nations Children's Fund
WHO	World Health Organization

Map 1 Map of Kenya 2020, with inset of field work locations in Kisumu County, in Taita town, located in Taita-Taveta County (Kassandra Hunt).

Introduction

Our bodies are our first homes. If we are not safe in our bodies, we are always homeless.[1]

In 2014, when I was working in Nairobi at the Kenya Human Rights Commission (KHRC), *The Nairobi Law Monthly* published an article entitled 'Female judicial officers fry in their hot temper'. The article went on to explain that 'science indicates that some women might, due to hormonal activities, be temperamental', a fact which needed 'to be accommodated by the vetting board'.[2] In Kenyan public life, women's bodies always need to be accounted for. The Kenyan public is constantly reminded that the experiential reality of living in a woman's body is something that would (and even should) often limit one's career prospects, and the reach of one's authority. For women in public office, or aspiring to public office, assumptions of the 'natural' weaknesses and limitations of womanhood need to be constantly refuted.

Although most women in Kenya are not lawyers, and do not aspire to public office, we know that Kenyan women as a group across the socioeconomic spectrum face serious challenges to their health, wellbeing and access to justice. In 1994, the prominent Kenyan women's rights advocate and scholar Maria Nzomo lamented the failure of the postcolonial era to provide women with improved access to their human rights. She argued that the twin forces of 'autocratic African governments' and 'underdeveloped economies built upon highly patriarchal societies' had contributed to generations of women with high rates of illiteracy and 'extremely low levels of gender, civil and legal rights awareness'.[3] Further, she argued, 'the trend in the status of women's human rights in Africa is increasingly one of violation rather than promotion of those

---

[1] Shailja Patel, as quoted in Ann Njogu, 'Alleged Sexual Violence Committed by Tony Mochama upon the Person of Shailja Patel', *Gukira*, blog post (14 September 2014), https://gukira.wordpress.com/2014/09/25/sexual-violence-committed-by-tony-mochama-upon-the-person-of-shailja-patel [accessed 15 July 2021].
[2] J. Osogo Ambani and H. Ombiti, 'Female Judicial Officers Fry in Their Hot Temper', *The Nairobi Law Monthly*, 4:4 (2014).
[3] Maria Nzomo, 'The Status of Women's Human Rights in Kenya and Strategies to Overcome Inequalities', *Issue: A Journal of Opinion*, 22:2 (1994), 17.

rights'.[4] The experiences of Kenyan women have not significantly improved in the intervening years.

Although recent national data sets are difficult to come by, the Kenyan Government's *Second Voluntary National Review on the Implementation of the Sustainable Development Goals* offers a collation of the available key statistical markers. The number of people living in absolute poverty has increased over the decade 2009–2019,[5] and maternal mortality is still high.[6] In the reporting period 2009–2014, almost 40 per cent of women and girls fifteen years and older had experienced physical violence from a current or former intimate partner, while almost half of all Kenyan women and girls aged over fifteen years reported experiencing physical, sexual or emotional/psychological abuse in the previous twelve months. Just over one-fifth of women (22 per cent) aged 15–49 experienced sexual abuse by a person other than an intimate partner.[7] These figures are almost certainly underestimates as data collection is affected by a culture of silence and hampered by serious ethical concerns about the safety of those who report violence in family settings.[8]

The latest Sustainable Development Goals (SDGs), published in 2020, note that a 'sizeable proportion of Kenya's population continues to suffer multidimensional poverty and exclusion from basic social and economic benefits and opportunities for sustainable livelihoods'. Forty per cent of the rural population lives in poverty, while almost 30 per cent of the urban and peri-urban population lives in poverty.[9] These phenomena have only been dramatically exacerbated by the COVID-19 pandemic: national school closures, loss of work and income, and the failure to designate gender-based violence support services as essential in the early days of the pandemic in Kenya have all contributed to spikes in already high rates of physical and sexual violence, particularly for women and girls. Gender-based violence hotline calls increased 775 per cent in the period March–April 2020 compared to the pre-COVID period.[10]

[4] *Ibid.*
[5] Although there was a reduction in the rate from 46.6 per cent in 2005/06 to 36.1 per cent in 2015/16 as reported in *Second Voluntary National Review on the Implementation of the Sustainable Development Goals* (Nairobi: National Treasury and Planning, 2020), https://sustainabledevelopment.un.org/content/documents/26359VNR_2020_Kenya_Report.pdf, 10.
[6] In 2014 Kenya reported 362 deaths per 100,000 people; see *Second Voluntary National Review on the Implementation of the Sustainable Development Goals*, 42, 102–03.
[7] Data from the baseline 2009–2014, *Second Voluntary National Review on the Implementation of the Sustainable Development Goals,* 102.
[8] Kenya Bureau of Statistics, *Kenya Demographic and Health Survey* (Nairobi: KBS, 2015), https://dhsprogram.com/pubs/pdf/fr308/fr308.pdf, 293.
[9] *Second Voluntary National Review on the Implementation of the Sustainable Development Goals*, 29.
[10] Neetu John, *et al.*, 'COVID-19 and Gender-Based Violence (GBV): Hard-to-

It is apparent, then, that for all the effort and attention Kenyan women receive from the international rights community and, at times, from their own government, human rights frameworks and policies promoting social and economic development have not significantly improved their lives. In an attempt to address this, a great deal of work has been done to monitor and evaluate human rights-based interventions, including tightening funding structures, making recipient organisations more accountable to donors[11] and assessing the progress of governments and non-government organisations (NGOs) in promoting human rights-based reform.[12]

Rather than assess individual projects or goals of aid, this book questions the assumptions that underpin these interventions. My purpose here is not primarily to offer a position on the efficacy of the international human rights system or its myriad forms of intervention but, rather, to examine the reception of these interventions and discourses by women on the ground, and the effects these programmes have on their lives. Following Sally Engle Merry's work on the proliferation and vernacularisation of transnational gender rights projects,[13] I argue that the local histories, understandings and hierarchies of gendered power must be understood in a much more nuanced and critical manner than we are currently doing. We need to look outside the mono-valence of human rights narratives to encourage other, more complex and challenging subject positions to be heard.

So often, women are depicted in the human rights imaginary as 'women as victims'. Even though women's experiences are so often at least partially defined by violence, as Veena Das argues, 'the for-

---

Reach Women and Girls, Services, and Programmes in Kenya', *Gender & Development,* 29:1 (2021), 55–71. The first case of COVID-19 was reported in Kenya in March 2020.

[11] For example, Mohga Kamal Smith, 'Enhancing Gender Equity in Health Programmes: Monitoring and Evaluation', *Gender & Development,* 9:2 (2001), 95–105; Hans-Otto Sano, 'Social Accountability in the World Bank: How Does It Overlap with Human Rights?' in *Closing the Rights Gap – From Human Rights to Social Transformation*, eds LaDawn Haglund and Robin Stryker (Berkeley: University of California Press, 2015), pp. 219–39; Casper Bruun Jensen and Brit Ross Winthereik, 'Monitoring Movements', in Casper Bruun Jensen and Brit Ross Winthereik (eds), *Monitoring Movements in Development Aid* (Cambridge: MIT Press, 2013), pp. 147–67.
[12] Sally Engle Merry, 'Measuring the World: Indicators, Human Rights and Global Governance', *Current Anthropology,* 52:S3 (2011), s83–s95.
[13] Sally Engle Merry, 'Constructing a Global Law – Violence against Women and the Human Rights System', *Law and Social Inquiry,* 28:4 (2003), 941–77; Sally Engle Merry, 'New Legal Realism and the Ethnography of Transnational Law' *Law and Social Inquiry,* 31:4 (2006), 975–95; Peggy Levitt and Sally Engle Merry, 'Vernacularisation on the Ground: Local Uses of Global Women's Rights in Peru, China, India and the United States', *Global Networks,* 9:4 (2009), 441–61.

mation of their subject positions, though mired in these constructions' of violence and victimisation, are 'not completely determined by them'.[14] These interventions fail to consider that a person's subjectivity is never completely determined by victimisation or suffering. Human rights interventions create and reinforce subjectivities which are constrained by assumptions of victimhood and a lack of agency, and are significant contributing factors to the limited gains of the human rights project. She is manifest, in victimhood, as a collection of needs and economic and political goals rather than as a multidimensional, complex, experiential and desiring subject.

As Kenyan women in the international human rights imaginary are primarily characterised as victims, this designation also defines the genres in which they can speak, and what of their speech can be heard. Indeed, suffering, as David Morris explains, 'tends to make people inarticulate … Many people who suffer the routine misery of famine, civil conflict and industrialised poverty have almost no status beyond the role of victim.'[15] The continued reproduction of subjectivities limited to material need and externally imposed goals, and the insistence that these subjectivities are taken up by the targets of these programmes, means that these human rights-based policies and programmes actually further embed existing power relations and even rely on these to function in communities, making long-term, substantive changes to power relations in women's lives and communities very difficult. This book seeks out Kenyan women's access to, and experiences of, civil and political rights and citizenship, beginning with the colonial encounter and following these legacies into the postcolonial period. This historical context reveals the persistent ways in which the 'imagination of the nation' is made visible 'as a *masculine* nation', and the effects this has on the subjectivity of women.[16] It is this gendered subjectivity, co-extant with the subjectivity of victimisation – 'woman-as-victim' – that forms the foundational identity categories available to Kenyan women in the international human rights imaginary and, as I explore below, in the Kenyan popular imagination.

---

[14] Veena Das, 'The Act of Witnessing: Violence, Poisonous Knowledge, and Subjectivity', in Veena Das *et al.* (eds), *Violence and Subjectivity* (Berkeley: University of California Press, 2000), pp. 205–25, 205.
[15] David B. Morris, 'About Suffering: Voice, Genre, and Moral Community', in Arthur Kleinman *et al.* (eds), *Social Suffering* (Berkeley: University of California Press, 1997), 28.
[16] Das, 'The Act of Witnessing', 205. Emphasis in original.

Gendered subjectivities

Wanjiku is a recurring figure in Kenya's popular history, an archetypal feminine symbol of the Kenyan citizen. She was born when Kenya's second president, Daniel Torotich arap Moi, was attempting to dismiss popular pressure to reintroduce multipartyism in the late 1980s. Moi quipped dismissively, disdainfully, 'what does Wanjiku want with a Constitution?'[17] Since then, Wanjiku has become a symbol of the Kenyan state's failure to consider the needs of its most vulnerable citizens. Although Moi was Kalenjin, Wanjiku is a classical Gĩkũyũ name and may be represented as a figure born in Central Province,[18] the geographical locus of the independence struggle and of the national capital, Nairobi. The Gĩkũyũ are the largest single ethnic group in Kenya (although not an absolute majority of the population) and thus Wanjiku also carries a kind of cultural privilege. Why do we ask about Wanjiku, but not other Kenyan women? Can Wanjiku stand for all Kenyan women? In seeking to dismiss her, 'Moi [had] unwittingly created [a] defiant and enduring symbol [and] Wanjiku was enthusiastically adopted by proponents of constitutional reform as the "anti-Moi"'.[19] Constitutional reform and a broad range of social justice demands were, and continue to be, campaigned for on her behalf. Wanjiku became ubiquitous in the Kenyan public imagination – a discursive gesture to 'public opinion', the 'common person' or the 'ordinary *mwananchi*'.[20] She is a kind of Kenyan 'everywoman', albeit inflected with the kinds of geographical and ethnic privilege that drives the waves of political tension and violence that have plagued the republic.

Wanjiku is deployed in modern Kenyan writing, political cartoons and editorials as a shorthand and as a foil for writers to respond to her plight. She has become a metaphor for the subject/citizens of the postcolonial Kenyan nation. If the citizen is sexed female, with what does the patriarch provide her? This natal narrative was explicitly mobilised by independence leader and inaugural president of the republic Jomo Kenyatta, who deliberately inscribed his Gĩkũyũ ethnicity and his role as patriarch into the national mythography. Upon the announcement of the long-awaited new Constitution in 2010, Willy Mutunga, Chief Justice of the Supreme Court, described the document as 'Wanjiku's

---

[17] Wambui Mwangi, 'Silence Is a Woman', *The New Inquiry,* blog post (4 June 2013), https://thenewinquiry.com/silence-is-a-woman [accessed 16 August 2021].
[18] The eight provinces of Kenya were replaced by 47 counties under the 2010 Constitution, articles 191 and 192, the fourth schedule of the Constitution, and the *County Governments Act* 2012.
[19] Mwangi, 'Silence is a Woman'.
[20] *Mwananchi* (Sw.) refers to a common person or ordinary citizen (plural: *wananchi*).

6 *Reimagining the Gendered Nation*

Figure 1 *MPs Salary Raise*, cartoon by Gado, 3 June 2013, http://gadocartoons.com/gado-on-mps-salary-raise (reproduced by permission of Gado Cartoons/bunimedia.com).

Constitution'. Mutunga CJ kept a half life-sized sculpture of Wanjiku on display in his chambers because 'Wanjiku is the boss'.[21]

Like all Kenyan women, Wanjiku works hard, but for all her rhetorical work she remains disembodied – a vessel to be filled by whomever has summoned her. Political cartoonist Godfrey Mwampembwa, who has done the most to popularise Wanjiku and her message of government critique, 'considers Wanjiku to represent the common woman/man. The man on the street, the mama mboga, the jua kali mechanic, the watchman, etc.'[22] Here, Mwampembwa has listed only one woman in a

---

[21] Mwangi, 'Silence is a Woman': 'The sculpture shows Wanjiku with a copy of the constitution in her *kiondo* (bag). [The sculpture is based on the rendering of Wanjiku by] Gado, the prominent political cartoonist, [who] frequently includes Wanjiku in his satirical images. She is a tiny figure in the corner, commenting wryly on political antics and the quirks of Kenyan society.'

[22] *Jua kali* (Sw., 'fierce sun'), informal workers who spend their days under the sun; *mama mboga* (Sw. 'vegetable woman'), a woman who sells vegetables at market stalls; Godfrey Mwampembwa, 'Who is Wanjiku? A Popular Analyst's View', in Naomi Shitemi and Eunice Kamaara (eds), *Wanjiku a Kenyan Sociopolitical Discourse* (Nairobi: Contact Zones, Kindle Edition, 2012).

list of jobs in which the masculine subject is the norm. Kenyan intellectual Keguro Macharia has explained that:

> Wanjiku started as a male political fantasy: an everywomen ... Wanjiku could never own herself. Women could never own Wanjiku. They might incarnate her, but she was so saturated with male fantasies of using Wanjiku, saving Wanjiku, speaking for Wanjiku, building a nation for Wanjiku that she could not exist.

One notes, for instance, that Wanjiku could never be a feminist; she could never critique the patriarchal state. She was too busy trying to survive. Even in political cartoons, she stands to the side, an outsider to a system that is, ostensibly, focused on her needs. Wanjiku, thus, incarnates an impossible woman, the impossibility of women within the state's political imaginary.[23]

Through the figure of Wanjiku, we can see the centrality of poor African women, both within local Kenyan popular discourse and mirrored in the international human rights imaginary. Indeed, her invocation as both national everywoman and metonym for the failings of international human rights interventions is emblematic of the symbiotic relationship between the ethno-patriarchal structures of Kenya's postcolonial state and the influence of globalised narratives addressing the feminisation of poverty. Where the human rights imagery has constructed Kenyans as potential human capital (the way out of poverty is to enter the market), Wanjiku does not fit this mould. Wanjiku is to be 'helped' – helped into participating in systems of capital generation, as quickly as possible.

A key tenet of this book is that the human rights imaginary has created and appropriated a Wanjiku-like figure for its own purposes. Here, she is a vessel for population-level statistics, maternal health outcomes, microfinance programming and rights awareness. For instance, assuming Wanjiku is Gĩkũyũ, she is Christian, has several children and is unmarried or separated, widowed, or in an unsatisfactory intimate relationship. She may be living with HIV and/or other chronic illnesses. Her children go to school when she can afford to send them, which is not often.[24] This Wanjiku also needs help, and what is so comforting

---

[23] Keguro Macharia, 'Wanjiku?, *Gukira* (blog), 26 December 2012, https://gukira.wordpress.com/2012/12/26/wanjiku [accessed 2 February 2021].

[24] Although the Mwai Kibaki administration announced free primary education in January 2003, the poor quality of primary education, and the fact that in 2015 two million primary school aged students were not in school, speaks to serious and unresolved issues with this programme and explains the rise of low-cost, poorly regulated private primary schools. See, for instance, Johnston Musungu, 'Free Primary Education in Kenya: A Critical Analysis', *International Journal of Humanities Social Sciences and Education,* 2:7 (2015), 65–77.

about her is that we do not need to ask her what she needs: her dire situation, captured in increasingly robust population statistical profiles, is obvious.

In the Kenyan case, whatever relationship precolonial Africans had to their bodies, gendered hierarchies were disrupted and remade in the colonial period, and the gender binary was established and entrenched by colonial governance. The essentialised idea of biological sex has so permeated Kenyan social and cultural life that eminent feminist advocates, policy specialists and leaders of women's rights movements and organisations have routinely relied on feminine traits of motherhood, nurturing, family creation and care to illustrate the value that women contribute to wider Kenyan society. The Nigerian historian and linguist Oyèrónkẹ́ Oyěwùmí has argued that:

> the cultural logic of Western social categories is based on an ideology of biological determinism: the conception that biology provides the rationale for the organisation of the social world. This cultural logic is actually a 'bio-logic'. Social categories like 'woman' are based on body-type and are elaborated in relation to and in opposition to another category: man; the presence or absence of certain organs determines social position.[25]

Oyěwùmí calls this kind of social organisation 'body-reasoning'. She argues that for African communities, 'the body was not the basis of social roles, inclusions, or exclusion; it was not the foundation of social thought and identity'.[26] Regardless of the precolonial organisation of African communities in the territory now defined as Kenya, the colonial project produced and entrenched the gender categories and foundations of the bio-logic seen today in Kenyan social and political life.

The gender politics and advocacy structures that have been set up around gender equality are a direct result of the internationalised, Western bio-logic of gender that has been entrenched as the dominant structure of inequality and community relations, and as a foundational explanation for women's experiences of violence, discrimination and structural inequality. In conjunction with the subject formation 'woman-as-victim', this project examines the ways in which the bio-logic of gender has been imported through the processes of colonisation. Western gender logic has been adopted and extended uncritically, not only by the structures and personnel at the heart of postcolonial African governance, but also, and more troublingly, by women and rights activists working to address gross structural inequalities. Through focus

---

[25] Oyèrónkẹ́ Oyěwùmí, *The Invention of Women: Making an African Sense of Western Gender Discourses* (Minneapolis: University of Minnesota Press, 1997), ix–x.
[26] *Ibid.*, x.

groups and interviews I conducted with women in the national capital, Nairobi, and across rural areas of Kisumu County in western Kenya, I engaged with the lived experiences of African women on their own terms. Setting our discussions about their lives in dialogue with the discourses of international human rights demonstrates that the frameworks and assumptions of the human rights project in fact reproduce the patterns, structures and hierarchies that are at the core of women's disenfranchisement and marginalisation.

This work addresses the constrained human rights-based subjectivity of Kenyan women using four thematic cases. Chapter 1 provides a broad public history of the late colonial period and the struggle for independence and traces the development of the ethno-patriarchy that has characterised modern Kenyan politics. Chapters 2–5 present case studies, each addressing an element of Wanjiku's identity as cast by the international human rights imaginary: of women as victims and objects of cultural violence (Chapter 2), myths of the sorority of African women (Chapter 3), women as victims of political and state violence (Chapter 4) and women as actors in national political processes (Chapter 5).

Chapter 2 examines the embodied history of African women in Kenya during the late colonial period and explores the diverse and sometimes conflicting ways in which these women resisted regime control and reasserted their agency against a complex system of cultural and colonial regulation. The chapter presents three instances of African women's embodied agency in the colonial period in which conflict over the validity and practice of female circumcision was a critical component. These examples complicate interpretations of women's agency in the Global South as always operating against patriarchy and in support of personal autonomy. The chapter argues that reading women's behaviour as exclusively resistive or supportive of patriarchal power produces narrow analytical frames that cannot capture the complexity and depth of women's strategies and goals. My critical reading of the archive, including recognising agency being deployed to achieve non-liberal aims, creates the possibility of more complex and, perhaps, ambivalent histories that attempt to take historical subjects on their own terms.

Chapter 3 addresses an abiding myth found in both human rights policy design and postcolonial African gender work – that African women support each other in ways that emphasise the communal bonds of cultural life and that are distinct from, and stronger than, affective gendered bonds in Western women's sororities. The chapter presents a colonial history of women's organising to contextualise modern formulations of women's self-help groups, and argues that they are a product of the combination of coercive policies of the late colonial government and a neoliberal development policy that seeks to encourage poor women to enter capital-generating activities to help themselves out of poverty. This chapter also engages with, and explores the limitations of, the body of postcolonial African scholarship, which privileges the bonds of motherhood as the primary social relation, and argues that the sorority of African women is a unique and politically powerful phenomenon. By setting interviews and focus group discussions with Kenyan women against the assumptions and policy decisions made by the colonial regime and, latterly, by the human rights industry, the chapter troubles key myths regarding the efficacy and continuity of women's traditional organisations through to the modern era. This chapter contests the popular notion that African women are a sorority of mothers (and future mothers) who work effectively together to address their lot in life, and instead shows how women's collective organisations construct women narrowly as entrepreneurial subjects, albeit collective ones.

Chapter 4 addresses the discursive treatment of Kenyan women as victims of the 2007 post-election violence in key human rights reports produced at the time, in the context of the high rates of physical, sexual, emotional and financial abuse with which women live in times of relative peace. By unpacking the reporting strategies human rights organisations deploy in addressing this violence, this chapter demonstrates their reliance on key assumptions, including that if women know their rights they will be able to access them; and that women need to be 'educated' and encouraged to use formal reporting mechanisms to address the significant violence and crime they experience. These assumptions are set against interviews and focus group conversations I conducted with women in Nairobi, and in rural areas of Kenya, which demonstrate the futility of formal reporting and the lack of support, and even abuse, from state security and welfare services. These conversations also shed light on the options that are actually available to women in times of crisis and provide insight into why women make the choices they do. Understanding these lived realities helps contextualise women's choices and, importantly, emphasises the need to make space for voices from these communities that speak outside accepted genres of victimhood and suffering. Further, listening to women in conversation around issues of police corruption, or intimate partner violence, it is imperative that rather than assuming victimhood, we actively seek agency, strategy and expertise in women's behaviour, remembering that, 'to be vulnerable is not the same as to be a victim'.[27]

Chapter 5 examines the treatment of women as members of parliament, and demonstrates the difficulties faced by women attempting to join Kenya's ethno-patriarchal political world. I examine the barriers that women face in vying for office in Kenya, and show that these barriers are not only formal and structural, but are also deeply embedded in Kenyan assumptions of gendered citizenship and heteronormative public life. Using embodiment as an analytical frame, I examine the

---

[27] Das, 'The Act of Witnessing', 209.

quality of citizenship that women experience. Women who seek public office in Kenya are frequently intimidated and controlled by threats and insults that are directed at their body, imputed desires, maternal and wifely responsibilities, and intellectual capacities.

These four chapters carry two overarching concerns. First, we need to challenge ourselves to locate women's agency within their own politics and goals rather than through what Saba Mahmood describes as the diagnostic and prescriptive lens of feminist analysis.[28] Second, although the initial focus on women's bodies as sites of political and cultural contest was critical in moving towards experiential and embodied histories and politics, we need to be vigilant that our continued attention to the bodies of women does not reinscribe the *embodiedness* of women and the *disembodiedness* of men – that is, that women cannot escape their bodies and men rarely inhabit theirs.

Witnessing and personal narrative are central to human rights advocacy and play 'a central role in the formulation of new rights protections, as people come forward to tell their stories'.[29] But these narratives are also central to building necessary critiques which challenge the monoculture of the international human rights agenda. By focusing on women's narratives, this project expands the understanding of Kenyan women's experiences, strategies and goals and, in so doing, interrogates the often mechanistic, linear approaches to rights protection, access and redress employed by the international rights community. It also seeks to trouble the aims of the international human rights project, which often fails to adequately consider the personal and cultural contexts within which rights protections and violations take place. Discussions with women about their experiences of violence and theft, as well as the more insidious violations by state authorities, such as denial of citizenship papers and voting rights and refusal of service at police stations, emphasise 'the manner in which everyday life is transformed in the engagement with violence'.[30] They also reveal the strategies women employ in order to live, and engage, with perpetrators of this violence, which is so routine that it often becomes unremarkable and, eventually, silent.

I am interested in the intersections between theories that have developed around the physical body as a site of experience, a site of evidence collection and a tool of corroboration, as well as the ways in which individuals and communities describe their experiences through

---

[28] Saba Mahmood, 'Feminist Theory, Embodiment and the Docile Agent: Some Reflections on the Egyptian Islamic Revival', *Cultural Anthropology*, 16:2 (2001), 206.
[29] Kay Schaffer and Sidonie Smith, 'Conjunctions: Life Narratives in the Field of Human Rights', *Biography*, 27:1 (2004), 3.
[30] Veena Das and Arthur Kleinman, 'Introduction', in Veena Das *et al.* (eds), *Violence and Subjectivity* (Berkeley: University of California Press, 2000), 1.

language-building, rebuilding and contesting individual identities and histories through speech, 'within and outside genres'.[31] Expansive modes of engagement are critical to encourage women to speak outside the restrictive genres of victimhood and suffering, such that women can offer insight into their experiences of intimate partner violence, and the relationships between this domestic violence and the ways women are denied access to their civil and political rights.

Read against the assumptions and narrative frames of international human rights discourse, the stories and experiences these women shared with me critique dominant frameworks and assumptions of international human rights scholarly and practitioner communities. Importantly, their narratives and insights illustrate the ways in which current human rights-based practice neglects the lived realities of women on the ground and thereby fails to offer programmes that support women to make the best choice for themselves in often hostile cultural and political environments. These discussions also offer a robust challenge to the axiom that 'women who know their rights are able to access them' and instead, in the event of rights violations or denial, compel a shift of focus to finding viable strategies in inhospitable environments 'through an attention to the concreteness of relations in which they [are] embedded'.[32] The material, embodied reality for these women comprises a number of shifting, fractured and even contradictory subject positions, which seek to balance intimate, cultural and social relations with the demands of democratic citizenship and the expectations of the international human rights imaginary.

Throughout this project, I have wrestled with my positionality with the work, in the field and in the academy. Certainly, there is a breadth of opinion and reception of foreign researchers working on issues pertaining to the experiences and delivery of human rights-based programmes on the African continent, and targeting African women in particular. I have the benefit of many years of scholars' introspections and the move of feminisms of the Global North towards a constant and necessary searching for collaboration and co-conspirators,[33] intersectionality and a diversity of voices. These complexities are critical to meaningfully engaging with material, issues and people whose lives exist in political, cultural and economic realities that are different from my own. There have been well-deserved and robust criticisms of the role of feminists,

---

[31] Das, 'The Act of Witnessing', 205.
[32] *Ibid.*, 209.
[33] Where co-conspiracy can be defined as 'a space of shared consequences and a willing loss of social, financial and human capital alongside white, cisgender privilege': Beth Hinderlier and Noelle Chaddock, 'A Rejection of White Feminist Cisgender Allyship', in Noelle Chaddock and Beth Hinderlier (eds), *Antagonizing White Feminism: Intersectionality's Critique of Women's Studies and the Academy* (London: Lexington Books, Rowman & Littlefield, 2019), 142.

situated across the Global North, in seeking to create a kind of global vision of women's rights – critiqued for its middle-class goals and heteronormative priorities, as well as the vision's 'whiteness' (a term that now has its own scholarship and critique[34]). All such postcolonial feminist critique draws attention to the existence of multiple centres and peripheries: of knowledge, of cultural and financial capital, and of communal and formal politics.

In examining the experiences of women in Kenya, and the national and local efforts to secure rights for women, I am acutely aware that the relationship between Western feminisms and African women's rights advocacy has been characterised by longstanding antagonisms. This is in part due to the reasonable perception on the part of African women's advocates and scholars that feminist agendas of the Global North have been imposed on African women's rights debates.[35] Many feminists working in cross-cultural contexts have responded to these critiques, in part with efforts to 'deconstruct the categories of "woman" and "gender"'.[36] The Western focus on the promotion of individual identities and rights at the expense of communal rights and obligations has also been vigorously critiqued by African scholars, who reject the colonial and neocolonial damning of Black and African men as violent and hypersexual.[37] As the Nigerian novelist Buchi Emecheta explains:

> I have never called myself a feminist. Now if you choose to call me a feminist that's your business; but I don't subscribe to the feminist idea that all men are brutal and we must reject them. Some of these men are my brothers and fathers and sons. Am I to reject them too?[38]

---

[34] See, for instance, Alfred J. López (ed.), *Postcolonial Whiteness: A Critical Reader on Race and Empire* (Albany: SUNY Press, 2012); Nicola Ginsburgh, *Class, Work and Whiteness: Race and Settler Colonialism in Southern Rhodesia, 1919–79* (Manchester: Manchester University Press, 2020); Philomena Essed et al. (eds), *Relating Worlds of Racism: Dehumanisation, Belonging, and the Normativity of European Whiteness* (Cham: Springer, 2018); and George Yancy, *Look, a White!: Philosophical Essays on Whiteness* (Philadelphia: Temple University Press, 2012).
[35] Joe Oloka-Onyango and Sylvia Tamale, '"The Personal is Political" or Why Women's Rights are Indeed Human Rights: An African Perspective on International Feminism', *Human Rights Quarterly*, 17:4 (1995), 691–731.
[36] Marie-Benedict Dembour, *Who Believes in Human Rights? Reflections on the European Convention* (Cambridge: Cambridge University Press, 2006), 212.
[37] For instance, Oloka-Onyango and Tamale, '"The Personal is Political"'; and Frank Rudy Cooper, 'Against Bipolar Black Masculinity: Intersectionality, Assimilation, Identity Performance, and Hierarchy', *UC Davis Law Review*, 39 (2005), 853–904.
[38] Buchi Emecheta, lecture at Georgetown University in Washington, D.C., 8 February 1994, as quoted in Gwendolyn Mikell, 'African Feminism: Toward a New Politics of Representation', *Feminist Studies*, 21:2 (1995), 406.

Women's rights advocacy in African contexts is also embedded in larger struggles and debates around post-independence nation-building[39] and the effects of postcolonial capitalism on women.[40]

The often adversarial relationship between Western feminists and African women's rights advocates is expressed in the now thoroughly critiqued culture/rights dichotomy – the most prominent effect of which has been to alienate African women who felt compelled to defend their cultural practice, their intimate relationships, and their fathers, brothers and sons from this neocolonial assault on Africa and Africans. This rejection of 'feminism' as a term, as well as the anti-male attitude with which Western liberal feminism was saddled (and, at times, actively promoted), led to alternative conceptions of African women's rights which distanced themselves from Western feminisms. As Gwendolyn Mikel has explained, the African discourse on feminism is manifested in part in the theorisation of alternative concepts to feminism, such as Mary Kolawole and Chikwenye Ogunyemi's conceptions of African womanism.[41] The Nigerian scholar, activist and writer Akachi Adimora-Ezeigbo, and many others, speak of 'African feminism' to express their ambivalence at being located within the network of a global feminism, and to instead focus on concepts emerging from the concrete social and cultural constellations of African societies.[42]

One of the most forthright and incisive critiques of Western feminisms' human rights-inflected intrusions into African societies was developed by Nigerian historian and linguist Oyèrónkẹ́ Oyěwùmí, whose seminal work *The Invention of Women* remains critical reading for its innovative and scathing critique of the foreign, gendered gaze and its effects on target populations. Oyěwùmí argues that, because there is a 'clear epistemological foundation to cultural knowledge', we must endeavour to examine the foundations of this knowledge to reveal 'the most basic but hidden assumptions, making explicit what has merely been implicit, and unearthing the taken-for-granted assumptions underlying research concepts and theories'.[43] This approach led Oyěwùmí to declare that the 'the so-called "woman question" … is a

[39] Mikell, 'African Feminism', 405–24; see also Akosua Adomako Ampofo *et al.*, 'Women's and Gender Studies in English-speaking Sub-Saharan Africa: A Review of the Research in the Social Sciences', *Gender and Society*, 18:6 (2004), 686.
[40] Pepe Roberts, 'Feminism in Africa: Feminism and Africa', *Review of African Political Economy*, 27/28 (1983), 175–84.
[41] Naomi Nkealah, '(West) African Feminisms and their Challenge', *Journal of Literary Studies*, 32:2 (2016), 61–74.
[42] Susan Arndt, 'Perspectives on African Feminism: Defining and Classifying African-Feminist Literatures', *Agenda: Empowering Women for Gender Equity*, 17:54 (2002), 32.
[43] Oyěwùmí, *The Invention of Women*, ix.

Western-derived issue – a legacy of the age-old somatocentricity in Western thought'.[44] While the totalising categories of 'Western' and 'African' have their own limits, Oyěwùmí's key point is important, because it draws attention to the ways in which the priorities and theoretical frameworks of an 'African research agenda on women and gender' are identified,[45] a process which is often presented as obvious, or as a logical response to collections of evidence.

However, this theoretical point has remained largely peripheral to human rights discourse and programme design; not only is the centrality of gender as a foundational category of organisation never questioned, but it is constantly reinscribed though the largest and most visible international organisations, in global human rights priorities, funding and strategies. When lamenting the massive failures and underperformance of programmes designed to target and 'empower' women across the Global South, critiques of failed programmes rarely, if ever, look to larger foundational, structural and discursive factors.

Field work – 'Daima kuna vumbi ama matope'[46]

This research is based on thirteen months of field work in Kenya across two trips, August 2012 to April 2013 and August to December 2014, and supplemented by further trips in 2016 and 2019. On these trips I was based in Nairobi and conducted field trips outside the national capital, predominantly in Kisumu County, using Kisumu town as a base.[47] Although I initially planned to interview women across a range

---

[44] *Ibid.*, ix.
[45] Claire Robertson, 'Putting the Political in Economy: African Women's and Gender History, 1992–2010', in Pamela S. Nadell and Kate Haulman (eds), *Making Women's Histories: Beyond National Perspectives* (New York: New York University Press, 2013), 61.
[46] 'There is always either dust or mud' (Sw.).
[47] From August 2012 to April 2013 I was a research associate with the Kenya Human Rights Commission (KHRC). I worked with the Gender and Equality team, and with the Civic Participation and Election Monitoring team in the lead up to the April 2013 General Elections, and I monitored these elections with KHRC. I later worked with the KHRC as a consultant on their Gender and Equality programme and represented the KHRC at consultations for the CEDAW Universal Periodic Review for Kenya. I was also KHRC's representative in joint advocacy efforts involving national Kenyan and African regional organisations and advocates of the rights of Sexual Orientation, Gender Identity and Expression (SOGIE), including the effort to challenge the Ugandan Anti-Homosexuality Law at the East African Court of Justice. I also monitored the 2014 General Election in Botswana with the KHRC African Regional Elections Monitoring Team and wrote the Election Observation Report on the Civil and Political Rights of people of diverse sexual orientation, gender identity

of education levels, geographic locations and socioeconomic statuses, middle-class women, including women with whom I worked or who I met through social or work events were very reticent about being interviewed. I understood that they generally did not consider themselves to benefit from rights discourses in their own lives. Harri Eglund observes a similar phenomenon in his work in Malawi, where he notes that the employees of local human rights NGOs maintained 'the same distinctions toward "ordinary" subjects [their clients] as the elites'.[48] Certainly, these Kenyan women did not understand themselves to hold a human rights subjectivity – that is, I understood that these women did not identify with the subjectivity of woman-as-victim. Where these middle/upper-class women were working in the gender rights sector, they would frequently offer to put me in touch with their client base so that I could interview 'grassroots' or poor women.

Shortly after arriving in Nairobi I met Joseph Ochieng at a Gender-Based Violence Prevention conference at Kenyatta University. He was very keen to show me around Kibera where he was living and working as a community health and human rights educator and outreach worker, and to introduce me to his work with young people – thespians and community outreach workers educating the community about gender-based violence and healthy family dynamics. Kibera is the largest urban slum in Africa, and home to up to a contested estimate of almost a million people. Growing from a population of 250,000 at independence, Nairobi is now a city of over five million of which an estimated three million live in slum communities.[49] UN Habitat projects that more than half of the total population of Kenya will be living in urban areas by 2025.[50]

We arranged to meet at the shopping complex, Nakumatt Prestige, a mall on the arterial Ngong Rd and for me, newly arrived in the city, a rare familiar marker in the complex and sprawling urban landscape of Nairobi. Prestige also hosted a *matatu* stage, where Joseph and I could ride a *matatu* – mini-buses of varying age, serviceability, and driver quality and aggression, often blasting African popular and gospel music and boasting bold artwork across their doors – into Kibera together. Yvonne Adhiambo Owuor writes so arrestingly of Nairobi that reading her novel *Dust* on my return to Australia, I vividly recalled the energy

---

and/or expression, and sex characteristics (SOGIE/SC) in Botswana.
[48] Harri Eglund, *Prisoners of Freedom: Human Rights and the African Poor* (Berkeley: University of California Press, 2006), 8.
[49] Thomas Meredith and Melanie McDonald, 'Kibera Integrated Water Sanitation and Waste Management Project' (UN Habitat, 2014), 23 https://unhabitat.org/sites/default/files/download-manager-files/Kibera%20Evaluation%20Report%20FINAL.pdf [accessed 20 August 2021]
[50] United Nations Human Settlements Programme, 'Kenya Overview', https://unhabitat.org/kenya [accessed 24 April 2022].

and chaos of those city streets. As readers move with the protagonist through Nairobi, Owuor writes of the 'the stench of decay, the perfume of earth hoping for rain, habits and dreams of Nairobi's people: smoke, rot, trade, worry, residues of laughter, and overbrewed Ketepa tea'.[51] That long, hot day spent walking around Kibera visiting the Pillars of Kibera Youth Group, meeting Joseph's colleagues and fellow volunteers, and being invited to his house in Kisumu Ndogo (Little Kisumu), a village within Kibera named for the predominance of Kenyans from Kisumu County in western Kenya, was my first of many visits to Kibera and the beginning of Joseph's and my rich collaboration, and friendship.

Joseph introduced me to the Pillars of Kibera Women's Group, with whom I met several times during my visits to Kibera and who agreed to be interviewed as a group for this work. Occasionally, I would meet a local who would ask about what I was doing in Kibera and, pointing to a slum improvement project, perhaps a concrete gutter which had been overrun with silt and rubbish, would explain that the government prefers to leave Kibera substantially as it is, as the shock of witnessing the conditions there was always highly motivating for international donors. 'But what happens to all the donor money?' I would ask, and the answer was always the same – 'it is eaten', an idiom so ubiquitous in Kenya to describe the rampant corruption and looting of state coffers that it occurs in the title of a book on this subject, Michela Wrong's *It's Our Turn To Eat*.[52] Joseph was similarly insistent that I meet his mother and family in Bar Ober, deep in Kisumu County. As I was keen to speak with women outside Nairobi, in time we planned a trip from Nairobi to Bar Ober, stopping to spend time with women's groups in Ugunja, Butere, Bumala, and Bar Ober. These travels and discussions were critical to the development of my thinking and, crucially, to my understanding of Kenya outside Nairobi.

My first travels outside Nairobi, however, were on trips as part of the Kenya Human Rights Commission's (KHRC) field work team to Ahero in Kisumu County, a small town outside the county capital, Kisumu; and, later, to Taita-Taveta County. On these trips, the KHRC reconnected with the Commission's human rights network partners (HuRiNets) and conducted a series of interviews for KHRC projects on gender empowerment strategies in rural locations. HuRiNets act in their communities as points of knowledge dissemination and peer-to-peer education on pressing human rights issues, and were formed by the KHRC over a period of several years. Many of the women in these groups hold long-term links to human rights education programmes and are identified as human rights advocates in their communities. Prior to being

---

[51] Yvonne Adhiambo Owuor, *Dust* (London: Granta Books, 2015), 9.
[52] Michela Wrong, *It's Our Turn to Eat: The Story of a Kenyan Whistle-Blower* (New York: Harper Perennial, 2010).

involved in the HuRiNets programme, many had also been advocates in efforts to support women experiencing family violence, to prevent the circumcision of girls, to provide access to education particularly for girl children, and to combat local corruption. I also conducted some initial scoping interviews for my own research on this trip with these groups, and it was on this first trip to Kisumu County, over two hours on increasingly bad roads outside Kisumu town, that I met Caren Omanga, a formidable human rights organiser based in Aweyo Canteen. This encounter formed the beginning of a long and fruitful collaboration with Caren and her human rights organisation, the Nyabende Human Rights Network. I was fortunate to stay with Caren and her family when I visited Kisumu and, with her introduction, to be welcomed into the homes of members of the Nyabende Human Rights Network for frank and important conversations across Kisumu County over the last several years.

At the same conference at which I met Joseph in 2013, I also met Stanley Ngara, 'Sweet Stan', the self-styled 'Condom King' of Nairobi, a safe-sex educator and community outreach worker with Liverpool Voluntary Counselling and Testing (LVCT), an NGO dedicated to testing for HIV and counselling Kenyans who are HIV positive. Stan is a bombastic feature of Nairobi city life and on my last trip to Nairobi in October 2019 I could still glimpse him across the crowded city streets due to the homemade cardboard crown he wears, with a prodigious variety of condoms and packets of lubricant glued to it. I was keen to know more about LVCT's outreach work with street families and sex workers in Nairobi, and to be introduced to parts and people of the city I would never have otherwise met. Stan invited me to a regular ride-along with the outreach team as they drove around the city centre of Nairobi at night. The LVCT van drove around the city, picking up street children and families who were interested in a health check, and drove them to a clinic in the affluent suburb of Westlands for a check-up, a meal and safe-sex education delivered in Stan's signature style. It was on these travels around the city at night that I learned one of the most common protestations against condom use – 'Why lick a lolly with the wrapper on?' On one of these trips, we stopped at the health centre in Kangemi, a low-income suburb not far from Westlands. Here I was introduced to Camilla Mwenda, a community health worker attached to the health centre and a dynamic and resourceful leader of a women's support group for women living with HIV. HIV positive herself, Camilla has an undetectable viral load and her three children are HIV negative. She continues to be committed to supporting other women to live with HIV the way she has learned, and to provide trusted health education to her community. Camilla facilitated focus groups for me with her women's group and interviews with women living in Kangemi, and continues to be a dear friend and collaborator.

By centring the lived experiences and views of Kenyan women, as told to me during these conversations and interviews, this study critically evaluates the efficacy and effects of human rights discourses and projects in local contexts and contributes to postcolonial feminist efforts to explore the complex and intersecting dimensions of gender, race and culture. The project acknowledges what Akosua Ampofo and others have called the 'misrepresentation and silencing of African women', including their cultural, political and bodily agency and seeks to bring African women's voices into conversation and contestation with international human rights orthodoxies.[53] Instead, my work offers insight into the formation of the fractured and complex subject positions which cohabit with woman-as-victim.

[53] Ampofo, 'Women's and Gender Studies', 685–714.

1
The Kenya Colony in British East Africa: A History of Ethno-patriarchy

'The transformation of Kenya from a polyglot of strangers into a coherent state was the work of force.'[1]

The histories of the peoples of East Africa and, latterly, those who were geographically contained within the territory that is now the Republic of Kenya, extend centuries before the Portuguese built the critical trading port of Fort Jesus in Mombasa in 1593.[2] Indeed, ancient Greek documents date trade from Greece and Rome with Lamu and Zanzibar islands as early as AD 100.[3] Despite the length and complexity of this precolonial history, it is the short but cataclysmic period from contact with British trading interests in the 1880s to independence in December 1963 that continues to significantly influence Kenya's modern identity. It is this period that will be examined here, so that the beginnings of the gendered nation can be understood in their historical context, and we can trace the legacies of that history through the postcolonial period.

Motivated by a combination of tantalising trading opportunities and increasing missionary interest in 'civilising' the East African coast, the British established a presence in parts of East Africa in the 1880s.[4] The Imperial British East Africa Association (IBEAA) began its economic exploration of the territories of East Africa in 1884, although it initially failed to secure backing from the British government. The IBEAA was reformed as the Imperial British East Africa Company (IBEAC) and was granted a royal charter in 1888, at least partly in response to the increasing German domination of the East African coast. Although the IBEAC was in control of Kenya

---

[1] William Robert Ochieng' and Eisha Stephen Atieno-Odhiambo, 'On Decolonization', in Bethwell A. Ogot and William R. Ochieng' (eds), *Decolonization and Independence in Kenya 1940–93* (London: James Currey, 1995), pp. xiv–xv.
[2] Roland Oliver and Gervase Matthew (eds), *History of East Africa*, vol. 1 (Oxford: Clarendon Press, 1963), 140.
[3] *Ibid.*, 94–95.
[4] 'The Colony and Protectorate of Kenya', *The Geographical Journal*, 56:5 (1920), 403–11.; Kenneth Ingham, *A History of East Africa*, 2nd edn (London: Longmans, 1963), 25–28.

and Uganda, the Company quickly realised that it could not meet its administrative costs. Nor was it able to pursue its goals of eradicating the slave trade in East Africa, opening the territory to a *laissez-faire* economic system and taking advantage of the economic opportunities for trade that were thought to exist in the interior.[5] Persuaded to keep the territories out of the hands of the Imperial German Government, the Foreign Office took over responsibility for Uganda in 1893 and East Africa in 1895, renaming it the British East Africa Protectorate.[6] By an Order in Council dated 11 June 1920, the East Africa Protectorate was annexed to the British Dominions under the name of the Colony of Kenya.[7]

To secure the land along the Mombasa–Kampala railway, a key trading route, and to promote the civilising mission in East Africa in the early years of the twentieth century, British autocrats began to encourage English subjects to settle in East Africa, using extensive grants of arable land to entice prospective migrants. However, rather than following the strategy adopted in West Africa, where the land was 'regarded as belonging to the native population, the [colonial] government [of Kenya] declared all land in [their] territories the property of the Crown which [could] be alienated at pleasure'.[8] Between 1900 and 1920, the British colonial government in Kenya alienated without compensation the lands of the Gĩkũyũ, Kamba, Nandi and Mijikenda (formerly known as the Wanyika) peoples to grant arable land to British settlers.[9] For similar reasons, it moved the Maasai from the Rift Valley after what Buell described as 'questionable negotiations'.[10] The numerically superior dispossessed African communities were moved to reserves to provide the white settler agricultural economy with cheap labour.[11]

---

[5] Eisha Stephen Odhiambo, T.I. Ouso and J.F.M. Williams, *A History of East Africa* (Hong Kong: Longman Press, 1977), 113–15; Olive and Matthew, *History of East Africa*, 353–55.
[6] William R. Foran, *The Kenya Police Force 1887–1963* (London: Robert Hale, 1962), 4.
[7] 'The Colony and Protectorate of Kenya', 403.
[8] Odhiambo and Williams, *A History*, 130.
[9] Caroline Elkins, *Imperial Reckoning: The Untold Story of Britain's Gulag in Kenya* (New York: Henry Holt and Company, 2005), 2–3.
[10] Raymond Leslie Buel, *The Native Problem in Africa* (New York: Macmillan Company, 1928), 409.
[11] Elkins, *Imperial Reckoning*, 15; Robert Gregory, *Sidney Webb and East Africa: Labour's Experiment with the Doctrine of Native Paramountcy* (Berkeley: University of California Press, 1962), 5, as quoted in Christopher P. Youe, *Robert Thorn Coryndon: Proconsular Imperialism in Southern and Eastern Africa, 1897–1925* (Waterloo: Wilfrid Laurier University Press, 1986), 160.

The tree of liberty must be watered with blood

Early African resistance did not begin as a nationalist movement agitating for a Kenyan nation-state. Rather, it began as resistance to colonial rule, with a view to restoring precolonial community organisation and autonomy.[12] By the time African political associations were formed in the early 1920s to articulate their grievances against the colonial government, the list was extensive: being forced off ancestral, agriculturally productive lands; deliberately increasingly burdensome taxation that forced men and women into town centres away from their families to seek waged labour; and a series of social welfare and education polices that were interpreted as direct attacks on the cultural and organisational foundations of particular tribes.[13] In addition to the mass alienation of tribal lands, the proximal causes included the introduction of forced labour for women and men; the establishment of the *kipande*, a system of labourer registration that compelled male labourers to carry cards bearing their fingerprints to enable settlers to keep track of their labourers; and the doubling of Hut and Poll taxes.[14] In addition to being abuses in their own right, the compulsory acquisition of land and resources, as well as oppressive taxation and labour migration, disrupted community organisation, intergenerational wealth accumulation and family formation.

The disenfranchised African population increasingly mobilised to resist the catastrophic harms inflicted by the Imperial Government using several strategies, including strikes, go-slows, sabotaging settler equipment and illegally cultivating their own crops.[15] Resistance was also manifested in the form of religious sects that propagated anticolonial sentiments among their adherents. For example, in Kisii, in the south-west, and parts of Luo land in western Kenya, the Mumbo Cult sprung up and counted women among its leaders.[16] Gĩkũyũ women

[12] Even oathed members of the Mau Mau movement, which emerged in the late 1940s, had divergent ideas of what the slogan 'Land and Freedom' entailed. For instance, for some it meant freedom from British rule; for others, the reclamation of precolonial tribal organisation; and for others again it represented freedom from forced labour and access to the fertile White Highlands. See Elkins, *Imperial Reckoning*, 28.
[13] Elkins, *Imperial Reckoning*, 15–16.
[14] Gordon H. Mungeam, 'Masai and Kikuyu Responses to the Establishment of British Administration in the East Africa Protectorate', *The Journal of African History*, 11:1 (1970), 127. See also Audrey Wipper, 'Kikuyu women and the Harry Thuku Disturbances: Some Uniformities of Female Militancy', *Africa*, 59:3 (1989), 302; Elkins, *Imperial Reckoning*, 15–16.
[15] Elkins, *Imperial Reckoning*, 17–18.
[16] Robert M. Maxon, 'The Establishment of Colonial Economy', in William R. Ochieng' and Robert M. Maxon (eds), *An Economic History of Kenya* (Nairobi: East African Publishers, 1992), pp. 63–74; and Audrey Wipper, *Rural Rebels* (Nairobi: Oxford University Press, 1977), 1.

formed their own Muumbi Central Association (after the Gĩkũyũ myth of Eve) to 'jolt men into accepting them as full ... members' of African political organisations, including the Kenya Central Association.[17]

The first East African advocacy organisation was the Gĩkũyũ Association, established in 1920 by chiefs and headmen – men who owed their current position of authority to the colonial government. Due to its membership, the Gĩkũyũ Association failed to inspire confidence in the wider Gĩkũyũ community.[18] In 1921, the Young Gĩkũyũ Association was established, but was quickly renamed the East African Association (EAA) in a bid to appeal to a broader African constituency. As the original name suggests, the EAA was formed by young, educated Gĩkũyũ men who were unconvinced that the chiefs and headmen of the Gĩkũyũ Association were capable, or indeed inclined, to lead the kind of radical advocacy for Gĩkũyũ and African interests that they felt necessary.[19] It was led by an ambitious and idealistic Harry Thuku and joined the following year by Johnstone Kamau, later known as Johnstone Kenyatta.[20]

Thuku mobilised support for the EAA both in Kenya and Britain and travelled through rural areas in Kenya to speak to large gatherings.[21] Thuku and the EAA protested the forced labour and rape experienced by African women and girls. The issue of forced female labour was particularly serious – at the request of a settler, the District Commissioner would task local headmen with providing the requisite number of women and girls, who would be selected by the headmen's enforcers and forcibly taken from their communities to work on the commercial farming interests of English settlers. Many of these women returned from forced labour pregnant, often because of assaults by the headmen's officers.[22]

As a result of Thuku's activism and leadership, forced labour for women ended in 1921 and, by the beginning of 1922, Thuku was encouraging men to burn their *kipande*s and only pay a fraction of the required taxation. It was clear that Thuku had very quickly become a direct threat to colonial rule, and he was arrested on 14 March 1922.[23] Thuku's championing of women during the forced labour campaign earned him

---

[17] Bruce Berman and John Lonsdale, *Unhappy Valley: Conflict in Kenya and Africa*, Book 2 (Nairobi: Heinemann Kenya, 1992), 387.
[18] Ingham, *A History of East Africa*, 280.
[19] *Ibid.*, 281.
[20] Mungeam, 'Masai and Kikuyu Responses', 127; Ingham, *A History of East Africa*, 280; Jeremy Murray-Brown, *Kenyatta* (London: Allen and Unwin, 1972), 85.
[21] Wipper, 'Kikuyu Women', 302.
[22] *Ibid.*, 112.
[23] *Ibid.*, 303–05.

the popular title of 'Chief of Women' among the Gĩkũyũ, and Gĩkũyũ women returned his commitment with deep loyalty.[24]

The forced mobilisation of African troops by the British to fight for the Empire in the Second World War produced a population of Africans who had been deployed across the Middle East and India–Burma and returned to Kenya only to watch their 'British counterparts receiving demobilization support from the colonial government ... [and] ex-servicemen from Britain ... coming to the colony through soldier settlement schemes'.[25] Rather than returning to them the recognition and support that their role in the war effort had led them to expect, following the war Gĩkũyũ ex-servicemen, and the Gĩkũyũ population more broadly, saw their quality of life decline.[26] Caroline Elkins has credited the advent of the Second World War with 'galvaniz[ing] Gĩkũyũ discontent, and channel[ling] it into a mass peasant movement called Mau Mau'.[27] Indeed, Waruhiu Itote, an ex-soldier who would come to be known as General China within the Mau Mau movement, returned from the war to find women being forced to terrace the land in reserves, a scheme 'that had caused great hardship and considerable social and family upheaval'. Itote joined the resistance organisation Anake a 40, or Kiama Kia 40 (The Forty Group), to protest this policy. Anake a 40 had several thousand members and achieved some notable successes, including the 'comparative failure of the compulsory terracing plan'.[28]

'He who is hit with a club returns, he who is hit with justice never comes back': Mau Mau, the Emergency and early colonial constitution-making

Initially, the colonial government sought to contain the growing frustration of the African population by offering constitutional amendments aimed at providing a minimum level of representation for Africans in the local government.[29] From the perspective of the colonial government, the introduction and development of local representation and the first, solitary African representative on the Legislative Council, Eliud Mathu in 1944[30] began as a series of shields against the threat of African political dominance in the dying days of the colony.

24 Ibid.
25 Elkins, *Imperial Reckoning*, 24.
26 Ibid.
27 Ibid., 22–23.
28 Waruhiu Itote, *'Mau Mau' General* (Nairobi: East African Publishing House, 1967), 37–38.
29 Anthony J. Hughes, *East Africa: The Search for Unity* (Baltimore: Penguin Books, 1963), 129.
30 Ibid., 113.

These early constitutional debates centred on the distribution and focus of African labour, the allocation of forcibly alienated African land and the formal representation and political influence of the three races living in the colony at the time: the Anglo-British settlers, the Indian population (Asians) and the numerically superior indigenous African population. The colonial government introduced the experience of constitution-making to the colony as an exercise in expedience. More concerned with strategic, racialised power-sharing arrangements than good governance, these early constitutions introduced an insidious kind of 'institutionalized tribal discrimination'.[31] The content and repeated modification of these colonial constitutions throughout the 1950s and early 1960s was explicitly designed to protect the commercial and governance interests of the anxious settler population and mollify increasingly implacable African and Asian political leaders.[32] Indeed, as Mahmood Mamdani has argued, the tactic of governing populations on the basis of their native or non-native status 'effectively fragmented the colonized majority into so many administratively driven political minorities'[33] and swiftly became a strategy central to the 'technology of colonial governance'.[34]

As the first constitutions were primarily concerned with racial representation, they were accepted or rejected by interested parties based on the representation of their group compared with others, and the perceived 'fairness' of the racial allocation of seats. For example, the 1954 Lyttleton Constitution, tabled by Colonial Secretary Oliver Lyttleton, was 'designed to produce a multi-racial Council of Ministers containing, in addition to civil servants, six unofficial members, three Europeans, two Asians, and one African'.[35] The African representatives rejected the proposals and demanded at least parity with Asians. European settlers protested Asians and Africans participating in government at all.[36]

In 1956, Secretary of State for the Colonies Alan Lennox-Boyd proposed 'further constitutional advance ... including [an increase of] six additional African elected members', but the newly elected African representatives protested the inadequacy of this new level of representation and 'all pledged to refuse government office and to oppose the new Lennox-Boyd constitution' in its entirety, demanding that an overall majority of seats be allocated to African representatives.[37] As Mamdani has explained, this organisation of political life by race and tribe:

[31] Mahmood Mamdani, *Define and Rule – Native as Political Identity* (Cambridge: Harvard University Press, 2012), 53.
[32] Hughes, *East Africa*, 129.
[33] Mamdani, *Define and Rule*, 45.
[34] Ibid., 46.
[35] Hughes, *East Africa*, 120.
[36] Ibid., 121.
[37] Ibid., 122.

not only distinguished between the colonizing *master race* (Europeans) and colonized *subject races* (Asians, Arabs, Colored, and so on) and discriminated in favor of the former against the latter, it also split the colonized population into two groups privileging non-native subject races in relation to native tribes ... it grounded rights – and thus discrimination – in a discourse on origin (nativism).[38]

This abiding colonial preoccupation with racial representation or, viewed structurally, the concern that the Constitution was a document that would, by its provisions alone, define minority groups and protect them from marginalisation, has persisted throughout Kenya's history.[39]

It is also worth noting that in response to the Indian government's request that all British subjects with an educational qualification be enfranchised (representing 10 per cent of the Indian population of Kenya at the time),[40] the white settlers seriously contemplated armed revolt.

[T]heir contemplated uprising, planned down to the details of where the kidnapped Governor was to be held, and how to operate the telegraph system, decisively influenced the British government in their favour. Indeed, the treatment of the seditious Vigilance Committee was in marked contrast to that shown to the most minor signs of disaffection among the African population. Not one European was arrested, charged, deported, or detained as a result of the preparations for revolution. Not surprisingly, the readiness of the British government to make concessions in the face of violence or threats of violence, was noted by those in the African community who would later use similar pressures in pursuit of constitutional advance.[41]

The constitutional concessions did nothing to quell African resistance. Gĩkũyũ demands for self-government and African independence became increasingly militant, and members of political associations sought to engender solidarity and trust by employing 'oathing' rituals – a familiar cultural practice among the Gĩkũyũ, but one that was viewed with suspicion by other tribes and Europeans.[42] An armed resistance movement formed alongside the political struggle against the colonial regime by those who were frustrated at the slow pace of negotiations,

---

[38] Mamdani, *Define and Rule,* 50–51. Emphasis in original.
[39] Tracking the ethnicity of members of cabinet and other high-profile public officers has followed the analysis of Kenyan governance into the postcolonial period, as evidenced in the tables of members of cabinet and other high-profile public service positions listed against their ethnicity in Charles Hornsby's 2012 modern history of Kenya, *Kenya: A History Since Independence* (New York: Palgrave Macmillan, 2013), 124–25, 231–22; and D. Pal Ahluwalia's *Post-Colonialism and the Politics of Kenya* (New York: Nova Science, 1996) 18–20.
[40] Hughes, *East Africa,* 99.
[41] *Ibid.*, 99.
[42] Elkins, *Imperial Reckoning,* 26.

the attitude of the British towards African demands and the perception that African representatives were acquiescing to British demands to protect their own interests.

Following organised resistance to the forced resettlement of Gĩkũyũ squatters from the Gĩkũyũland of the Mau plateau and an increase in murders of Europeans committed by Gĩkũyũ gangs, Jeremy Murray-Brown posited that the term 'Mau Mau' came into usage, 'purporting to belong to an underground terrorist movement pledged to kill every white person in Kenya'.[43] Throughout the late 1940s and early 1950s, governance and constitutional development was increasingly frustrated and challenged by the emergence and growth of Mau Mau. Beginning as a predominantly Gĩkũyũ cultural and political independence movement, Mau Mau swiftly grew into a violent, anticolonial guerrilla force[44] that has had a lasting effect on the style of governance preferred by postcolonial African governments.[45] The fact of the Mau Mau commitment to violent action to overthrow the British colonial government also split already constantly fracturing African alliances. This rift was felt most acutely within the Gĩkũyũ community itself, from whose ranks came the majority of the movement's guerrilla fighters, as well as several key moderate proto-nationalists explicitly against violent action. These Gĩkũyũ loyalists were joined by members of the Embu and Meru ethnic groups and formed a significant proportion of the Home Guard, defending the colony against predominantly Gĩkũyũ liberation fighters, who were also joined by Embu and Meru fighters.[46] As a result of this conflict, a brutal bifurcation of Gĩkũyũ, Embu and Meru communities developed in the late 1950s, which has only increased since independence.[47]

Jomo Kenyatta had been involved with groups that sought Kenya's independence from the British since the establishment of the Young Gĩkũyũ Association in the 1920s, but the movement had been forced underground during the Second World War.[48] In the intervening period, Kenyatta sought to position himself as leader not only of the

---

[43] Murray-Brown, *Kenyatta*, 240–41.
[44] Elkins, *Imperial Reckoning* 2005; Moritz Feichtinger, '"A Great Reformatory": Social Planning and Strategic Resettlement in Late Colonial Kenya and Algeria, 1952–63', *Journal of Contemporary History*, 52:1 (2016), 49–50.
[45] Ahluwalia, *Post-Colonialism and the Politics of Kenya*, 18–20.
[46] Daniel Branch, 'The Enemy Within: Loyalists and the War Against the Mau Mau in Kenya', *The Journal of African History*, 48:2 (2007), 291–315.
[47] Elkins, *Imperial Reckoning*, 13–14, 24–33; Branch, 'The Enemy Within', 291–315; Ahluwalia, *Post-Colonialism and the Politics of Kenya*, 20. See also Carl G. Rosenburg and John Nottingham, *The Myth of Mau Mau –Nationalism in Kenya* (Nairobi: East African Publishing House, 1961), 234–76.
[48] Elkins, *Imperial Reckoning*, 24–25.

Gīkūyū but of all African Kenyans in their struggle for independence.[49] Such was his prominence in public life that Europeans began to attribute actions against the colonial regime to his influence, regardless of the evidence. Returning to Kenya from study and advocacy in Britain in 1946, Kenyatta was elected President of the Kenya African Union (KAU). Although Kenyatta shared the objective of liberating Africans from colonial rule, he publicly rejected violence and illegal activity and encouraged Africans to build their own future through hard work, eschewing 'idleness' and giving up 'thuggery ... graft and corruption'.[50] Kenyatta particularly tried to distance himself from both the splintering KAU and the growing, and recently outlawed, 'Mau Mau Association'. Speaking at Nyeri in July 1952 at a rare government-sanctioned meeting, Kenyatta affirmed the rights of Africans to rule their own lands, but he also rejected Mau Mau:

> God said this is our land, land in which we are to flourish as a people. We are not worried that other races are here with us in our country, but we insist that we are the leaders here, and what we want we insist we get ... We do not want the fat [of the land] to be removed to feed others ... KAU speaks in daylight. He who calls us the MAU MAU is not truthful. We do not know this thing MAU MAU.[51]

Murray-Brown reported that:

> At this point ... an African District Officer, one of the few in government service, asked Kenyatta what he was going to do about Mau Mau. Kenyatta said: 'I think Mau Mau is a new word. Elders do not know it. KAU is not a fighting union that uses fists and weapons ... Remember the old saying that he who is hit with the clubs returns, but he who is hit with justice never comes back.'[52]

Despite this public repudiation of Mau Mau, Kenyatta was arrested in October 1952 and tried and convicted in 1953 with five others (known as the Kapenguria Six), to whom the British attributed the organisation and rise of Mau Mau. He spent seven years in prison and three in exile in Lodwar, almost 700km north of Nairobi.[53]

The British allocation of particular areas of land in the colony to Africans of different tribes to better supply white settlers with agricultural labour, combined with regulations that permitted local but not national political organisation, created a tribalised political culture that continues to grip Kenyan politics. As A.J. Hughes has noted, 'Kenya's particular form of indirect rule, the demarcation of tribal land units and the

---

[49] Murray-Brown, *Kenyatta*, 225–54.
[50] *Ibid.*, 234–35.
[51] *Ibid.*, 244 (capitalisation in original).
[52] *Ibid.*
[53] *Ibid.*, 257–95.

administration's hostility to African nationalism, had already encouraged tribal politics'.[54] The ban on African political organisations during the Emergency (1953–1955) exacerbated these tendencies, and continues to affect the dynamics of political organisation in postcolonial Kenya. Through the web of competing allegiances and political philosophies that developed during this period, the true contest for the shape and leadership of the independent Kenyan state emerged.

> Coming at such a vital time, it stamped a pattern. Every kind of local separatism was encouraged ... tribalism was entrenched as the basis of political organization and thinking ... The regulation also meant that dominant local leaders could arise, free from the restraints of having to work with others of equal stature in a national body.[55]

Although Mau Mau failed to force the British government out of the colony, the resistance movement encouraged British interests to seek African representation in government and to permit some regional political parties to develop.[56] However, the entrenchment of tribalism as the geographic and cultural basis for national politics has persisted in the post-independence period. Answering his own question, 'Did tribe exist before colonialism?' Mamdani has argued that, although

> ethnic group[s] with a common language did exist in the precolonial period, 'tribe' as an administrative entity that distinguishes between natives and non-natives and systematically discriminates in favour of the former and against the latter – defining access to land and participation in local governance and rules for settling disputes according to tribal identity – certainly did *not* exist before colonialism.[57]

The reification of 'cultural identity [as] an administratively driven political identity'[58] was thought to be integral to the democratic success of an independent territory of Kenya. In his opening remarks at the 1959 Lancaster House Conference, then Colonial Secretary Iain Macleod

> declared that the aim of the conference should be to build a nation based upon parliamentary institutions, of the Westminster type, and to achieve a general acceptance by all of the right of each community to remain in Kenya and to play a part in public life. For a time the interests of minorities might have to be guaranteed by constitutional safeguards.[59]

---

[54] Hughes, *East Africa*, 123.
[55] *Ibid.*, 123.
[56] *Ibid.*, 20.
[57] Mamdani, *Define and Rule*, 73.
[58] *Ibid.*, 53.
[59] Hughes, *East Africa*, 129.

Although the Mau Mau guerrilla resistance movement was brutally suppressed, the colonial government understood that its future presence in East Africa was unsustainable. A consequence of Mau Mau was the elevation of non-violent African loyalists to positions of local and colonial influence during and following the Emergency in the early 1950s.[60]

Thus, on the cusp of independence, the Africans (almost exclusively men) who were poised to take the reins of the new state in 1963 were those who had either avoided the stigma of too close an association with Mau Mau or, in the case of Jomo Kenyatta, been too prominent an advocate for self-determination on the African and international stage to be sidelined by the outgoing British government. The new Kenyan state was therefore in the hands of men who were politically conservative and broadly appreciative of the achievements and goals of the colonial regime of which they were, on occasion, beneficiaries.[61]

Occurring during a period of political and physical resistance, this process of state formation created new cultural and political identities.[62] These men sought to preserve the colonial legacy and insert themselves within it[63] rather than to remake Kenya as a kind of pan-African socialist ideal, as other independence leaders in the region aspired to do.[64] The result was an African leadership group that was

---

[60] It is no small irony that the atrocities committed by the British regime during the Mau Mau insurgency between the early 1950s and the declaration of independence in 1964 took place in the period in which key international human rights instruments were being developed, including the *Forced Labor Convention* in 1930, the *Convention on Human Rights* adopted by the Council of Europe in 1950, the 1948 United Nations *Universal Declaration of Human Rights*, 1951 *Convention Relating to the Status of Refugees* and 1948 *Convention on the Prevention and Punishment of the Crime of Genocide*. See Australian Human Rights Commission, 'Timeline – Major Human Rights Treaties' (n.d.), www.humanrights.gov.au/publications/timeline-major-international-human-rights-treaties [accessed 4 July 2021].

[61] Murray-Brown, *Kenyatta*, 312–13.

[62] Mahmood Mamdani, 'Beyond Settler and Native and Political Identities: Overcoming the Political Legacy of Colonialism', *Comparative Studies in Society and History*, 43:4 (2001), 651.

[63] Hughes, *East Africa*, 116–45. After his release from prison, Jomo Kenyatta married into the prominent Koinange and Muhoho families and built relationships with wealthy clan leaders, and opened communication with former opponents including James Gichuru, Julius Kiano and a young technocrat from Nyeri, Mwai Kibaki. J.A. Widner, *The Rise of a Party-state in Kenya: From 'Harambee' to 'Nyayo'* (Berkeley: University of California Press, 1993), 56; see also Ahluwalia, *Post-Colonialism and the Politics of Kenya*, 22–23.

[64] Kenyatta's biographer, Jeremy Murray-Brown, explains that Kenyatta 'took part in the Pan-African movement, as he did in anything which might suit his purpose, but with a down-to-earth approach which sometimes worried his more doctrinaire colleagues': *Kenyatta*, 217, 312.

sympathetic to British colonial economic interests, expressly conservative in its aspirations for independence and not nearly as invested in the radical programme of dismantling the colonial state as its rebel counterparts might have been. In his postcolonial history of Kenyan independence politics, D. Pal Ahluwalia observed that the nascent independent Kenyan government inherited two oppositional styles of governance – the first, that of the 'executive dominance' of the Governor, supported by 'extensive powers ... [and] a pervasive and effective administrative state structure', and the Westminster system developed through the Lancaster House negotiation process in preparation for independence.[65]

During his years in prison and exile, Kenyatta gave an interview in 1961, in Maralal, roughly halfway between Lodwar and Nairobi. Kenyatta explained that 'we want to rule ourselves ... I shall always remain an African nationalist to the end'.[66] His conception of the 'absolute right' to self-government 'did not depend on any political theories originating in Moscow or Westminster'.[67] On the cusp of independence, this guiding belief was further developed by then member of the Kenya African National Union (KANU, the resurrected KAU, which had been banned during the Emergency) and Minister for Justice and Constitutional Affairs, and one of the most prominent independence advocates, Tom Mboya, in a strident speech in July 1963, who asserted:

> the countries of Africa emerging from political subjection are entitled to modify, to suit their own needs, the institutions of democracy as developed in the West. No one has the right to cavil at this so long as all citizens – irrespective of their racial, tribal or religious affiliations – are treated alike.[68]

The Westminster ideal that there exists 'a special connection between the democratic form of government and the party system, such that one cannot exist without the other' was explicitly rejected by Kenyatta and KANU.[69] In his biography of Kenyatta, Murray-Brown characterised the president's belief in a one-party state as, 'the expression of the people's new found unity'.[70] Kenyatta justified his resistance to the uncritical uptake of the Westminster system in Kenya by characterising the British push to implement a Westminster system as a neocolonial impulse to control the newly independent state through its institutions.

---

[65] Ahluwalia, *Post-Colonialism and the Politics of Kenya*, 20.
[66] Murray-Brown, *Kenyatta*, 305.
[67] *Ibid.*, 312.
[68] Tom J. Mboya, 'The Party System and Democracy in Africa', *Foreign Affairs*, 41:4 (1963), 658.
[69] *Ibid.*, 650.
[70] Murray-Brown, *Kenyatta*, 313–14.

Just as it had been throughout the colonial period, expeditious constitutional amendment and the placating of marginalised racial and tribal groups through constitutional recognition were also prominent features of the new Kenyan republic, founded in 1963. What had begun as a colonial preoccupation with formally providing for disenfranchised groups through constitutional amendment – initially to address racial (and tribal) representation – has persisted. The following year, addressing an issue that would come to haunt the political landscape of the independent state, Mboya stated categorically that:

> it would be entirely false for anyone in Britain ... to set themselves up at this very late stage as the only source of safeguard and protection for the minorities in Kenya. There is no alternative to the fact that when Kenya becomes independent in December this year, the only safeguard, the only protection that any minority tribe or community can enjoy in Kenya is that which comes out of the good will and understanding of the Kenya Government. Nobody today can run away from that fact. It would be undesirable that anyone should insist rigidly on the false assumption that by merely writing some rigid provisions in the constitution you protect the minorities or the minority tribes. In the end, I believe you destroy their chances.[71]

Writing on the formation of political parties prior to independence, Mboya explained that KANU was formed to express a national African political organisation and 'was created as soon as Africans were permitted to form national political organisations'. Mboya deftly situated KANU as a catalysing force within the progressive discourse of Uhuru (Sw., Freedom), which was built on the pre-independence slogan in which the freedom of Kenyatta from exile became synonymous with the impending liberation of the territory with the release of the living symbol of this struggle, 'Uhuru na Kenyatta' (Freedom and Kenyatta).[72] Disparaging of both the British inclination for multiparty democracy as a good in its own right, and the need for minority tribes to be protected through such political organisation, Mboya poured scorn on the 'traditional regard shown by British politicians and the press for the interests of the so-called downtrodden minority tribes or communities' and emphasised that Kenya only had room for one liberating African organisation.[73]

The treatment of the 'Uhuru na Mashamba' (Independence and Land) movement illustrates the limits of liberation and the market-driven priorities of the new African government. Although Uhuru na Mashamba was promoted during the struggle for independence, Kenyatta failed to support the movement once in office, requiring Africans to purchase land

---

[71] Tom Mboya, 'The Future of Kenya', *African Affairs*, 63:250 (1964), 6–12.
[72] Murray-Brown, *Kenyatta*, 303.
[73] Mboya, 'The Party System and Democracy', 651.

that Europeans owned. Again, this pitted Mau Mau fighters, who had survived years of brutal conditions both in the forest and in the detention camps, against political operatives who were now in control of the government. One of Kenyatta's fellow Kapenguria Six detainees formed a public organisation, popularly called Mituikire (The Ragged Ones), to protest the government's position on land redistribution.[74]

The third and final Lancaster House Conference in 1963 was marked by significant disagreement over the procedure for amending the independence Constitution. The 1963 Constitution deliberately included significant barriers to its amendment, which were expressly designed to protect the negotiated constitutional guarantees. In the last days of the colony, Mboya complained that the Constitution Kenya had been given was 'rigid ... perhaps the most inflexible anywhere in the Commonwealth'.[75] Citing costly, parallel administrative requirements and the prohibitive 90 per cent majority required for constitutional amendment to pass the Senate, Mboya argued that the Constitution was in fact an impediment to 'unity and stability in the country'.[76] To modify the Constitution, Kenyatta would need the support of his own party, KANU, and the support of the major opposition party, KADU, which was led by fellow independence campaigner Ronald Ngala. Among other provisions, KADU had consistently advocated for the prohibitive majorities required in both houses to achieve constitutional change as part of their platform of Majimboism (regionalism), which sought to 'appease the fears of minority ethnic groups ... and reconcil[e] deep rifts caused by the colonial experience'.[77] As the opposition was unlikely to vote against its hard-won gains at Lancaster House, Kenyatta quickly came to see multipartyism as an impediment to his presidential vision.

The expression of the people's new-found unity

Benedict Anderson has contended that nation states need to be 'emotionally plausible and politically viable'.[78] Majimboism was discredited as emotionally implausible – perhaps because it unintentionally confirmed the British understanding of African tribes as incapable of working together under a centralised government and reinforced the backwardness of tribalism expressed as regionalism rather than 'the objective modernity of [nation]'.[79] In the Kenyan case, the 'affective bonds of

[74] Geoff Lamb, *Peasant Politics* (London: Julian Friedman Publishers, 1974), 31–36.
[75] Mboya, 'The Future of Kenya', 6.
[76] *Ibid.*
[77] Ahluwalia, *Post-Colonialism and the Politics of Kenya*, 26.
[78] Benedict Anderson, *Imagined Communities: Reflections on the Origin and Spread of Nationalism*, 2nd edn (London: Verso, 2006), 51–52.
[79] *Ibid.*, 5.

nationalism',[80] which were critical to the success of the immediate postcolonial period, came to be associated with, and dependent upon, the personality and tribe of the liberator.

That the imaginary Kenyan nation could be defined by an *absence* of tribal politics was belied by the symbiotic relationship the Gĩkũyũ had developed with the ideas of freedom and 'nation-ness'.[81] The alliance of Gĩkũyũ independence with Kenyan independence is derived partially from the targeting of almost the entire ethnic group during the Emergency, either through the military campaign and the gross abuses associated with its detention and interrogation programme, or through forced villagisation.[82] The impression that Gĩkũyũ nationhood was synonymous with anticolonial resistance was further entrenched by the facts that the largest ethnic group in Kenya formed the majority of the resistance force and the inaugural president was Gĩkũyũ, and by the reclamation of Gĩkũyũ land in the political heart of the new nation by political elites. As Anderson has argued, 'all communities are imagined. Communities are to be distinguished, not by their falsity/genuineness, but by the style in which they are imagined.'[83] Thus, the impression that the Gĩkũyũ identity is tied to the new imaginary of the Kenyan nation exists as a kind of fundamental symbiosis, and has created lasting resentments among the remaining ethnic communities. Just as the administrative and political identity of tribes and races contributed to the colonial imagery, so has the Gĩkũyũ resistance become the foundation of the postcolonial nation.

The mythic power of this symbiosis of Gĩkũyũ and Kenya is also gendered. As Gĩkũyũ women were increasingly moving to Nairobi to engage in waged labour, leaving their rural homes and responsibilities, Gĩkũyũ men understood 'female, urban' Nairobi to be a direct threat to their 'masculine ethnicity'.[84] An insight into the historical depth of Gĩkũyũ patriarchy can be found in an origin myth, which is reimagined here in an explanation given by Chege to his son in Ngũgĩ wa Thiong'o's novel, *The River Between*:

> Long ago women used to rule this land and its men. They were harsh and men began to resent their hard hand. So when all the women were pregnant, men came together and overthrew them. Before this,

[80] *Ibid.*, 64.
[81] *Ibid.*, 6. For discussion of the extension of imagined communities to those which consume not only print media, in this case kinds of food and alcohol, see Paul Nugent, 'Do Nations Have Stomachs? Food, Drink and Imagined Community in Africa', Continuities, Dislocations and Transformations: 50 Years of Independence in Africa, *Africa Spectrum*, 45:3 (2010), pp. 87–113.
[82] Feichtinger, '"A Great Reformatory"'; Elkins, *Imperial Reckoning*, 154–91.
[83] Anderson, *Imagined Communities*, 6.
[84] Lonsdale and Berman, *Unhappy Valley*, 381.

women owned everything. The animal you saw was their goat. But because the women could not manage them, the goats ran away. They knew women to be weak. So why should they fear them? It was then Waiyaki understood why his mother owned nothing.[85]

Upon achieving independence, the mantra of Uhuru na Kenyatta (Independence and Kenyatta) was augmented with the addition of Kenyatta as the father of the nation, and it was around the symbolic and physical body of Kenyatta that the nation of Kenya was built. Kenyatta's party, KANU, developed a 'patrimonial authoritarianism' that fed Kenyatta's personal power and encouraged the 'informalisation of the state, and its systemic deployment of predatory activities'.[86]

After forming the first independent parliament in 1963, Kenyatta and KANU inherited a governance system of which they fundamentally disapproved.[87] Rather than moving towards a kind of modern expression of territorial and political unity, Kenyatta and the new government were faced with a populace divided by class, political alliances, geography and inter-tribal grievances. These fractures were produced and manipulated by the outgoing colonial regime and exacerbated by a vicious and traumatising struggle for independence. The grievances, discourses and decisions made during the transition period from colony to nation continue to haunt the modern Kenyan nation. Faced with a fractured and fragile state, Kenyatta developed a unifying, to the point of assimilationist, rhetoric, and his motto of *harambee* (come together) was enthusiastically taken up by the new government.[88]

Although Kenyatta positioned himself as a leader for all Kenyan tribes and races, he had built his reputation as a defender of African custom and identity partly through his role in establishing the Young Gĩkũyũ Association, and later through his polemical thesis dissertation *Facing Mount Kenya*, a masterful work positioning him as an authority on Gĩkũyũ custom and cultural life.[89] Anderson has suggested that it is the 'decline of sacred communities, languages and linages [which prompted] a fundamental change ... in modes of apprehending the world, which more than anything else, made it possible to "think" the nation'.[90] In this sense, Kenyatta's Gĩkũyũ identity and the great burden of Mau Mau carried by the Gĩkũyũ community centred Gĩkũyũ identity at the heart of the

---

[85] Ngũgĩ wa Thiong'o, *The River Between* (London: Penguin Random House, 1965), 15; see also Brendon Nicholls, *Ngugi wa Thiong'o, Gender and the Ethics of Postcolonial Reading* (Farnham: Ashgate, 2010).
[86] Rok Ajulu, 'Thinking Through the Crisis of Democratization in Kenya: A Response to Adar and Murunga', *African Sociological Review*, 4:2 (2000), 133.
[87] Robert M. Maxon, 'Constitution-Making in Contemporary Kenya: Lessons from the Twentieth Century', *Kenya Studies Review*, 1 (2009), 14–15.
[88] Murray-Brown, *Kenyatta*, 309.
[89] Jomo Kenyatta, *Facing Mount Kenya* (New York: Random House, 1962).
[90] Anderson, *Imagined Communities*, 22.

new nation, but the process of building a nation inherited from strangers asked the other tribes to become 'tribeless' Kenyans.

Kenyatta began a campaign of coercive persuasion, luring members of the opposition, the Kenya African Democratic Union (KADU) by offering government positions to defectors while making it increasingly difficult for the party to conduct its affairs.[91] Once KADU had 'bowed to the inevitable',[92] dissolved itself and joined KANU, the government seized the opportunity to effect a reduction of the amendment threshold through the *Amendment Act* (1965) providing a 65 per cent majority threshold in both the lower and upper houses to effect an amendment to the Constitution.[93] As historian George Bennett noted in 1963, 'the rapid succession of Constitutions – 1954, 1957 and 1960 – had given many of [Kenya African National Union's] leaders a feeling that Constitutions could be as easily broken as made'.[94] This culture of strategic constitutional modification fast became a recurring feature of postcolonial Kenyan politics.

Following the assassination of Tom Mboya, a Luo, by a Gĩkũyũ assassin in Nairobi on 5 July 1969, Kenyatta delivered a television address to quell inter-tribal violence:

> I appeal to you to identify ourselves as Kenyans, to unite together as one people, and one big tribe of Kenya ... We should not be thinking in terms of 'I come from that place of that district of that tribe' because all of us are of one tribe, and that tribe is Kenya.[95]

This strategy is well known to Kenyans today in sometimes futile attempts to quell unrest in periods of stress – for instance, the repeated violence of election periods, or terrorist attacks.

Upon Kenyatta's death in office in August 1978, he had ruled the nation for fifteen years and had never been directly elected. He had been handed the KANU leadership in 1961 and run unopposed for the presidency in 1962, 1963, 1969 and 1974. During the Kenyatta regime, constitutional amendments were used as either an attempt to strengthen the president's powers or to limit the opposition's capability to effectively compete. The primary effect of the amendments was that the electorate's ability to make a free, fair and informed decision was significantly curtailed.[96] Henry Amadi has argued that the Kenyatta government 'set in motion a series of constitutional amendments that had

---

[91] David Goldsworthy, *Tom Mboya: The Man Kenya Wanted to Forget* (London: Heinemann Educational, 1982), 232–48.
[92] Murray-Brown, *Kenyatta*, 313–14.
[93] Hornsby, *Kenya: A History Since Independence*, 163.
[94] Bennett, 'Political Realities in Kenya', 296.
[95] Murray-Brown, *Kenyatta*, 244.
[96] For further discussion of the effects of constitutional amendments under Kenyatta, see for instance Ahluwalia, *Post-Colonialism and the Politics of Kenya*, 37.

weakened the existing checks and balances leading to the emergence of an imperial presidency'.[97] Kenyatta's successor, Vice President Daniel arap Moi, was unanimously endorsed as KANU's presidential candidate in 1978 and was elected unopposed the following year. In addition to electoral fraud, intimidation and state-sponsored violence,[98] Moi continued the tradition of expedient constitutional modification and buttressed his hold on state power through the repression of political and civil society opposition and an aggressively entrenched autocracy. He is also credited with allowing social and political violence to seep into the community in the form of politically aligned, ethnically derived gangs.[99] By the time the Kenyan polity was demanding multiparty democracy in the late 1980s and early 1990s, 'disillusionment with the Moi government was widespread'[100] and Kenya's post-independence Constitution had been amended more than thirty-two times.[101]

While the struggle for independence was marked by an increasingly cohesive call for the creation of Kenya as a geographically located nation, Ochieng and Atieno-Odhiambo have argued that:

> it is generally accepted that independent Kenya did not effect a major ideological, or structural, break with the colonial state ... This has often lead to Kenya being labelled a 'neo-colonial' state in economic, political and cultural fields ... while the neo-colonial appellation is generally regarded in Kenya as offensive, it is, nevertheless, important to recapitulate the salient features of the colonial state, for Kenya has borrowed substantially from it.[102]

As I explore in later chapters, the dynamics of modern Kenyan politics, including gender and social welfare policies, and engagement with and influence of international human rights frameworks and discourses, continue to be informed by these colonial legacies. The promise of the new nation and the myths of its creation have remained foundational. The early independence years under Kenyatta and then Moi were characterised by short periods of momentarily strengthened governance followed by years of civic decay, from which it was difficult for the fledgling democratic state to recover. The everlasting hope, that

---

[97] Henry Amadi, 'Kenya's Grand Coalition Government: Another obstacle to Urgent Constitutional Reform?' *Africa Spectrum,* 44:3 (2009), 149–64, 151. See also Alfred Anangwe, 'From Kenyatta to Kenyatta: The Evolution of the Kenyan Presidency', *The Nairobi Law Monthly,* 4:11 (2013), 72–75.
[98] David Throup, 'Elections and Political Legitimacy in Kenya', *Africa: Journal of the International African Institute* 63:3 (1993), 389.
[99] Michael Bratton and Mwangi S. Kimenyi, 'Voting in Kenya: Putting Ethnicity in Perspective', *Journal of Eastern African Studies,* 2:2 (2008), 272–89.
[100] Throup, 'Elections and Political Legitimacy', 389.
[101] Amadi, 'Kenya's Grand Coalition Government', 151.
[102] Ochieng' and Atieno-Odhiambo, 'On Decolonization', xiii.

the best election is ahead for Kenya, has energised civil society and the occasional progressive politician to advocate for a new era of national solidarity, manifested in support for free and fair elections and equitable governance and resource distribution. The new nation has also demanded a new narrative, arranged 'around the metaphor of struggle', a narrative that

> entails seeing [Kenya's] history of the past fifty or so years a moral enterprise: against the injustice that is colonialism; against poverty, ignorance and disease; against the drudgery of rural life; against the foreignization of the cultural ecology; against the intervention of alien ideas in the indigenous discourses of nation building. [103]

Since independence there have been peaks and troughs in a fundamentally linear narrative of democratic progress – moments that were thought to be catalysing in the pursuit of the 'model East African democracy' and high points in the struggle. In the modern era, repeated constitutional modification and corrupt, autocratic governance have contributed to a popular understanding in Kenyan politics that constitutions and legislation can be drafted and expediently modified at will, and that *it is this modification alone* that is the necessary and sufficient condition of policy reform and change in the culture of politics. This reliance on legislative and constitutional reform rather than implementing radical personnel, governance, service delivery and policy change continues to materially affect the Kenyan government's ability to govern and its motivation to protect and promote the rights of minority and disadvantaged groups.

Constitutional reform has long served as a proxy for substantive political change in Kenya, cynically manipulated by politicians to protect politico-ethnic cabals. Reform has also been a rallying cry of civil society campaigning for the restoration not only of the primacy of the Constitution as a foundational document, but also for constitutionalism – the system of values that includes the separation of powers, the rule of law, the protection of fundamental rights and freedoms and the promotion and protection of institutions that support democracy.[104] Engaged in recording and making sense of Kenya's turbulent history, Atieno-Odhiambo observes that:

> [t]he historian in postcolonial Kenya has recognized that daily living is always the site of struggle ... It is these struggles [for land, health

---

[103] Eisha Stephen Atieno-Odhiambo, 'The Invention of Kenya', in B.A. Ogot and W.R. Ochieng' (eds), *Decolonization and Independence in Kenya 1940–93* (London: James Currey, 1995), 2.
[104] Paul Tiyambe Zeleza, 'The Protracted Transition to the Second Republic in Kenya', in Godwin Murunga *et al.* (eds), *Kenya: The Struggle for a New Constitutional Order* (London: Zed Books, 2014), 36.

water, housing, for the environment] that have constituted rural and urban political discourses; the self-same struggles that have also remained the core agenda for the developmental state, and for the many constituencies of the civil society that have continually urged the politics of vision as an attainable reality within our lifetimes. [105]

The uses of the Constitution by politicians and civil society accustomed Kenyans to expect little from their democratic institutions and, paradoxically, to look to a utopian future in which institutional and constitutional reform could fundamentally change the political culture. This reliance on reform rather than governance continues to profoundly and negatively affect Kenya's ability to promote and protect the rights of minority and disadvantaged groups, including women.

---

[105] Atieno-Odhiambo, 'The Invention of Kenya', 2.

2

Bodies as Battlefields, Bodies as Weapons: The Colonial Regulation of Women's Bodies

'In the village, most of Zakariah's circumcision mates were already married and they used to boast to him about their beautiful wives and even more about their children ... [I]t was true that they had attractive young and charming wives who made them feel like men. These women were friendly but shy, ready to obey and attended their husbands with respect. They never answered back their husbands like Mrs Smith. Their husbands were little lords in their houses, and not babysitters like Mr Smith. Indeed, there were many things to envy these men for. Still, many wives had a lot to learn about looking after babies, cleanliness, and being able to talk.'[1]

Throughout the colonial period, both indigenous communities and the colonial authorities fought for control of the bodies of African women and girls in Kenya, as women's bodies were (and remain) primary sites of cultural identity formation and expression. Indeed, the level of control over women's reproductive potential, labour, migration, hygiene, health and clothing became indicators of the success of the British civilising mission.[2] Both the ritual and the results of body modification have served as conscious markers of difference not only between Kenyans and colonialists, but also within and between indigenous Kenyan ethnic groups. Given the unrelenting focus on women's bodies, the regulation and attempted eradication of female genital

---

[1] Muthoni Likimani, *They Shall Be Chastised* (Nairobi: East African Literature Bureau, 1974), 55.
[2] See, for instance, Hilda Hendrickson (ed.), *Clothing and Difference: Embodied Identities in Colonial and Post-colonial Africa* (Durham: Duke University Press, 1996); Carolyn Martin Shaw, *Colonial Inscriptions: Race, Sex and Class in Kenya* (Minneapolis: University of Minnesota Press, 1995), 60–89; Brett Shadle, *Girl Cases: Marriage and Colonialism in Gusiiland, Kenya 1890–1970* (Portsmouth: Heinemann, 2006); Beth Maina Ahlberg, *Women, Sexuality and the Changing Social Order: The Impact of Government Policies on Reproductive Behaviour in Kenya* (Philadelphia: Gordon and Breach, 1991); Claire C. Robertson, *Trouble Showed the Way: Women, Men and Trade in the Nairobi Area, 1890–1990* (Bloomington: Indiana University Press, 1997), 91–101, 190–238; Luise White, *The Comforts of Home: Prostitution in Colonial Nairobi* (Chicago: University of Chicago Press, 1990).

cutting (FGC) is, unsurprisingly, a recurring theme in the history of colonial Kenya and was at the centre of existential struggles between the colonial regime and the ethnic communities that practise it.[3] In the Kenyan context, resistance to FGC and the promotion and perpetuation of the practice have been interpreted as the two halves of a dichotomy. However, Kenyan women's motivations are much more complex than merely supporting either colonial or cultural authority.

Here, I examine three instances in which female genital cutting was a central issue in political contests during the colonial period, focusing on how women's public, political statements relied upon their sexed bodies and gendered identities. These alternative accounts trouble earlier histories which interpreted these acts as statements of proto-feminist autonomous action, directed towards the liberation of African women from the compound patriarchal burdens of both the colonial regime and their own ethnic communities. Rather than seeking (and almost inevitably locating) a rights-based feminist agency, I explore alternative motivations for women's actions, centring women's cultural and political priorities, and demonstrate the centrality of women's bodies in the larger political and cultural struggles against the colonial regime. Through these events I interrogate the ways in which African women used strategies of embodied resistance, as well as the ways in which

---

[3] This chapter will use the term 'female genital cutting' (FGC) because the object is to refrain from arguing for or against the practice and instead to examine the role that FGC played in defining the anticolonial struggle and the centrality of women's bodies in this struggle. It is also the term used in the *Kenya Demographic and Health Survey 2014*, https://dhsprogram.com/pubs/pdf/fr308/fr308.pdf, 331 [accessed 16 August 2021]. Although control of women's bodies has dominated the discourses on body modification, it is important to acknowledge that men's genital modification also has a contested history and remains a central theme in the cultural and political fractures in Kenya's modern politics. For instance, a study on the circumcision of boys and men in historical and modern contexts noted the forced circumcision/castration of Luo men by Kikuyu rioters after the 2007 elections. See Beth M. Ahlberg, Kezia Njoroge and Pia Olsson, '"We Cannot Be Led by a Child": Forced Male Circumcision during the Post-election Violence in Kenya' (Uppsala: Department of Women's and Children's Health, Uppsala University and Karaborg Institute for Research and Development, 2011). Further, adult men are now encouraged to undergo circumcision in order to curb the spread of HIV, in spite of cultural proscriptions against the practice: Stuart Rennie, Adamson S. Muula and Daniel Westreich, 'Male Circumcision and HIV Prevention: Ethical, Medical and Public Health Tradeoffs in Low-income Countries', *Journal of Medical Ethics*, 33:6 (2007), 357–61; see also World Health Organization, *Voluntary Medical Male Circumcision for HIV Prevention in 14 Priority Countries in Eastern and Southern Africa*, Progress Brief (2017), https://apps.who.int/iris/bitstream/handle/10665/179933/WHO_HIV_2015.21_eng.pdf [accessed 16 August 2021].

their bodies became battlegrounds for larger debates around British control of African bodies.

The relationship between Western feminism and African women's rights advocacy has been characterised by a deep antagonism on the part of many African activists to the imposition of Western feminist agendas on African women's rights debates.[4] Indeed, while Joe Oloka-Onyango and Sylvia Tamale heralded the 'arrival' of international feminism, they argued that the phenomenon of the internationalisation of feminism was in fact the emergence of 'domestic Western feminism ... as dominant on the international stage'.[5] This Western discourse is criticised for its focus on the promotion of individual identities and rights at the expense of communal rights and obligations. Further, the framing of African women's rights as a struggle grounded in the postcolonial period ignores the central roles of women in resisting colonial rule, as well as their foundational contributions to post-independence nation-building,[6] and the effects of postcolonial capitalism on women.[7]

The culture/rights dichotomy has been rigorously critiqued for alienating African women. The move of Western feminisms (themselves a collection of culturally bounded ideologies) to set themselves in opposition to African culture and traditions, compels many African women to reject these 'rights' in order to defend their male relatives and their culture. Responding to a dire need for African women's voices in the 'third world' women's rights debate, and to counter scathing and uncontextual criticism of non-Western cultures, a variety of discourses have been developed by African feminists and activists seeking to restore value to African cultures and cultural practice. This move has been taken up by women and other marginalised groups across the Global South seeking to navigate a course between conservative cultural forces at home and critical voices abroad. Framing women's rights within 'traditional' discourses is also useful in pre-empting nationalist, conservative criticism of women's rights programmes. As Geraldine Heng has observed:

> the strategic response of a third world feminism under threat must be, and has sometimes been to assume the nationalist mantle itself: seeking legitimation and ideological support in local cultural history,

[4] Joe Oloka-Onyango and Sylvia Tamale, '"The Personal is Political" or Why Women's Rights are Indeed Human Rights: An African Perspective on International Feminism', *Human Rights Quarterly*, 17:4 (1995), 691–731.
[5] *Ibid.*, 696.
[6] Akosua Adomako Ampofo, Josephine Beoku-Betts, Wairimu Ngaruiya Njambi and Mary Osirim, 'Women's and Gender Studies in English-speaking Sub-Saharan Africa: A Review of Research in the Social Sciences', *Gender and Society*, 18:6 (2004), 686.
[7] Pepe Roberts, 'Feminism in Africa: Feminism and Africa', *Review of African Political Economy*, 27/28 (1983), 175–84.

by finding feminist or proto-feminist myths, laws, customs, characters, narratives and origins in the national or communal past or in strategic interpretations of religious history or law.[8]

In essence, such an approach seeks to articulate women's rights concerns within a framework that is palatable to conservative local commentators.

The rejection of 'feminism' as a term, as well as the anti-male attitude that it is seen to endorse, has led to alternative conceptions of African women's rights. As Mikel explains, the African discourse on feminism is manifested in part in the theorisation of alternative concepts – for example, Mary Kolawole and Chikwenye Ogunyemi's formulations of African womanism.[9] Nigerian scholar, activist and writer Akachi Adimora-Ezeigbo, along with others, speaks of 'African feminism' to express ambivalence towards being located within the network of a global feminism, and to focus on 'concepts emerging from the concrete social and cultural constellations of African societies'.[10] The African feminist project re-centres the feminine subject, who is at both the heart and the margins of Western feminist narratives, and troubles the centrality of feminine victimhood as a discovery, and project, of modern international rights advocacy. In focusing here on gendered agency and embodied experience, I illustrate the centrality of initiation rites to the politics of identity and cultural reproduction[11] – particularly where 'the female body is implicated in the crises of nation [and] citizenship'.[12]

Women's sexuality rights in general, and genital cutting in particular, is one of the most contentious areas of rights discourse, as the sexual behaviour and regulation of women sits at the heart of domestic

[8] Geraldine Heng, '"Great Way to Fly": Nationalism, the State, and the Varieties of Third World Feminism', in M. Jacqui Alexander and Chandra Talpade Mohanty (eds), *Feminist Genealogies, Colonial Legacies, Democratic Futures* (London: Routledge, 1997), 34.
[9] See, for example, their seminal works: Mary E. Modupe Kolawole, *Womanism and African Consciousness* (Asmara: Africa World Press, 1997); Chikwenye Okonjo Ogunyemi, *Africa Wo/Man Palava* (Chicago: University of Chicago Press, 1995).
[10] Susan Arndt, 'Perspectives on African Feminism: Defining and Classifying African-Feminist Literatures', *Agenda: Empowering Women for Gender Equity*, 17:54 (2002), 32; Susan Arndt, 'African Gender Trouble and African Womanism: An Interview with Chikwenye Ogunyemi and Wanjira Muthoni', *Signs: Journal of Women in Culture and Society*, 25:3 (2000), 709–26; Ama Mazama, 'The Afrocentric Paradigm: Contours and Definitions', *Journal of Black Studies*, 31:4 (2001), 387–405.
[11] Wambui Mwangi, 'Silence Is a Woman', *The New Inquiry*, blog post (4 June 2013), https://thenewinquiry.com/silence-is-a-woman [accessed 20 August 2021].
[12] Kathleen Canning, 'The Body as Method? Reflections on the Place of the Body in Gender History', *Gender and History*, 11:3 (1999), 507.

and cultural life. As Tamale reminds us, 'the ideological domestic site of the family is a gendered space closely associated with women (albeit headed by men)'.[13] A further complexity is that sexual rights are not recognised as a separate category but are a collection of rights related to human sexuality, including bodily integrity, privacy, the spacing and timing of children and equal protection of the law.[14] In this context, a focus on individuated rights 'is not only insidious and illegitimate, but can lead to a truncated and incomplete social existence'.[15]

In response to sustained and pertinent criticism of their didactic and cultural imperialist approach to women's sexuality – and specifically FGC – Western feminists have recently worked to develop a more inclusive frame of reference for their politics. This has included recognising multiple cultural and political centres and their associated peripheries, and recognising that rights hierarchies and preferences vary – for example, acknowledging that rights to culture may appear to compete with rights to bodily integrity. In spite of the reframing of African women's agency, limitations remain in the ways in which bodily agency is characterised as either resistive to or supportive of patriarchal authority, and colonial and cultural control. This nexus is rarely more apparent than in the discourse around FGC.

Attempts to claim African women's actions in the colonial archive for feminist and other human rights-based agendas appropriate women's lives to support narratives outside these women's own historical and cultural contexts. Efforts to write women into linear, incremental narratives of rights attainment also mistakenly assume that the motivations and voices of these women exist in the archive, waiting for discovery; that is, that 'the subaltern consciousness, voice or agency can somehow be retrieved through colonial texts'.[16] Thus, the women suffer under dual narrative oppressions. First, African women are oppressed by the assumption that their voices exist to be excavated from a colonial archive that was, in fact, designed to control and silence them.[17] Second, they are read only in proto-feminist terms: even in the absence of *'explicit* feminist agency',[18] African

---

[13] Sylvia Tamale, 'The Right to Culture and the Culture of Rights: A Critical Perspective on Women's Sexual Rights in Africa', *Feminist Legal Studies*, 16 (2008), 51.
[14] *Ibid.*, 46.
[15] Oloka-Onyango and Tamale, '"The Personal is Political"', 712.
[16] Premesh Lalu, 'The Grammar of Domination and the Subjection of Agency: Colonial Texts and Modes of Evidence', Theme Issue, *History and Theory*, 39 (2000), 68.
[17] *Ibid.*, 68.
[18] Saba Mahmood, 'Feminist Theory, Embodiment and the Docile Agent: Some Reflections on the Egyptian Islamic Revival', *Cultural Anthropology*, 16:2 (2001), 206–07. Emphasis added.

women's disorderly voices and actions are read as being deliberately disruptive of patriarchal and colonial authority, and are therefore imputed to evince a 'nascent feminist consciousness'.[19] In this way, it is possible to weave historical events and actors into a narrative that culminates in progress towards familiar modern Western gender and rights goals. This appropriation of the agency of these historical women creates the possibility that Kenyan women *have always been* advocating for the kinds of rights and protections the modern human rights community now advocate for on their behalf.[20]

British reordering of African regulatory structures emphasised the kind of masculine authority to which the coloniser was accustomed, making it difficult in the postcolonial period to excavate precolonial matriarchal forms of authority. In addition to national histories of women's experience, anthropologists have studied the social organisation and ritual practice of African communities in colonial and postcolonial contexts. These studies have explored complex communal regulations[21] and ritual practices, as well as explicitly observing the gender relations evident in communities.[22] Many scholars have emphasised what they interpret as a local African preference to entrench patriarchal authority within both domestic and public arenas. Studies have often noted that men's rights are privileged in key aspects of community life, including polygynous marriages, inheritance, bride wealth, access to schooling and labour migration.[23]

Many of these anthropological studies have implicitly sought what Saba Mahmood described as 'expressions and moments of resistance that may suggest a challenge to male domination'.[24] These agentive fragments are used as evidence that women who have, for instance, become the second or third wife of a man, undergone FGC, and who may have participated in the circumcision of their girl children,[25] in

---

[19] *Ibid.*, 206–07.
[20] For a robust examination of this phenomenon in the Indian context, see Ratna Kapur, *Erotic Justice: Law and the New Politics of Postcolonialism* (London: GlassHouse, 2005).
[21] For example, Margarethe Silberschmidt, *'Women Forget that Men Are the Masters': Gender Antagonism and Socio-economic Change in Kisii District, Kenya* (Stockholm: Elanders Gotab, 1999).
[22] For instance, Henrietta L. Moore, *Space, Text and Gender: An Anthropological Study of the Marakwet of Kenya* (New York: Guilford Press, 1996); An-Magritt Jensen, 'Poverty, Gender and Fertility in Rural Kenya', *Forum for Development Studies,* 42:2 (2015), 311–32.
[23] See, for instance, Brett Shadle, 'Bridewealth and Female Consent: Marriage Disputes in African Courts, Gusiiland, Kenya', *The Journal of African History,* 44:2 (2003), 241–62; Shadle, *Girl Cases.*
[24] Mahmood, 'Feminist Theory', 206.
[25] For instance, Shraboni Patra and Rakesh Kumar Singh, 'Attitudes of Circumcised Women towards Discontinuation of Genital Cutting of their Daughters in

fact believe that these practices circumscribe female agency, bodily autonomy and sexual pleasure. A small number of later studies that seek to privilege oral history, as well as autobiographical accounts from Kenyan women, have partially succeeded in complicating these colonial and neocolonial narratives and have gone some way to restoring women's agency[26] – particularly in instances in which such agency is read as operating outside feminist expressions of agency. Mahmood offers insights into the impetus that authors have to locate the 'liberatory potentials' of women's actions, even (perhaps especially) when these actions appear to support or reinscribe their own subordination.

What is often forgotten in the search for these 'slumbering embers' of resistance is that this argument presumes the 'universality of the desire – central for liberal and progressive thought, and presupposed by the concept of resistance it authorises – to be free from relations of subordination and, for women, from structures of male domination'.[27] Thus, feminist readings are often both analytical and proscriptive, 'identifying both the situation of women within particular societies and offering a *prescription* for changing the situation of women who are understood to be marginal, subordinate, and oppressed'.[28] In order to acknowledge and contribute to countering these assumptions, I offer here what Premesh Lalu has termed a 'critical history' – that is, I take up the 'opportunity to reconstitute the field of history by addressing the sites of its production and also its practices'.[29] By examining several instances in which FGC became the focal point of larger political and cultural contests, I illustrate the tensions between coloniser and colonised and take up Lalu's challenge 'to mark ... sites [within the colonial archive] where other stories may have taken place'.[30] This frame highlights the ways in which feminist histories seek to claim women's agency for the progressive project of rights attainment, rather than situating women's actions within their own political worlds and assessing their effectiveness against their own contemporaneous political and cultural goals. It also allows for new, albeit necessarily incomplete, readings of the archive that are not tied to the excavation of feminist agency but, rather, suggest the possibility of reframing women's autonomous actions within local culturally and politically relevant narratives and assessing their success on this basis.

Kenya', *Journal of Biosocial Science*, 47:1 (2015), 45–60.
[26] Jean Davison, *Voices from Mutira: Changes in the Lives of Rural Gikuyu Women, 1910–1995* (Boulder: Lynne Rienner, 1995).
[27] Mahmood, 'Feminist Theory', 206–07.
[28] *Ibid.*, 206–07. Emphasis in original.
[29] Lalu, 'The Grammar of Domination', 45.
[30] *Ibid.*, 68.

A great deal of work has been undertaken to acknowledge the effects of the colonial encounter on Kenyan women[31] and to include the perspectives of women in the historical and cultural record. These histories counter the masculine and disembodied history which characterises the great majority of historical accounts of the late colonial and independence periods. Centring women's experiences allows us to historicise the regulation of women's bodies and the ways in which women responded to and resisted this regulation on their own terms. Frustratingly, this excellent literature and its abiding focus on women's bodies in order to reclaim their voices can have the paradoxical effect of narrowing the scope of women's historical presence. The first reclamation and acknowledgement of women's resistance through asserting their bodily and intellectual integrity can be productively disruptive. However, the repetition of this move can imply that this embodied resistance is *the most significant way* in which women have resisted oppression. As argued above, while women typically escape their bodies, men rarely inhabit theirs. In focusing on women's bodies as sites of political and cultural contest, we should avoid essentialising this gendered framing.[32] The issue of embodiment also speaks to the quality of citizenship that women experience. Women who seek public office in Kenya (see Chapter 6) are frequently intimidated and controlled by threats and insults directed at their bodies, imputed desires, maternal and wifely responsibilities, and intellectual capacities. The emphasis on the materiality of bodies may have unintended consequences for modern policy and advocacy platforms that continue to focus almost entirely on bodily manifestations of disadvantages for women – for instance, reproductive and sexual health and exposure to physical violence – while the complexity of women's political action has not often permeated modern human rights discourses.

Modern rights-based approaches predominantly, and frequently ahistorically, focus on the undisputed burdens that Kenyan women bear rather than on creating a space for women's agency to be acknowledged on its own terms. Further, modern human rights discourses seek to provide answers from *within* their self-generated, internationalised

---

[31] For example, Tabitha Kanogo, *African Womanhood in Colonial Kenya 1900–1950* (London: James Currey, 1987), 79; Claire C. Robertson, 'Grassroots in Kenya: Women, Genital Mutilation and Collective Action 1920–1990', *Signs: Journal of Women in Culture and Society,* 21:3 (1996), 615–42; Susan Pedersen, 'National Bodies, Unspeakable Acts: The Sexual Politics of Colonial Policy-making', *Journal of Modern History,* 63:4 (1991), 647–80.

[32] As Luce Irigaray has argued, 'men are distanced from their bodies' in building a public world that is 'further and further removed from their relation to the corporeal': Luce Irigaray, *The Irigaray Reader,* ed. Margaret Whitford (Massachusetts: Blackwell Publishers, 1995), 49.

rights history rather than drawing strength and knowledge from the large variety of examples and styles of vernacular and contemporaneous women's agency and modes of resistance. This inability to appreciate women's agency and priorities in demanding rights and services is pervasive, as is the lack of recognition of the innovative ways women have demanded, and continue to demand, equality in the modern push for women's rights access.

While women have resisted the colonial regime in several ways, the following examples demonstrate that these modes of resistance are complicated by their desire to preserve their cultural identities not only *in opposition* to colonial governance, but *in spite of it*. These aims situate women's agency outside the simple duality of colonial support or resistance and compel us to develop frames of agency that do not rely on the liberal rights project for legitimacy.

'Something savage and barbaric, worthy of only heathens who live in perpetual sin under the influence of the Devil': A note on female genital cutting

There is prodigious international literature on rituals and typologies of FGC. Much of this work attempts to quantify the physiological implications for women who undergo circumcision in terms of maternal health outcomes and childbirth complications. Far fewer studies have directly addressed the sexual pleasure of women who undergo a circumcision experience – or, indeed, the sexual desire and experiences of African women more broadly,[33] – despite the fact that a central claim of the human rights case against FGC is the loss of sensation and an often assumed diminution in the experience of sexual pleasure.[34] My purpose here is not to reiterate these debates but, rather, to examine these contests around FGC in Kenya as instances in which women's agency is explicit, although often manifested in political frames that are not based on a foundation of modern gender rights. These contests are central to the resistance of

---

[33] With the notable exceptions of Nana Darkoa Sekyiamah, *The Sex Lives of African Women* (London: Random House, 2021) and Rachel Spronk's work, including, *Ambiguous Pleasures: Sexuality and Middle Class Self-Perceptions in Nairobi* (Oxford: Berghahn, 2012) and 'Female Sexuality in Nairobi: Flawed or Favoured?' *Culture, Health & Sexuality*, 7:3 (2005), 267–77.

[34] Lori Leonard, '"We Did It for Pleasure Only": Hearing Alternative Tales of Female Circumcision', *Qualitative Inquiry*, 6:6 (2000), 212–28; Laura M. Carpenter and Heather Kettrey, '(Im)perishable Pleasure, (In)destructible Desire: Sexual Themes in U.S. and English News Coverage of Male Circumcision and Female Genital Cutting', *The Journal of Sex Research*, 52:8 (2015), 841–56.

colonial domination and reassertions of autonomous, African ethnic identities.

Four main types of female circumcision are delineated by the World Health Organization (WHO).[35]

> Type I: Partial or total removal of the clitoris and/or the prepuce (clitoridectomy).
>
> Type II: Partial or total removal of the clitoris and the labia minora with or without excision of the labia majora (excision).
>
> Type III: Narrowing of the vaginal orifice with creation of a covering seal by cutting and appositioning the labia minora and/or the labia majora with or without excision of the clitoris (infibulation).
>
> Type IV: All other harmful procedures to the female genitalia for non-medical purposes (e.g., pricking, piercing, incising, scraping and cauterisation).

Sylvia Tamale has written persuasively on the eurocentrism of the WHO's guidelines and the deliberate ignorance of African women's perspectives in the formulation of the classification of FGC. Tamale took particular offence to Type IV in the classification,[36] arguing that the Ganda customs of genital modification (such as stretching the labia majora) contribute to the health, wellbeing and identity of Baganda women.[37] However, other African scholars have argued that genital modifications other than cutting have also been reported by African women to limit or constrain their sexual expression.[38]

Rates of circumcision are always difficult to ascertain.[39] Tabitha Kanogo reports that during the colonial period, FGC was practised by 'Kikuyu, Embu, Meru, Elgeyo, Nandi, Kipsigis, Okiek and Terik communities, among others'.[40] In the modern period, it is estimated that 20–28 per cent of Kenyan women have undergone some form of FGC (about 12.4 million women).[41] Prevalence varies greatly across

---

[35] World Health Organization (WHO), 'Classification of Female Genital Mutilation', *Sexual and Reproductive Health,* 3 February 2020, www.who.int/newsroom/fact-sheets/detail/female-genital-mutilation [accessed 26 August 2021].
[36] *Ibid.*
[37] Tamale, 'The Right to Culture', 47–69.
[38] Mathabo Khau, 'Exploring Sexual Customs: Girls and the Politics of Elongating the Inner Labia', *Agenda: Empowering Women for Gender Equity,* 23:79 (2009), 30–37.
[39] Ian Askew, 'Methodological Issues in Measuring the Impact of Interventions against Female Genital Cutting', *Culture, Health and Sexuality,* 7:5 (2005), 463–77.
[40] Kanogo, *African Womanhood in Colonial Kenya,* 79.
[41] Lillian Mwanri and Glory Joy Gatwiri, 'Injured Bodies, Damaged Lives: Experiences and Narratives of Kenyan Women with Obstetric Fistula and Female

50 Reimagining the Gendered Nation

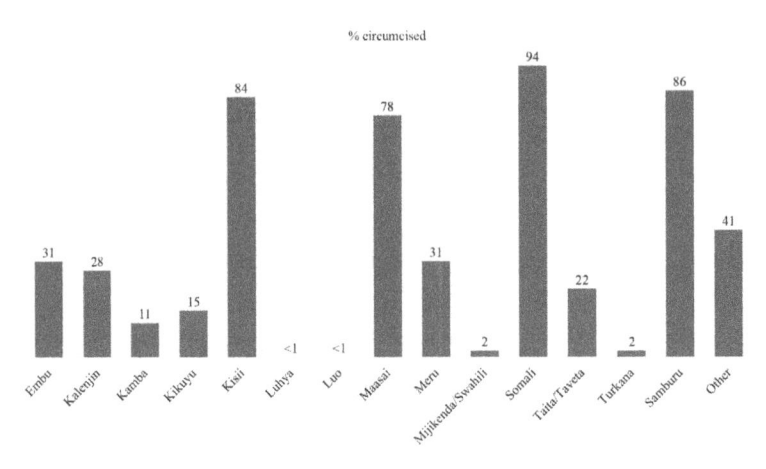

Figure 2 Rate of female genital cutting among women aged 15–49, by ethnic group in Kenya (Kenya Demographic and Health Survey, 2014, 333).

ethnic groups in Kenya and is also affected by religious affiliation. For instance, the Kenyan Somali ethnic group retain high rates of infibulation, whereas the Gĩkũyũ and other Christian ethnic groups that have traditionally circumcised as part of their initiation rites have, in general, gradually reduced the prevalence of female circumcision, although rates of male circumcision remain high.[42] The most recent Kenya Demographic and Health Survey (2014)[43] reported that the prevalence of FGC is based on intersecting ethnic and religious identities.

Significantly, the United Nations Children's Fund (UNICEF)'s data summary on FGM lists 'ethnic group with highest prevalence (98 per cent), ethnic group with lowest prevalence (0.2 per cent)' and then the rates of circumcision among religiously affiliated Kenyans: 'Muslim (51 per cent), no religion (33 per cent), Roman Catholic (22 per cent) and other Christians (18 per cent)'.[44] What is not clear from these sta-

---

Genital Mutilation/Cutting', *Reproductive Health,* 14:38 (2017), 1–11; United Nations Fund for Population Activities (UNFPA) and United Nations International Children's Emergency Fund (UNICEF), *UNFPA/UNICEF Joint Programme on Female Genital Mutilation (FGM) in Kenya – Accelerating Change 2014–2017* (2017), www.unfpa.org/publications/unfpa-unicef-joint-programme-female-genital-mutilationcutting-accelerating-change [accessed 10 August 2021].

[42] This is the result of a programme to increase the rates of male circumcision: Jennifer Galbraith *et al.* 'Status of Voluntary Medical Male Circumcision in Kenya: Findings from 2 Nationally Representative Surveys in Kenya, 2007 and 2012', *Journal of Acquired Immune Deficiency Syndrome,* 66 (2014), 37–45.

[43] *Kenya Demographic and Health Survey 2014,* 333.

[44] UNICEF, *Kenya: Statistical Profile on Female Genital Mutilation/Cutting* (2020).

tistical analyses is the correlation between particular ethnic groups, their religious affiliation *and* their relationship to the Kenyan state. For instance, Kenyan Somalis on the border with Somalia are also Muslim and have experienced decades of abuse and mistreatment following their unsuccessful bid for more than 100,000 square miles of historically Somali-occupied territory (including Garissa, Mandera and Wajir) to be united with Somalia in the last days of the Kenya Colony.[45] The concerted campaign against Somali Kenyans has continued throughout the independence period, characterised by mass atrocities committed by Kenyan state security forces and a sustained and deliberate lack of infrastructure and development funding.[46] This situation has been exacerbated by the increase in cross-border terrorist attacks perpetrated by Somali nationals in recent years.[47]

Of the 28 per cent of Kenyan women who have been circumcised in the modern period, according to the Kenya Demographic and Health Survey 2014, 8 per cent have undergone infibulation – the most severe form of the operation – which involves the:

> narrowing of the vaginal orifice with creation of a covering seal by cutting and appositioning the labia minora and/or the labia majora, with or without excision of the clitoris (infibulation) ... Infibulation is most common among girls whose mothers are Muslim (13 percent), have no education (11 percent), or are themselves infibulated (25 percent).[48]

Academic and policy literature continues to focus on strategies to reduce, and eventually eradicate, the practice in all its forms.[49] It is interesting to note that, while adult male circumcision is being promoted in Kenya, because it contributes to a reduction in the rates of HIV

---

[45] Alphonso A. Castagno, 'The Somali–Kenyan Controversy: Implications for the Future', *Journal of Modern African Studies*, 2:2 (1964), 165–88; David E. Kromm, 'Irredentism in Africa: The Somali–Kenya Boundary Dispute', *Transactions of the Kansas Academy of Science*, 70:3 (1967), 359–65; Jon D. Holtzman, *Killing Your Neighbours: Friendship and Violence in Northern Kenya and Beyond* (Berkeley: University of California Press, 2017), 101–06, 98, 117, 106, 121.

[46] Charles Hornsby, *Kenya: A History Since Independence* (New York: Palgrave Macmillan, 2013), 78, 97, 179, 369.

[47] 'Kenya: Garissa University Massacre', *Africa Research Bulletin: Political, Social and Cultural Series*, 52:4 (2015), 20539–41; E.S. Odhiambo et al., 'The Reprisal Attacks by Al-Shabaab against Kenya', *Journal of Defence Resources Management*, 4:2 (2013), 53–64.

[48] WHO, 'Classification of Female Genital Mutilation'.

[49] See, for instance, Sarah R. Hayford, 'Conformity and Change: Community Effects on Female Genital Cutting in Kenya', *Journal of Health and Social Behaviour*, 46 (2005), 120–40.

transmission,[50] any form of female genital modification, even that which adult women choose to undergo, is characterised as damaging and classified as a human rights violation.

'Burning their modesty like firewood': Women's bodies as sites of contestation

In the dominant narrative of the late colonial period, the issue of female circumcision was a continuing point of tension and resistance to British rule. British attempts to regulate and ultimately eradicate female circumcision were a recurring catalyst for popular protests during the early twentieth century. Three colonial instances are examined here: the Harry Thuku Riot (1922), the Female Circumcision Controversy (1928–1931) and the Ngaitana ('I will circumcise myself')[51] movement (1956).[52] These cases are all important for their contribution to African resistance to colonial rule, which culminated in the Mau Mau uprising (1952–1960). The earliest of these, the Thuku riot, is now understood to be the beginning of Gĩkũyũ women's 'participation in public arena politics'.[53] Cora Ann Presley has argued that between the Thuku riot in 1922 and the 1930s, early women nationalists began recruiting thousands of other women to their cause.[54] This momentum, and the rising political consciousness of African women, led them to demand better representation in African political organisations and to establish their own.

---

[50] Melinda Pavin et al., *Assessing Two Strategies for Expanding Coverage of Adult Male Circumcision in Nyanza Province, Kenya* (New York: EngenderHealth, 2011), 6.
[51] From the KiMîîrú language, a collection of dialects spoken by Ameru people.
[52] Although the third case study addresses an instance in which Meru girls responded to the ban on circumcision in the final months of the Mau Mau resistance, the history and commentary drawn upon in this chapter is predominantly focused on the experiences and political organisation of the Gĩkũyũ community. This is because of the early and continued contact that Gĩkũyũ communities had with the British colonial regime, the centrality of Kenyatta and his own promotion of the Gĩkũyũ identity as integral to Kenya's independence mythmaking, the fact that at the time the Gĩkũyũ were a community which circumcised women, and the comparative sizes of the Gĩkũyũ, Meru, and Embu communities, in which the Gĩkũyũ were (and remain) a clear numerical majority.
[53] Cora Ann Presley, 'The Mau Mau Rebellion, Kikuyu Women, and Social Change', Special Issue: Current Research on African Women, *Canadian Journal of African Studies*, 22:3 (1988), 507.
[54] Ibid., 508.

As Mau Mau became a guerrilla movement, women were integral to maintaining the supply chain to the forest and information gathering, and were also frontline fighters and prisoners of the colonial regime.[55] Presley also notes that women officiated and participated in oathing ceremonies. Women's participation in public politics, as well as the administration and taking of oaths, was previously alien to Gĩkũyũ custom, but women 'joined the nationalist associations to improve their economic status, to gain access to the political process, to further their education, and to abet the return of alienated land'.[56] As Muthoni wa Gachie, member of the Kikuyu Central Association (KCA) and the KAU explained in an interview with Presley, 'we were fighting so we would know how to become independent'.[57] The ethnic groups that were most involved with Mau Mau were the similarly linguistically and geographically contiguous Christian Gĩkũyũ, Meru and Embu communities, groups which also traditionally included female circumcision as part of their initiation rites. Each case study explores the relationships between circumcision and initiation rites, as well as strategies that resisted colonial rule.

Female initiation through *mariika* – circumcision organised in generational age-sets (Gĩkũyũ) – engendered solidarity by enduring the ritual cutting and healing process together:[58] 'the history of the tribe, and one's place in it, are written into the body through circumcision and clitoridectomy. The ritual teaches, the scar reminds'.[59] Age groups acted as associations for mutual aid; they also served to enforce the distinctions of status and behaviour prescribed for their members at different stages of life.[60] Thus, women often understandably identified clitoridectomy as the 'most important – if also the most painful – experience of their lives'.[61] However, although initiation fostered unity across gendered age-sets, as Lynn Thomas argues, 'reproductive rituals and processes were as much about constituting and enforcing differences among females as creating a shared sense of womanhood'.[62] Thus, it

[55] See, for instance, Caroline Elkins, *Imperial Reckoning: The Untold Story of Britain's Gulag in Kenya* (New York: Henry Holt and Company, 2005); Presley, 'The Mau Mau Rebellion'; Katherine Bruce-Lockhart, 'Unsound Minds and Broken Bodies: The Detention of "Hardcore" Mau Mau Women at Kamiti and Gitamayu Detention Camps in Kenya, 1954–1960', *Journal of Eastern African Studies*, 8:4 (2014), 590–608; Lynn M. Thomas, *Politics of the Womb: Women, Reproduction and the State in Kenya* (Berkeley: University of California Press, 2003), 84.
[56] Presley, 'The Mau Mau Rebellion', 507–08.
[57] Ibid., 508.
[58] Robertson, 'Grassroots in Kenya', 622.
[59] Shaw, *Colonial Inscriptions*, 63.
[60] Kanogo, *African Womanhood in Colonial Kenya*, 79.
[61] Pedersen, 'National Bodies, Unspeakable Acts', 649.
[62] Thomas, *Politics of the Womb*, 17.

is important to note that these organisational structures also operate through exclusion and hierarchy.

Focusing on FGC centres women's agency by examining the ways in which Kenyan women deploy traditional forms of protest. The case studies also illuminate the assumptions of much of the feminist analysis of women's agency and strategies of political engagement, which seek to frame women's agency within recognisable opposition to, or rejection of, patriarchy through the reclamation of ritual practices as modes of resistance. Kenyan sociologist and historian Wairimu Njamibi explains that:

> becoming a woman or man in Gĩkũyũ isociety was not determined by birth but by a series of initiation ritual markings that would continue to take place throughout one's lifetime, beginning with *irua* (circumcision) ... in this sense, *irua ria atumia na anake*[63] played an important cultural and political role of situating both women and men in various social and political positions as both members of their society and as guardians of their history and culture inscribed through this body practice.[64]

Mahmood has outlined the limitations of this approach, arguing that focusing on whether women are undermining systems of male domination encumbers the process of analysis by framing it as a 'binary of resistance and subordination', and that it 'is also insufficiently attentive to motivations, desires, and goals that are not necessarily captured by these terms'.[65] Exploring these more expansive frames, which include non-liberal modes of agency, allows us to examine the uses of African women's bodies in larger discourses, as well as the positionality of women as subjects and agents within contests over their bodies.

Critically, some of the best-known battles over the eradication of female circumcision in Kenya have been contested primarily between the Gĩkũyũ, Meru and Embu ethnic groups and the British colonial government and missionaries. Thus, as one of the most visible of the ethnic groups to the colonial government, and one of the most vocal within the colonial record, the history of FGC in Kenya is predominantly the story of circumcision practices among the Gĩkũyũ. Here again, a Gĩkũyũ-centric narrative of resistance to an attack on the integrity of intergener-

---

[63] *Irua ria atumia na anake* denotes the initiation ritual of becoming women and men among the Gĩkũyũ people: *irua* refers to an initiation ceremony, while *atumia* translates as 'women' and *anake* is 'men'. Note that the word for initiation itself does not carry a gender. Wairimú Ngarúiya Njambi, 'Irua Atumia and Anti-Colonial Struggles Among the Gĩkũyũ of Kenya: A Counter Narrative on 'Female Genital Mutilation', *Critical Sociology*, 33:4 (2007), 691.
[64] Njambi, 'Irua Atumia and Anti-Colonial Struggles Among the Gĩkũyũ of Kenya', 696.
[65] Mahmood, 'Feminist Theory', 209.

ational communal identity formation is taken up as a proto-nationalist narrative. The centrality of the Gĩkũyũ perspective on FGC here results from two key ethnographic studies of the Gĩkũyũ community: Louis Leakey's *The Southern Kikuyu before 1903* (published posthumously in 1974) and Jomo Kenyatta's ethnography of the Gĩkũyũ people, *Facing Mount Kenya* (1938), which includes detailed descriptions of FGC based on accounts of his aunt, who was an 'operator'.[66] Indeed, Kenyatta claimed personal experiential expertise in every aspect of Gĩkũyũ life about which he wrote, describing himself as a 'member of the warrior class ... [and] the leader of his [initiate] age group', as well as being proficient in the practice of magic rites, since his grandfather was a 'seer and a magician, and in traveling around with him and carrying his bag of equipment [Kenyatta] served a kind of apprenticeship in the principles of the art'.[67] As Wambui Mwangi has explained, *Facing Mount Kenya* 'is so iconic in post-colonial Gĩkũyũ culture that now it does not so much describe as generate Gĩkũyũ identity'.[68] This work, then, is an account that has become not only a record of Gĩkũyũ's cultural life but also the authoritative statement of Gĩkũyũ identity.

It is pertinent to address Kenyatta's attention to clitoridectomy in *Facing Mount Kenya* given that, as Shaw has observed, he 'devotes considerably less attention to women, and to sexual morality' than does the canonical paleoanthropologist and archaeologist Louis Leakey, 'making women almost disappear except for the discussion of clitoridectomy and as their roles and statuses intersect with those of men'.[69] In his defence of African culture against colonial attitudes towards African life, Kenyatta uncritically took on the British characterisation of women's roles and cultural place in an attempt to elevate African women to the 'civilised' status of British women, explaining that 'women are essentially the home makers, as without them there is no home in the Gikuyu [*sic*.] sense of social life'.[70] As explored below in the section, 'The Female Circumcision Controversy', Kenyatta's position on the promotion or eradication of the practice was guided by a cynical political pragmatism, and not at all by his personal views. Shaw argued that Kenyatta's early 'gradualist, pro-choice position' is in stark contrast to his pro-clitoridectomy argument in *Facing Mount Kenya*, when the need for Gĩkũyũ solidarity and mobilising the rural Gĩkũyũ base had become critical to the success of the independence movement.[71]

[66] L.S.B. Leakey, *The Southern Kikuyu before 1903* (London: Academic Press, 1977); Jomo Kenyatta, *Facing Mount Kenya* (New York: Random House, 1962), xix.
[67] *Ibid.*, xix–xx.
[68] Mwangi, 'Silence is a Woman'.
[69] Shaw, *Colonial Inscriptions*, 63.
[70] Kenyatta, *Facing Mount Kenya*, 180.
[71] Shaw, *Colonial Inscriptions*, 63.

'You take my dress and give me your trousers – you men are cowards!' Mary Muthoni Nyajiru and the Harry Thuku Riot[72]

The increasing pressures of excessive taxation and abusive labour practices in the early years of the twentieth century galvanised opposition to the British regime across urban and rural African populations. Key issues for Harry Thuku and the East African Association (EAA) included fighting the extension of forced labour to women, a policy driven by the British settler demand for labour to develop their expanding land holdings, and which further exposed African women and girls to rape and sexual exploitation by African officials when the women were working British land holdings, or while they were away from their villages on work parties.[73] After a concerted African campaign, forced labour for women was abolished in 1921. In the latter months of 1921, Thuku was involved in an incident in Pangani, a village in Nairobi, that resulted in police shooting into the crowd, killing twenty-five people. Thuku travelled to Murang'a where his supporters at the Anglican Missionary Society hailed him as their 'living God' and characterised the local chiefs as 'Judas' for denying Thuku support.[74] By the beginning of 1922, Thuku was encouraging men to burn their *kipande*s and only pay a fraction of the required taxation. Thuku had quickly become a direct threat to colonial rule and was arrested on 14 March 1922 and incarcerated at Nairobi police station.[75]

---

[72] The authoritative account of the participation of women in what has become known as the 'Harry Thuku Riot' remains Audrey Wipper's thorough and still fruitful gendered analysis of the riot and its fatal consequences: Audrey Wipper, 'Kikuyu Women and the Harry Thuku Disturbances: Some Uniformities of Female Militancy', *Africa*, 59:3 (1989), 300–37; and Audrey Wipper, 'Riot and Rebellion among African Women: Three Examples of Women's Political Clout', in Jean O'Barr (ed.), *Perspectives on Power: Women in Africa, Asia, and Latin America* (Durham: Duke University Press, 1982), pp. 50–72. However, the riot appears only rarely in later work dealing with Kenyan history or Kenyan women's history – perhaps most notably in Claire Robertson's 1997 book, *Trouble Showed the Way*. Wipper's cogent argument – that women's leadership had a decisive effect on the outcome of the Harry Thuku Disturbances – has not penetrated later academic work on women's agency during the late colonial period. For instance, Kanogo did not mention the disturbances in her seminal history of Kenyan women, *African Womanhood in Colonial Kenya 1900–1950*. Therefore, the narrative presented here is largely drawn from Wipper's and Robertson's work and supplemented by my own archival research.
[73] Wipper, 'Kikuyu Women', 303–05.
[74] Bruce Berman and John Lonsdale, *Unhappy Valley: Conflict in Kenya & Africa, Book Two: Violence and Ethnicity* (Nairobi: Heinemann Kenya, 1992), 380.
[75] Wipper, 'Kikuyu Women', 303–05.

News of Thuku's arrest promoted the EAA to call a strike for the following day, and a crowd of several thousand workers presented at the police station, prayed for Thuku for a time and, at the request of the protest leaders, most then dispersed. The next day, the crowd grew to between seven and eight thousand people, including 'a large party of [probably 150] native women'.[76] We do not know what brought these women to Nairobi. Some scholars think they may have been sex workers, and certainly many women in Nairobi were engaging in sex work, prompting Kikuyu Central Association General Secretary George Ndegwa to exclaim in a letter to the EAA that the women were 'burn[ing] their MODESTY LIKE FIREWOOD'.[77] However, these women may also have been beer brewers protesting the new prohibition on private beer brewing, and the establishment of a municipal brewery in 1921. In either case, these women were in Nairobi to work.[78]

A delegation of African men invited to speak with the Colonial Secretary returned and assured the crowd that Thuku was not being mistreated and would be given a fair hearing before any decision was made. African and colonial sources generally agree that at this critical juncture the women protesting Thuku's arbitrary detention became agitated, expressing their frustration at the continued incarceration of Thuku and accusing the male delegation of accepting bribes.[79] As the Nairobi Resident Magistrate B.A. Crean testified at the coronial inquest into the subsequent riot deaths:

> the repeated warnings to disperse, not only from Government Officers but from their own leaders, had been disregarded, and the excitations of agitators and the taunts of the women had by then raised the ugliest passions ... the crowd had got up to move off after being addressed by the deputation, and I have no doubt would have done so had it not been for the unfortunate interference by the women of the crowd.[80]

The Director of Public Works reported that while the rest of the crowd were 'very orderly', 'the women made a great noise ... [and] very slowly the women made towards the corrugated fence. They came to within a yard of the bayonets'.[81] But an African man, Job Muchuchu, an eyewitness to the riot, founding member of the East African Associa-

---

[76] Wipper, 'Riot and Rebellion among African Women', 10.
[77] Berman and Lonsdale, *Unhappy Valley*, 386, quoting KCA member George Ndegwa (capitalisation in the original).
[78] Robertson, *Trouble Showed the Way*, 36. See also Janet Bujra, 'Ethnicity and Religion: A Case Study from Pumwani, Nairobi', Institute of African Studies Discussion Paper 13 (October 1970).
[79] Wipper, 'Riot and Rebellion among African Women', 8.
[80] Wipper, 'Kikuyu Women', 314–15.
[81] *Ibid.*, 315.

tion and politician from Mary Nyanjiru's area of Fort Hall,[82] described the incident differently. When the delegation of six that spoke with the Colonial Secretary

> returned at mid-day, they spoke to the crowd, telling them that the Government had promised to give Thuku a fair trial and that they should now disperse. But the temper of the crowd was by now too high. They accused the delegation of having been bribed, and the women in particular became very excited. Mary Muthoni Nyanjiru ... leapt to her feet, pulled her dress right up over her shoulders and shouted to the men: 'You take my dress and give me your trousers. You men are cowards. What are you waiting for? Our leader is in there. Let's get him'. Hundreds of women trilled their *ngemi* [a high-pitched cry] in approbation and from that moment on trouble was probably inevitable.
>
> Mary and the others pushed on until the bayonets of the rifles were pricking at their throats, and then the firing started. Mary was one of the first to die.[83]

Mary Nyanjiru was one of four women and eighteen men to die, with a further twenty-eight people injured.[84] The official sources agree that there was no order to fire. It appears the first shot was fired in a scuffle between a protestor and the commander of the *askaris* (native police) guarding the prison grounds. This apparently precipitated spontaneous volleys from the police, who had been on duty for more than twenty-four consecutive hours at the time of the disturbance.[85]

Like many stories of Kenyan women's agency and political engagement, Mary Nyanjiru is only a historical object lesson, so little is known of her life before Thuku's arrest; the sum of her contribution is taken to be these last hours of her life, rising to prominence moments before being shot. In African retellings, Nyanjiru became emblematic of the unity and bravery of African resistance.[86] Recalling the incident later,

---

[82] Wipper, 'Riot and Rebellion among African Women', 10.
[83] Wipper, 'Kikuyu Women', 315.
[84] Wipper, 'Riot and Rebellion among African Women', 11.
[85] *Ibid.*, 9–10.
[86] Nyanjiru's demand that men act was one of several such acts led by women across the colony. Moraa wa Ngiti was an elderly prophetess of the Abagusii ethnic group, who urged resistance to alien rule and protested the repeated confiscation of Gusii cattle by the colonial administration. Moraa was famous for 'denigrating the valour of young men who seem to be afraid of a single white man'. She was thought to be the power behind her foster son, the warrior Otenyo, who tried to assassinate then District Commissioner G.A.S. Northcote and the Assistant District Commissioner in 1908 following a series of violent and punitive raids instigated by Northcote against the Abagusii. This plan reflected the belief that Northcote was *in fact* the British administration and that his death would topple the colonial regime: Robert M. Maxon, *Conflict and Accommodation in Western Kenya: The Gusii and the British* (Rutherford:

Thuku noted that 'the death of the woman Mary showed that women were in the forefront of Kenya's fight for freedom'.[87]

Reports of the Thuku riot reflected a prevalent assumption – especially in this early period of anticolonial Kenyan resistance – that African women were not politically active; therefore, their behaviour was frequently attributed to the agency and direction of others. For instance, *The Times*'s correspondent in Nairobi reported that:

> the mob advanced toward the police palisades waving flags and shouting. The men pushed their womenfolk in front of them, expecting that this would prevent the police from firing. Upon seeing the King's African Rifles approaching, the mob rushed the palisades, though they had been previously warned of what the consequences would be. Fire was then opened with ball cartridge.[88]

However, there is agreement in the eyewitness sources that the women were instrumental in escalating the situation and were vocal in their criticism of the nominated male delegates. That 'the women were seen as heroines in African eyes' is evident in the song *Kanyegenuri*, which commemorated the events of the riot and the bravery of Nyanjiru.[89] Wipper has suggested that it is possible that the audacity and unity demonstrated by the women at the Thuku riot may, in part, have been the result of an oathing ritual that:

> undoubtedly raised the women's level of political consciousness and helped create the discipline and unity required to spearhead the rescue attempt ... The oathing of women was a step in the direction of treating women as equals rather than as juveniles.[90]

Importantly, uncircumcised men or women could not be oathed. They had not undergone the cultural training of the physical ordeal of becoming adult; therefore, they were not fit to be involved in tribal business.

Then there is the rather striking scene of a woman with her skirt up around her shoulders yelling insults at the male delegation in front of a large crowd. Nyanjiru was invoking the Gĩkũyũ insult of *guturamira ng'ania* ('the curse of nakedness', or 'showing your mother's secrets').[91]

Fairleigh Dickinson University Press, 1989), 30–31. See also Wanyiri Kihoro, *The Price of Freedom: The Story of Political Resistance in Kenya* (Nairobi: MvuleAfrica, 2005), 15.

[87] Wipper, 'Kikuyu Women', 316.
[88] 'Fatal Rioting At Nairobi', *The Times* (London, 18 March 1922), 10.
[89] Wipper, 'Kikuyu Women', 316. A detailed search was conducted for the text of the *Kanyeguri* in the Kenya National Archive, academic databases, printed scholarly materials and online without success.
[90] Wipper, 'Kikuyu Women', 318.
[91] Alexandra Tibbetts, 'Mamas Fighting for Freedom in Kenya', *Africa Today*, 41:4 (1994), 36–37.

It is only available to women and involves displaying one's genitals to the person or thing cursed.[92] The historian Audrey Wipper explains that:

> the gesture indicated the end of social intercourse with the person or persons thus insulted, or, in the case of a man, the women's refusal to any longer recognise his authority. Only on rare occasions when extremely provoked did women use this curse.[93]

Significantly, this curse was not available to all women; motherhood in this case is a political resource when combined with the respect accorded to older women.[94] Robertson has argued that the impact of the act 'rested on the reference to women's reproductive power that men would be betraying the source who gave them life if they continued to misbehave'. *Guturamira ng'ania* thus demonstrates the 'paradoxical nature of women's power, that avoidance and sexual taboos could be reversed to confer power on those who are normally regarded as inferior ... [and] that initiation provided girls with an induction into how to exercise authority independent of men, or in limited cases, over men'.[95]

Authority for both men and women within Gĩkũyũ society was derived from the combination of circumcision and oathing. To take an oath, one must have gone through initiation or *irua ria atumia na anake*. Even as part of the *irua* process, the new initiates had to take an oath committing them to a code of behaviour to which they vowed to adhere as Gĩkũyũ adults. Wipper reports that Mary Nyanjiru's stepdaughter, Elizabeth Waruiru, had taken an EAA oath the night prior to the demonstration, and it is likely that Nyanjiru was oathed at the same

---

[92] This act of protest has continued to be deployed by Kenyan women in the postcolonial period, most notably during the successful deployment of *guturamira ng'ania* by women in 1992 at the march at Freedom Corner in Nairobi to free political prisoners held by the Moi regime. For an authoritative account, see Tibbetts, 'Mamas Fighting for Freedom in Kenya', 27–48: 'On the last day of February 1992, a group of rural, elderly, Kikuyu women descended on Nairobi with a potent demand. Empowered by a tradition of female activism and collective activity, a group of mothers of political prisoners acted on principles of care and justice and strategically employed motherhood to demand the release of their sons, who were imprisoned in October 1990 for advocating multipartyism. In order to reach their aim they staged a hunger strike and three elderly mothers stripped ('*guturamira ng'ania*', to curse a person by stripping) when they were attacked by the police. The Mamas' protest was an important causal factor in the release of the prisoners in June 1992 and January 1993. The author argues that although the experience of mothering shapes what issues women choose to address and the ways they express them, the motivating force of women's political action is not limited to the "care ethic". The mothers also made rights-oriented arguments and exhibited concern for abstract principles such as justice and freedom'.
[93] Wipper, 'Kikuyu Women', 319.
[94] Robertson, *Trouble Showed the Way*, 36.
[95] *Ibid.*, 244–45.

time. Given the support Nyanjiru received from women in the crowd following her demonstration, and that 'the women trilled their battle cry and followed Nyanjiru's lead as she advanced toward the police guarding the station',[96] it would appear that she was indeed accessing a familiar and accepted method of insult and protest. Thus, although Nyanjiru was the only woman named of the estimated 150 women who attended the protest, we know she was a leader within her community and therefore initiated.

The protest was initially aimed not at the colonial authorities but at the Gĩkũyũ men, leaders and participants who were losing the stomach for the fight. Although historians who have examined this incident – Audrey Wipper and Claire Robertson in particular – have concluded that these women were exercising their growing political influence in Nairobi, Nyanjiru's protest was a contingent one: 'the women were trying to force the men to play their proper role in making the protest successful'.[97] Women insulting 'men who behave like women' has a long tradition in Kenya, which has continued into the postcolonial period. Indeed, recent and prominent examples of such 'feminising' insults occurred during the 2007 post-election violence. Wanjiku Kihato has argued that 'the[se] slights go right to the heart of understanding how gender influences the production and reproduction of violence' and demonstrate women's complicity in 'fuelling violence even when they are not actively involved in it themselves'.[98] The audacity of Nyanjiru also spoke to the fragility of Gĩkũyũ men, who were already threatened by the loss of ancestral lands and economic power – the 'idea of an ordered masculine tribe was under threat from unruly women'.[99] The fact that women were moving to Nairobi to work – in some cases as sex workers – was more evidence of the inability of Gĩkũyũ men to financially support their families.

The colonial government referred to these labour-seeking, urban, migrant women as 'detribalised natives' – that is, Africans who were disconnected from their communities and culture. Gĩkũyũ men had already demonstrated their disdain for these women; indeed, the men of the KCA had:

> anointed themselves guardians of Gĩkũyũ 'seed', alarmed that women in Nairobi were breaking what seems to have been an entirely new expectation of patriotic Gĩkũyũ motherhood … The behaviours of Nairobi women threatened male power and Gĩkũyũ posterity, politics

[96] Wipper, 'Kikuyu Women', 318–19.
[97] Robertson, *Trouble Showed the Way*, 36.
[98] Wanjiku Kihato, '"Go Back and Tell Them Who the Real Men Are!" Gendering Our Understanding of Kibera's Post-Election Violence', *International Journal of Conflict and Violence*, 9:1 (2015), 19.
[99] Berman and Lonsdale, *Unhappy Valley*, 3.

and production. Delinquent women shamed Gĩkũyũ men. Men who could not control women were heathen, *acenji*.[100]

Nyanjiru was speaking and acting in front of a number of audiences. The public record of the riot perpetuated the assumption that women are stripped of agency in all circumstances, even where a woman was universally reported as the instigator of the events that followed. Nyanjiru mobilised her cultural authority through being initiated, in conjunction with her new, modern authority as a migrant worker in the city. She created this space to speak, not to accrue further power to herself, but to convince people she felt *should* be the true leaders – the male delegation – to lead the protestors to more satisfactory action. The complex mix of traditional and modern authority that Nyanjiru mobilised is emblematic of the ways in which Kenyan women would move into the late colonial period and demonstrates the reductive nature of arguments which seek to claim such actions as evidence of a nascent women's rights movement in the late colonial period.

The Female Circumcision Controversy

Only four years later, female initiation, and female circumcision in particular, came to explicitly occupy the colony's political consciousness. In 1926, in response to pressure from missionary groups and 'some level of official concern about the prevalent practice of clitoridectomy', governors of the East African dependencies met to develop a strategy to mitigate the practice. The governors favoured a shift from the 'brutal' practice of removing 'the entire external genitalia' to 'simply clitoridectomy [a] ... "less brutal" form'.[101] The decision was adopted by the meeting, and regulations were circulated to native councils. Three years later, in 1929, the decision by some missions to enforce this regulation by 'refusing communion to all Christians unwilling to forswear the practice led to the largest outbreak of popular protest among the Kikuyu that the British Government had yet faced'.[102]

The 'Female Circumcision Controversy' began when three key Protestant missions issued a formal declaration that they required all of their African followers to sign a simultaneous disavowal of the practice of female circumcision and of membership of the proto-nationalist KCA, whose members were typically educated, urban Gĩkũyũ,

---

[100] *Ibid.*, 386. Note that Mary Njeri Kinyanjui translates *acenji* as 'illiterate', in opposition to *athomi*, 'mission educated elite': Mary Njeri Kinyanjui, *African Markets and the Utu-Ubuntu Business Model: A perspective on Economic Informality in Nairobi* (Cape Town: African Minds, 2019), 80.
[101] Pedersen, 'National Bodies, Unspeakable Acts', 647.
[102] *Ibid.*

including their secretary, the young Jomo Kenyatta. The African response was swift. The KCA argued that the 'ban on female circumcision was but the beginning of an assault on all Gĩkũyũ traditions'.[103] The immediate result of the declaration was a massive boycott of mission schools and churches; 'one missionary society reported they had lost 90 per cent of the congregation and 80 per cent of its students' and, shortly afterwards, Gĩkũyũ leaders formed independent schools and churches.[104] Missions across the colony had been campaigning against female circumcision in Kenya for several years. The importance of this particular declaration was in the association of circumcision with membership of an African political organisation, and the simultaneous banning of both.

The KCA further politicised the circumcision issue by linking it to the land grievances of the Gĩkũyũ, suggesting that this attack on Gĩkũyũ tradition would jeopardise the tribal organisation of land – 'uncircumcised Kikuyu girls would not find husbands among the Kikuyu men and, therefore, would turn to Europeans who would not only take the women but also would take Kikuyu land'.[105] However, 'if prostitution was banned [by the colonial government] as KCA members wanted, then their president was quite willing to discuss clitoridectomy. Until whites cleaned up Nairobi their attack on female initiation could only encourage the heathendom they affected to despise'.[106] In September 1929, a missionary's refusal to grant communion to those who had not rejected circumcision sparked large demonstrations. The *Muthirigo* became a popular protest song in Gĩkũyũ areas, which illustrated 'how a defence of sexual order became entangled with a revolt of younger Kikuyus against British and their African collaborators'. The song claimed the church was collaborating with the colonial government to 'corrupt Kikuyu customs, to seduce young women, and to take away the land'.[107] Indeed,

> the mission's insistence that one could not both be a good Christian and respect traditional customs struck many African Christians as hypocritical and baffling, especially when the vernacular translations of the Bible prepared by the missions themselves often used the terminology of initiation rites to describe Christian rituals.[108]

---

[103] Theodore Natsoulas, 'The Politicization of the Ban on Female Circumcision and the Rise of the Independent Schools Movement in Kenya: The KCA, the Missions and the Government', *Journal of Asian and African Studies*, 33:2 (1998), 140.
[104] *Ibid.*, 144, 137–38.
[105] *Ibid.*, 144.
[106] Berman and Lonsdale, *Unhappy Valley*, 3.
[107] Pedersen, 'National Bodies, Unspeakable Acts', 653.
[108] *Ibid.*, 652.

As many Gĩkũyũ had attended mission schools and read the Bible in their vernacular,[109] they were:

> not convinced that the mission insistence on monogamy and the abandonment of some traditional customs was essential for the practice of Christianity. They found no specific prohibition on polygamy, and, in fact, it was widespread in the Old Testament. They also discovered other 'heathen' practices such as animal sacrifice and circumcision in the Bible. The Gĩkũyũ word for circumcision *kurua* does not distinguish between male and female, and as circumcision was a part of the Christian tradition, the Gĩkũyũ felt the missions had ulterior motives for campaigning against the practice.[110]

Although the Female Circumcision Controversy was a clash of cultures, this is only one element of the conflict. The Gĩkũyũ position, expressed through the masculine KAU, was to defend the tribe at all costs against the feminine corruptions of detribalisation.[111] Jomo Kenyatta discussed the Circumcision Controversy in *Facing Mount Kenya*:

> 'a gentlemen's agreement' was reached between the Government and the missionaries. The ban on children attending the schools would be lifted, but the missionaries maintained that teachers may be only those who had denounced the custom, for they hoped that teachers with this qualification would be able to mould the children in a way favourable to the missionary attitude. People were indignant about this decision and at once demanded the right to establish their own schools where they could teach their children without interference with the group custom. The cry for schools was raised high, and the result was the foundation of Gikuyu [*sic*.] independent schools and Kareng'a schools. These schools are entirely free from missionary influence, both in educational and religious matters.[112]

Although a significant proportion of the KCA's natural constituency – educated, urban Africans – were in fact *against* female circumcision, the KCA advocated *for* it in a strategic decision that allowed them to mobilise a previously disengaged, conservative, rural base. The announcement was seen as a direct attack on the integrity of Gĩkũyũ cultural systems and values that the KCA used to its advantage, characterising the ban as a 'political conflict uniting all Gĩkũyũ against the

---

[109] Natsoulas, 'Politicization of the Ban on Female Circumcision', 144.
[110] *Ibid.*, 145; see also John Lonsdale, 'Kikuyu Christianities', *Journal of Religion in Africa*, 29:2 (1999), 206–29; Derek Peterson, 'Colonizing Language? Missionaries and Gikuyu Dictionaries, 1904–1914', *History in Africa*, 24 (1997), 257–72.
[111] Berman and Lonsdale, *Unhappy Valley*, 248.
[112] Kenyatta, *Facing Mount Kenya*, 130–31.

combined forces of British imperialism'.[113] Culture was relied upon as a reflex gesture in a moment of political advantage.

In the face of the erosion of traditional forms of cultural authority, such as the alienation of tribal lands, the establishment of 'native reserves' and restrictive taxation systems, initiation stood as one of the powerful remnants of Gĩkũyũ cultural identity and social organisation.[114] The combined ban on female circumcision and membership of the KCA reenergised the Gĩkũyũ tradition of female initiation, situating the practice and the circumcised Gĩkũyũ woman at the centre of an increasingly politically aggressive cultural nationalism.[115] Defence of *irua*, 'always the sign of a "true Gĩkũyũ" ... came to be seen as a mark of loyalty to the incipient, as yet imaginary, nation',[116] with the ritual and mark of circumcision 'a gestural and graphic inscription of ritual on the body'.[117] This new association of a precolonial, cultural practice with an expressly modern, proto-nationalist movement 'endowed this ostensibly timeless and immutable practice with new, and highly political, meanings'.[118] Simultaneously, the reinvigorated, politicised practice of *irua* demonstrated that 'even the lives of "the modern" could never be fully detached from older hierarchies rooted in local notions of gender, generation, and wealth'.[119] Thus, in the late colonial period, the ideological battle between colonial and anticolonial forces was fought primarily on the physical and figurative terrain of the body of the Gĩkũyũ woman. In this context, the cultural and organisational power of *irua* was immense.

Ngaitana: I will circumcise myself

In 1956, at the end of the Mau Mau Rebellion (although the state of Emergency was in place until 1960),[120] the Meru council of elders, Njuri Ncheke, banned female circumcision. Methodists had given up attempting to ban circumcision among the Gĩkũyũ following the disaster of the Female Circumcision Controversy in 1928–1931. The new ban in Meru was promoted by the District Commissioner J.A. Cumber as a way for the Meru to distinguish themselves from the Gĩkũyũ, and to repay the government for creating a Meru land unit, apart from the

---

[113] Pedersen, 'National Bodies, Unspeakable Acts', 662.
[114] *Ibid.*, 648.
[115] Natsoulas, 'Politicization of the Ban on Female Circumcision', 154.
[116] Pedersen, 'National Bodies, Unspeakable Acts', 663
[117] Deepak Mehta, 'Circumcision, Body, Masculinity: The Ritual Wound and Collective Violence', in Veena Das *et al.* (eds), *Violence and Subjectivity* (Berkeley: University of California Press, 2000), 80.
[118] Pedersen, 'National Bodies, Unspeakable Acts', 663.
[119] Thomas, *Politics of the Womb*, 186.
[120] *Ibid.*, 80.

Gĩkũyũ land unit, by 'setting a good example to other Tribes in Kenya who persist in the enforcement of this iniquitous Tribal Tradition'.[121]

The complexity and ambiguity of women's agency is perhaps most evident in what came to be known as the Ngaitana movement in Meru. Here, Meru girls insisted that they be circumcised because, like all African women, they had been raised to believe that initiation – which for Meru girls included circumcision – was necessary to pass through all other life stages, including marriage and motherhood. However, stripped of the ritual practices and teaching that had surrounded the ritual of circumcision for the Meru community prior to the state of Emergency, the girls of Ngaitana were, in fact, ridiculed by their own community. Interviewing Meru women in the 1990s, Lynne Thomas[122] reported that when she asked the women what they thought of the Ngaitana phenomenon, the question 'drew chuckles of laughter or, on occasion, head-shakes of knowing disapproval from those who could recall the time of the ban ... Those who remembered or learned of Ngaitana often spoke of it as a preposterous undertaking, simultaneously absurd and amusing'.[123] The source of amusement was the very idea that the girls involved could ever think that cutting their own genitals was ever going to be considered an acceptable form of initiation.

The great irony of the movement was that in their insistence that they become Meru women, these girls had in fact, committed a cultural faux pas. Without the involvement of a *mutani* (a woman trained in circumcision and other initiation rites) and her iron-wedge knife, initiation was considered impossible. Thomas reported that the women interviewed felt that 'Ngaitana was a travesty that ruined initiation in Meru', explaining that it had '"spoiled" female initiation by omitting the meaningful teachings and celebrations and reducing it to the practice of excision'.[124]

Defiance of the circumcision ban imposed by the Njuri Ncheke spread quickly and promoted the formation of a movement, nicknamed Ngaitana ('I will circumcise myself'). Adolescent girls circumcised each other and occasionally themselves in defiance of the ban. The girls who were part of Ngaitana departed from the traditional practice in several critical respects: they were using razor blades bought at the store, rather than the 'iron-wedge knife' used by *atani* (the plural of *mutani*) who would otherwise have performed the ritual; and as the cutting was now done in secret, the rituals which would have accompanied the circum-

---

[121] *Ibid.*, 83.
[122] Reflecting the comparative attention paid to Gĩkũyũ history and forms of resistance in scholarly literature in English, Lynn M. Thomas is probably the only scholar writing in English who has provided a detailed account of the movement itself and its place in Meru oral history.
[123] Thomas, *Politics of the Womb*, 100.
[124] *Ibid.*, 100.

cision were absent, including other ritual tattooing of the abdomen and wide holes in the earlobes (which were rejected at least partly because these were much more visible signs of initiation).[125] As this forbidden circumcision was no longer accompanied by the public spectacle and necessary bodily markings, 'it was reduced to the clandestine performance of excision'.[126]

This dramatic response to the ban was not well received by their fellow Meru. The nickname Ngaitana was given by their elders intended to emphasise the 'absurdity of their undertaking'.[127] Importantly, the girls circumcising themselves performed operations on each other that 'fell far short of excision'. A woman who was part of the movement explained that a combination of a lack of fortitude and a lack of knowledge prevented them from completing the excision of the clitoris. Other reasons these circumcisions were less invasive include the fact that the razor blades the girls were using were more fragile than the iron-wedge knives used by the *atani*, the pain of the procedure deterring girls from proceeding with cutting their companions, and, possibly, some girls not wanting the full procedure performed on them. Finally, Thomas suggests that perhaps these girls performed a simple cut to prompt the older women to complete the operation for them.[128] The content of the label 'I will circumcise myself' contains a series of possibilities – some girls attempted to circumcise themselves, although it is more likely that they attempted to circumcise each other; in other cases, girls who were arrested or fined for undergoing circumcision would claim to have circumcised themselves to protect their mothers or other elders who had helped them.[129]

Families whose daughters had defied the ban on circumcision were subjected to a range of punishments – in some instances, the girls themselves were forced to perform punitive manual labour on roads, plastering home guards' houses or digging drainage trenches and roads, whereas others paid fines to the Njuri Ncheke in bulls or goats, which the council slaughtered and ate. Others reported that punishments such as attending the national African women's organisation, Maendeleo ya Wanawake Organisation (MYWO) meetings were 'an effective instrument against subversive elements', while other headmen felt that attendance at MYWO meetings was a privilege and so banned Ngaitana girls from attending meetings for up to ten weeks (for the history and colonial origins of MYWO, see Chapter 4).[130]

[125] *Ibid.*, 79, 81–82.
[126] *Ibid.*, 90.
[127] *Ibid.*, 80.
[128] *Ibid.*, 91.
[129] *Ibid.*, 79.
[130] *Ibid.*, 98.

Occurring as it did in the waning months of Mau Mau and the Emergency, Thomas argues that, while it is tempting to situate this movement within the 'paradigm of resistance to colonialism',[131] this 'dyad of resister/oppressor is isolated from its context' and elides class, age, gender and other structural inequalities. Ngaitana also illustrates the complexities of identity formation and belonging within ethnic groups in Kenya, as well as between African Kenyans and the colonial government.[132]

Members of the Njuri Ncheke, whose authority had been seriously undermined by the resistance to the ban they had instigated, instead blamed people outside the Meru community, particularly well-educated, urban Gĩkũyũ, like Kenyatta, whom they accused of promoting circumcision for political purposes.[133] As was typical of the period, the clear motivation and organisation of these women was attributed elsewhere, so that the girls were characterised as the dupes of 'young men ... who encouraged girls to defy the authority of the Njuri Ncheke', continuing 'a long tradition of colonial officers interpreting female protests as male-instigated'.[134] Far from being instigated by outsiders or elders, the phenomenon was so compelling that women reported that circumcision occurred in waves, and girls of increasingly young ages were being circumcised between 1956 and 1959. During this period, girls who had been circumcised taunted uncircumcised girls, some of whom reported being beaten by circumcised girls, who called them 'cowards' and *nkenye* (uncircumcised), such that they 'sat down and decided to circumcise [themselves] ... through taunts and beatings, they made Ngaitana a movement, gathering even unsuspecting girls to its cause'.[135]

Here there are several competing agentive groups – the elder women who reject the clandestine circumcision as a travesty, the girls and young women who insist that they will be circumcised even if they must hide in the bush and circumcise each other in secret, and the younger girls and those who were bullied into being circumcised with a razor blade from the village shop. These are all Meru women and girls responding to the ban on circumcision (in the context of the brutal suppression of Mau Mau and the profound physical hardship and punitive attitude of the regime to anyone deemed a Mau Mau sympathiser) in very different ways. These contradictory positions taken up within the Meru community illustrate that the 'real motivations' so often attributed to marginalised groups are, in fact, what Mahmood described as 'real

---

[131] *Ibid.*, 80.
[132] Frederick Cooper, 'Conflict and Connection: Rethinking Colonial African History', *American Historical Review,* 99:5 (1994), 1516–45, as quoted in Thomas, *Politics of the Womb,* 81.
[133] Thomas, *Politics of the Womb,* 93.
[134] *Ibid.*
[135] *Ibid.*, 89–90.

motivations' ... authorised by the analysts' categories (such as social protest, economic necessity, anomie, utilitarian strategy).[136]

There are five critical dyads here – women in the Meru community who participated in Ngaitana and those who rejected it; Meru women and the colonial regime; Meru women and Meru men; Meru men and the colonial regime; and the overarching dyad of coloniser and colonised. Within these binaries, all Meru women express agency and self-determination against a force that seeks to control and regulate their bodies in ways designed to destroy their embodied identity as becoming-Meru women. Each relationship affects the others. Taking the dyads involving women demonstrates the complexity and unpredictability of attempting to locate women's agency through the colonial archive, as well as the contradictory ways in which agency was expressed during this incident among Meru women. For instance, one reading of the Ngaitana girls and Meru men might be that the girls were seeking to limit their own sexual and bodily agency by participating in the secret circumcisions because they felt their worth was found in their reception by future husbands – that these women sought to make their bodies fit for, and to maintain patriarchal cultural norms. But these very norms were ostensibly rejected by the cultural council itself. Perhaps the Ngaitana were positioning themselves as the true protectors of cultural identity in the face of the treachery of their elder men. This invites examination of the third dyad – Ngaitana women and elder women who rejected the movement in its entirety. This dyad rejects the notion that these young women and girls could participate in, and perform, the necessary rituals that would keep intergenerational Meru culture alive. Although Ngaitana has traditionally been read as the latest in a series of contests over women's bodies and the sites of cultural protection, rather than viewing it as

> something that merely mimicked these other ... episodes of anticolonial resistance, it is important to recognise how all three episodes emerged from a faith that linked women's fertility to the future of the land and situated excision as enabling proper procreation. It was this faith that girls and women defended when they defied the ban. The politics of the womb infused yet surpassed anticolonial resistance.[137]

The cultural and political significance of body modification

Genital cutting mobilised coloniser and colonised; and bodies, bodily modification, cultural identity and authority are at the centre of these incidents – implicitly in the Harry Thuku Riot (Nyanjiru could not have

[136] Mahmood, 'Feminist Theory', 209.
[137] Thomas, *Politics of the Womb*, 95.

shamed the men without her cultural capital as an initiated, elder, Gĩkũyũ mother) and explicitly in the 'Female Circumcision Controversy' and the Ngaitana movement. Colonial regimes misrepresent and dismiss 'Other' women in their interactions with them, and in the colonial archive. Thomas argues that 'the faith in the ability of excision to transform girls into women and ensure proper reproduction was something that both preceded and exceeded anti-colonial resistance'.[138] The Thuku riot was conveniently blamed on the uncontrollable 'jeering' women. The colonial accounts do not mention Nyanjiru's nakedness, as though this physical expression of identity and status was unseen or unknowable, achieving paradoxically, and simultaneously, a shaming nakedness and an affirmation of cultural authority through a performative reminder of the shared bond of *irua*, the respect of motherhood (showing your mother's secrets) and the authority of age.

All these women, in diverse and sometimes contradictory ways, were attempting to reposition themselves within these constantly shifting hierarchies. Throughout the colonial encounter, it has been women's task 'to protect the "national body" from internal enemies … disease, physical weakness and immorality'. These histories examine the effect of what Kathleen Canning terms 'the embodied deprivations of the home front'.[139] Women through the colonial period are caught between a new nationalism borne of armed resistance against colonial power (being Gĩkũyũ or Meru means undergoing initiation, including circumcision for men and women, and the Gĩkũyũ and Meru are warriors who freed the nation) and a momentary and selective cultural essentialism (circumcision is positive for women and is culturally valid). These examples show that women's sexuality is at the centre of understandings of culture and the identity of the nation-state, that 'the native woman became the symbol of the incipient … nation'.[140] The identity and roles of Gĩkũyũ women are narrowly and violently defined, bounded by a triumphal Kenyan nationalism and cultural proscription.

Locating women's agency both within and outside feminist notions of resistive agency creates a space for women to be understood more on their own terms. Concepts of 'self, moral agency, and discipline' are now able to be located in events that may have been previously characterised as supportive of oppressive hierarchies. Saba Mahmood has suggested that 'we think of agency not as a synonym for resistance to relations of domination, but as a capacity for action that histori-

---

[138] *Ibid.*, 81.
[139] Kathleen Canning, 'The Body as Method? Reflections on the Place of the Body in Gender History', *Gender and History*, 11:3 (1999), 508.
[140] Kapur, *Erotic Justice*, 29.

cally specific relations of subordination enable and create'.[141] In these instances of FGC and attempts to regulate the practice, each case and each woman responded to what she perceived to be her responsibilities in unique ways. Each incident contributed to the 'debate on what it was to be a man or a woman' – a debate that defines, 'perhaps more than any other issue, what it was to be Gĩkũyũ. It marked the boundaries of a mutually intelligible ethnic language of class, gender and virtue.'[142] Women's agency cannot be spoken about as a uniform set of authority, goals and strategies. Each woman has wielded her cultural and political power in distinctive ways. Parsing their choices to endure pain and censure, and to risk death through the single feminist lens of resistance to patriarchy, elides their layered subjectivities.

---

[141] Mahmood, 'Feminist Theory', 202.
[142] Berman and Lonsdale, *Unhappy Valley*, 3.

3
Myths of Sorority: Kenyan Women's Community Organisation

'Sometimes it's better to stay with your problems.'
(Pillars of Kibera Women's Group, focus group, October 2014)

One of the most enduring myths about Kenyan women is that they have a long tradition of gendered organising to achieve agreed goals. This myth is predominantly derived from the existence of age-set initiation rites in the precolonial period, when girls and boys were initiated into adulthood through a combination of cultural training, seclusion and (depending on the community) gendered circumcision ceremonies. Groups that passed through initiation rites at the same ceremony were given a name to delineate their age-set from others.[1] These culturally generated groups were organised to achieve community goals, and they often supported each other as they progressed through life milestones at similar times. Substantial work by historians and anthropologists has foregrounded the communal life of East African ethnic groups and their gendered social and political organisation.[2] Fundamentally,

---

[1] While there is value in trying to understand the precolonial period, it is outside the scope of this book to comment on the ways in which these precolonial cultures were altered by the colonial encounter. Ifi Amadiume has persuasively argued against the Eurocentrism of 'reducing centuries of African history to relations just with Europe and European scholarship' and for the need for an African 'classical period [that serves] as an archive which influences both the present and the future'. Nevertheless, this chapter focuses on the women's organisations that arose in the colonial period for two reasons: the organisations are well documented, albeit in the colonial archive, and this colonial history continues to profoundly affect postcolonial women's organising in Kenya: Ifi Amadiume, *Reinventing Africa* (London: Zed Books, 1997), 4. Authors who have provided an overview of precolonial cultural organisation in works dealing with the colonial encounter in Kenya include Carl G. Rosberg Jnr and John Nottingham, *The Myth of Mau Mau: Nationalism in Kenya* (Nairobi: East African Publishing House, 1966), 2–7; see also Valentin Y. Mudimbe, *The Invention of Africa: Gnosis, Philosophy, and the Order of Knowledge* (Bloomington: Indiana University Press, 1988).
[2] For example, Achola Pala Okeyo, 'Daughters of the Lakes and Rivers: Colonisation and the Land Rights of Luo Women', in Mona Etienne and Eleanor Leacock (eds), *Women and Colonisation: Anthropological Perspectives* (New York: Praeger Publishers, 1980), pp. 186–218; Regina S. Obeler, *Women Power*

these groups were generated through intergenerational cultural practices and worked to support and perpetuate the structures and values of ethnic communities.

The British colonial regime actively sought to remake this African tradition of gendered organisation to better suit the regulatory and labour needs of the colony. This process created new forms of gendered organisation that responded to the onerous demands of the regime. Latterly, two modern discourses – international human rights policy and members of the postcolonial African academy – have sought, in different ways, to claim the gendered organisation of women as a structure that is integral to African communal life.

I argue here that the motivations of women joining late-modern women's organisations and community groups in Kenya are much more closely related to economic imperatives and poverty than to 'traditional' modes of women's organisations. Further, drawing on interviews I conducted with Kenyan women, I interrogate key assumptions of both African women's history and human rights policy literature that women have *always* collectively organised, that women *naturally* turn to each other for support and guidance, that Kenyan women all want the same rights and are working towards the realisation of these rights as a united group, and that women will be able to access their rights once they are educated about them. The expectations of modern women's organisations are grounded in the colonial past, but they carry modern burdens.

Kenyan women's self-organisation took on fundamentally new forms through the latter phase of the colonial period in response to the new challenges and stresses with which the British colonial government burdened African communities. In contrast to the myth of Kenyan women's natural sorority, these colonial manifestations of gendered organising were both expressions of and reactions against a deliberate project on the part of colonial authorities to remake women's roles within the colony. As discussed in Chapter 3, African women living in the Kenya Colony organised to mount direct challenges to colonial authority, often by accessing authority through their ethnic identities and communities. In addition to these modes of resistance, which sought to preserve the ethnic and cultural integrity of African communities, African women built and joined organisations and groups with proto-nationalist membership and goals. Broadly, these organisations took two forms: grassroots groups that were opposed to oppressive labour demands and taxation, and groups that were explicitly affiliated with the colonial regime. Grassroots groups drew upon the camaraderie

---

and Economic Change: The Nandi of Kenya (Stanford: Stanford University Press, 1985); Melissa Llewelyn-Davies, 'Women, Warriors, and Patriarchs', in Sherry B. Ortner (ed.), *Sexual Meanings: The Cultural Construction of Gender and Sexuality* (Cambridge: Cambridge University Press, 1981).

of a common cause and burgeoning labour rights discourses to protest the labour conditions imposed on women. Colonially affiliated groups derived authority from transnational, racialised welfare discourses and the colonial government itself. These colonial groups were explicitly products of the regime and were designed to achieve regime-friendly coalitions of women across the country.

The existence of women's organisations in both the precolonial and colonial periods may have led modern human rights policymakers to assume that the substance and motivations of precolonial and colonial sororities were similar and were, therefore, expressions of continuous communal organising based on gender. More troubling though, is the myth of African women's solidarity reified in a discrete body of literature produced by members of the postcolonial African academy. Seeking to reclaim a space outside Western feminism and associated feminist development discourses, a number of African women's rights activists and academics have criticised the Western emphasis on individual rights to bodily autonomy over communal rights to cultural knowledge and practice; however, in doing so, they have uncritically adopted an invented colonial tradition. These critics attack the neoliberal development project and reject the reliance on policy frameworks that privilege individualist modes of support, arguing that many communities of the Global South prefer communal modes of organising and derive strength from indigenous modes of community support. In the Kenyan case, this centring of the communal approach is grounded in claims of precolonial, traditional modes of gendered organising. The gendered age-sets, which are central to initiation rites,[3] take on a new utility in the postcolonial period as evidence that Kenyan women have *traditionally* organised collectively, and in single-gendered groups, to achieve communally beneficial logistical and political goals.

But in fact, the increasing demands of the neoliberal state have refigured the centrality of these women's groups, moving away from culturally grounded, age-set initiation ('traditional model') towards more explicit economic bases of organisation and action ('neoliberal model'). I argue that modern women's organisations are built on a foundation of productivity and economic empowerment and are often designed to deliver 'goods' that support the neoliberal state's goal of improved economic productivity, as well as servicing their household's financial

---

[3] Corinne Ann Kratz, *Affecting Performance: Meaning, Movement and Experience in Okiek Women's Initiation* (Washington: Smithsonian Institution Press, 1994); Jomo Kenyatta, *Facing Mount Kenya* (New York: Random House, 1962). For an analysis of the ways in which colonial values have influenced community morals and organisations in the Samburu community in northern Kenya, see George Paul Meiu, 'Belonging in Ethno-erotic Economies: Adultery, Alterity, and Ritual in Postcolonial Kenya', *American Ethnologist*, 43:2 (2016), 215–29.

responsibilities, which are disproportionately allocated to women,[4] including school fees and child and maternal health. Here, I question the assumption of members of the African academy, donor priorities and NGO research regarding the utility of women's organisations in the lives of their members. Both colonial and postcolonial manifestations of sorority are driven by economic necessity and political pressure and are not directly linked to precolonial 'traditional' modes of organising. This is a critical distinction, as the efficacy of women's organisations is frequently assessed in the context of the myth of women's natural sorority and history of 'traditional' modes of organising.

Modern women's community groups therefore represent a kind of rapprochement between the 'cultural' and neoliberal positions by providing access to key neoliberal economic goals through 'traditional', local ways of organising. Rather than evidence of the unbroken history of Kenyan sorority, colonial women's organising is indicative of the propensity for external actors to co-opt traditional modes of behaviour for their own ends. This chapter presents women's voices from focus groups I conducted in Kenya between 2012 and 2014, with participants drawn from women's health, human rights and economic groups in Nairobi, Bar Ober, and Awayo Canteen. The experiences of these women offer insights into the current dynamics of grassroots groups, the motivations of the women who join them, and the benefits and stresses of membership. The interviewees had diverse experiences of women's organisations and women's communal support groups. Many could not recall their mothers or grandmothers participating in groups of this kind, thereby refuting claims of the perpetual existence of traditional ways that African women associate on the basis of gender.

'In traditional times':
Initiation, motherhood and African womanism

One of the methods used by members of the postcolonial African academy to reinscribe efficacy and authority in African cultural life is to turn to traditional modes of organisation as proof that gendered, community-level organisation is inherent in African culture.[5] These arguments

---

[4] Kalpana Wilson argues that neoliberal feminism in development has entrenched and reproduced gender inequalities in the pursuit of strengthening the process of global capital: Kalpana Wilson, 'Towards a Radical Re-appropriation: Gender, Development and Neoliberal Feminism', *Development and Change*, 46:4 (2015), 803–32. See also Edward Bikketi *et al.*, 'Gendered Division of Labour and Feminisation of Responsibilities in Kenya: Implications for Development Interventions', *Gender, Place and Culture*, 23:10 (2016), 1432–49.
[5] Amadiume, *Reinventing Africa*, 146–50. See also Annie Lebeuf, 'The Role of Women in the Political Organisation of African Societies', in Denise Paulme

do important work in the postcolonial academy by positing that indigenous modes of organisation have the capacity to be disruptive of hegemonic cultural and political structures, and supportive of progressive political goals. These arguments simultaneously validate and centre the cultural life of African communities, while also locating modern values of agency and autonomy within these traditional practices. In this way, women's traditional organising and ritual identity formation is often characterised as simultaneously revolutionary and traditional, fulfilling two key aims of the postcolonial project.[6] Historically, and as explored in Chapter 2, this framing is explicit in the reinvigoration of female circumcision during the Female Circumcision Controversy in the 1920s, and again during the Ngaitana movement ('I will circumcise myself') in the 1950s. Both cases emphasise women's agency and the importance of cultural identity in telling a story that centres women as autonomous agents in decisions about their bodies, as well as identifying culture as a source of strength against colonial oppression. Both cases defend the practice of female genital cutting (FGC) – a practice that, under other circumstances, might not have enjoyed such enthusiastic political or communal support. Women's age-sets were formed during the precolonial period through initiation rites but, as arguments against the promotion of FGC have grown in volume nationally and internationally, women's advocacy organisations and gender rights policymakers have relied increasingly on a decontextualised understanding of women's organising, separated from the culturally authoritative reasons for women's sorority. Decoupling initiation and women's sorority in this way moves modern women's organising even further from the origins of precolonial women's solidarities.

Of course, even where there is evidence of women's solidarity during the colonial period – as the FGC examples in this chapter illustrate – these incidents are bounded by the limits of the texts and memories that have survived. Premesh Lalu argues that historical evidence is 'produced under conditions of constraint … In other words, evidence is not necessarily a sign pointing to a prior reality but the very effect

---

(ed.), *Women of Tropical Africa* (Berkeley: University of California Press, 1963), pp. xx–yy; David Sweetman, *Women Leaders in African History* (London: Heinemann Educational, 1984); Chiekh Anta Diop, *Precolonial Black Africa: A Comparative Study of the Political and Social Systems of Europe and Black Africa from Antiquity to the Formation of the Modern States* (Westport: Lawrence Hill, 1987).

[6] One of the best-known examples of this reasoning is Sylvia Tamale's work on sexual education among Baganda women in Uganda: Sylvia Tamale, 'Eroticism, Sensuality and "Women's Secrets" Among the Baganda', *IDS Bulletin*, 37:5 (2006), 89–97. See also Sylvia Tamale, 'The Right to Culture and the Culture of Rights: A Critical Perspective on Women's Sexual Rights in Africa', *Feminist Legal Studies*, 16 (2008), 47–69.

of power, in the case of a colonizing project.'[7] As reliant as we are on the colonial record for knowledge of African cultural and communal organisation, any attempts to support modern arguments for women's communal practices through appeals to the precolonial past must be exercises in critical history rather than a resurrection of past practices. Further, Lalu reminds us that 'to claim that subaltern consciousness, voice, or agency can be retrieved through colonial texts is to ignore the organisation and representation of colonial subjects as a subordinate proposition within primary discourses'.[8] In order to address these silences, scholars have populated the historical record with the voices and experiences of women, which address the effects of colonialism on traditional life by contributing oral histories from women who were either interviewed contemporaneously[9] or later in life about their experiences of cultural life in the colonial period.[10]

In a classic example of the myth of women's precolonial organisation, Kenyan scholars Wilhemina Oduol and Wanjiku Kabira located the origins of women's community organising and social practice of sharing problems 'in traditional times':

> In traditional times women cooperated and mobilized themselves to assist one another through self-help groups; membership was based on friendship, kinship networks and common need ... This tradition of community self-help was practiced by ethnic groups throughout much of Kenya, providing a firm foundation for women's self-help activities and a strong women's movement.[11]

This characterisation proposes a revisionist history that places the modern women's rights movement within a homogenising, linear history beginning in the precolonial period. In this version, 'ethnic groups throughout much of Kenya' in the precolonial period are identified as precursors to the national women's organisations of the later colonial and independence periods. This move to locate cultural and individual strength of African women in the precolonial past nobly intends to create what Amadiume has called a 'resource of classical cultural heritage from

[7] Premesh Lalu, 'The Grammar of Domination and the Subjection of Agency: Colonial Texts and Modes of Evidence', *History and Theory*, 39:4 (2000), 51.
[8] Ibid., 68.
[9] For instance, Phoebe Musandu, 'Daughters of Odoro: Luo Women and Power, Re-examining Scripted Oral Traditions', *Women's Studies*, 41 (2012), 536–57; Jean Davison, *Voices from Mutira: Change in the Lives of Rural Gikuyu Women, 1910–1995*, 2nd edn (Boulder: Lynne Rienner, 1996).
[10] Cora Ann Presley, *Kikuyu Women, the Mau Mau Rebellion, and Social Change in Kenya* (Boulder: Westview Press, 1992).
[11] Wilhemina Oduol and Mukabi Kabira, 'The Mother of All Warriors and Her Daughters: The Women's Movement in Kenya', in Amrita Basu (ed.), *The Challenge of Local Feminisms: Women's Movements in Global Perspective* (Boulder: Westview Press, 1995), pp. 187–208.

which to counter European racism'.[12] However, phrases such as 'in traditional times' illustrate the self-perpetuated mythologies of African women derived from a largely inaccessible precolonial past. This move also appears to ignore the colonial text as a silencer of African women's voices while simultaneously mining it 'for subaltern agency', although the nature of the colonial archive means that this attempted retrieval of the 'silenced subject' can never succeed.[13]

Speaking at the first African Feminist Forum in 2006, Nigerian human and women's rights activist and lawyer Ayesha Imam alluded to traditional practices and structures that affirm women's power. She noted that, in addition to the 'many fundamentalisms' African women face, including 'religious, generic traditionalist ... and ethnic', they must also contend with three types of patriarchy: 'pre colonial, indigenous patriarchy; patriarchy in established religion, particularly monotheistic religions [and] ... the patriarchy that came with our colonisers'.[14] Imam argued that precolonial patriarchy thrived 'on selecting particular cultural norms and institutions (and ignoring those that, for example, valorised women's autonomy), mobilising the concept of ethnicity and resistance to western hegemony to impose [these patriarchal cultural norms] on us'.[15] Imam has argued that African women continue to struggle against the combination of these three kinds of patriarchy.[16] Oduol and Kabira have made a similar case – that during the late colonial period, African women were fighting on two fronts, against the colonial regime and also against an African 'patriarchal structure that provided all the opportunities to men while marginalizing women'.[17] For example, in the late 1920s, Gĩkũyũ women criticised the Kikuyu Central Association (the KCA) 'as chauvinistic in its approach toward issues and dominated by men, who assumed all the leadership positions and marginalized women', and left to establish their own Muumbi Central Association, named 'after the mythical mother of the Agikuyu'.[18]

Even where colonial actors justified their intervention on the basis that African women needed support to combat the African patriarchal structures, Robertson reminds us, it is:

> a common misperception among those unacquainted with African women's and gender history is that colonialism liberated African

---

[12] Amadiume, *Reinventing Africa*, 5.
[13] Premesh, 'The Grammar of Domination', 68.
[14] Ayesha Imam, 'Fundamentalism and Women's Rights in Africa', *Report of the First African Feminist Forum* (2006), 21–23, www.ritimo.org/IMG/pdf/Fundamentalism_20and_20women_20rights.pdf [accessed 15 August 2021].
[15] *Ibid.*, 22.
[16] *Ibid.*, 23.
[17] Oduol and Kabira, 'The Mother of All Warriors', 195–96.
[18] *Ibid.*, 195.

women. If the first generation of African women's historians definitively disproved that, more recent studies have made generalization about colonialism's impact more difficult and have demonstrated mixed impacts – none of them, however, involving 'liberating' women. If some women did take advantage of new opportunities, all too often colonial-induced economic privations drove them, and colonial and colonised men tried to impede their journeys.[19]

Nigerian scholars Oyěwùmí and Amadiume have each provided some of the most radical and cogent critiques of these gendered understandings of the colonial encounter. Both scholars reject the gendered organisation of precolonial African societies as they appear in European anthropology and government records, as well as the argument that social and political hierarchies were grounded in seniority and age-sets rather than gender. Amadiume draws on Kamene Okonjo's argument that traditional African political systems are 'dual-gender' systems, whereas the European system is a 'single-sex' system. Okonjo also contends that in the European 'single-sex' system, 'political status-bearing roles are predominantly the preserve of men [and] ... women can achieve distinction and recognition only by taking on the roles of men in public life and performing them well'.[20] Oyěwùmí also argues that the focus on gender in Africa is a product of a Western gaze that refigures community structures through European gendered frames of analysis applied to African societies rather than seeking indigenous modes of interpretation.[21]

These approaches are perhaps best understood as exercises in *nzagwalu*, an Igbo word meaning 'answering back [in reply to an insult you have suffered]'.[22] Amadiume distinguishes *nzagwalu* from protest because 'protest implies powerlessness, while nzagwalu affirms confidence and certainty'.[23] Scholars have defended the focus on gender as a strategy to foreground the power relations that exist between colonised and coloniser and the ways in which power relationships between men

---

[19] Claire C. Robertson, 'Putting the Political in Economy: African Women's and Gender History, 1992–2010', in Pamela S. Nadell and Kate Haulman (eds), *Making Women's Histories: Beyond National Perspectives* (New York: New York University Press, 2013), 82.
[20] Kamene Okonjo, 'The Dual Sex Political System in Operation: Igbo Women and Community Politics in Midwestern Nigeria', in Nancy J. Hafkin and Edna G. Bay (eds), *Women in Africa: Studies in Social and Economic Change* (Stanford: Stanford University Press, 1976), as quoted in Amadiume, *Reinventing Africa*, 147.
[21] Oyèrónkẹ́ Oyěwùmí, *The Invention of Women: Making an African Sense of Western Gender Discourses* (Minneapolis: University of Minnesota Press, 1997), 1–30.
[22] Amadiume, *Reinventing Africa*, 4.
[23] *Ibid.*, 4.

and women at intimate and community levels are affected by the colonial encounter. Indeed, Amadiume also argues that power is a multidimensional concept in the context of colonial history:

> One [dimension] is the imperialist sense, and therefore synonymous with violence. The other is in the sense of autonomy in self-determination. Here, gender-derived meaning seems to be the real issue that is the character of the culture and politics of gender.[24]

In the Kenyan case, Carolyn Shaw provides a nuanced view of Gĩkũyũ gender power relations and the sources and limitations of the power that Gĩkũyũ women exercised in their precolonial communities. She explains that 'the power they had to make others comply was based on their spiritual powers, strength of character, ability to use kin lines of influence to their advantage, and knowledge of the indispensability of their household services'.[25] Thus, while women wielded some significant cultural and political power, even where we can historically locate evidence of this women's power was bounded by sexed roles and responsibilities.

Answering Oyěwùmí's critique of Western scholarly engagement with gender categories in African contexts, Robertson argues that rather than merely focusing on gender,

> the overarching focus of this literature is power. A generalized politicization of historical studies of women and gender is evident, where, no matter the subject, most works examined power and authority ... Whereas Oyěwùmí's presumption that 'Western' and 'African' female scholars have different and conflicting agendas, this literature that politicizes African women's and gender history does not demonstrate such a division. To the contrary, oral historians, of whatever origin, showed themselves willing to reflect accurately their informant's priorities, even when that meant abandoning dearly held scholarly assumptions.[26]

Robertson makes a strong argument here that the agendas of scholars of both 'Western' and 'African' politics are broadly working towards understanding gender within the context of an array of power relationships, including power relations within the global academy. Nevertheless, it is true that African scholars who describe themselves as womanists or proponents of womanism centre their politics around an Afrocentric theoretical frame which centres motherhood and the 'role of African mothers as leaders in the struggle to regain, reconstruct, and create a cultural integrity that espouses the ancient Maatic[27] prin-

---

[24] Ibid., vii.
[25] Carolyn Martin Shaw, *Colonial Inscriptions: Race, Sex and Class in Kenya* (Minneapolis: University of Minnesota Press, 1995), 46.
[26] Robertson, 'Putting the Political in Economy', 82.
[27] From the Egyptian Goddess, Maat. Nah Dove, 'African Womanism: An

ciples of reciprocity, balance, harmony, justice, truth, righteousness, order, and so forth'.[28] Thus, one of the most abiding points of difference between Western feminist frameworks and African women's rights movements is that Western frameworks have tended to be critical of binary gender roles and essentialised identities based on sex characteristics, whereas African women's rights movements and activists have often embraced the qualities associated with womanhood as a biological identity and motherhood as key elements of their advocacy platform. For instance, Nah Dove has sought to develop a 'tool of analysis for understanding the nature of African women's experiences' that 'specifically address[es] culture as a weapon of resistance and as a basis for defining a new world order'. Dove emphasises the validity of the experiences of mothers, who look to their re-Africanisation as the solution to challenging alien social structures and inappropriate values and behaviours among African women and men.[29] One prominent proponent of womanism, Amadiume, argues that the 'recognition of the motherhood paradigm' provides a strategy to challenge the patriarchy, and it presents motherhood as a state that precedes the patriarchy. This framing argues that patriarchies are 'disputable, since fatherhood is a social construct',[30] whereas motherhood is 'concrete and material'.[31] Women's collective action is different from that of other interest groups for several reasons. Tripp argues that the:

> differences lie not only in [the] goals [of women's collective action], but also in the size of the movements, their inclusiveness, the unique ways they link the personal and the political and the use of motherhood as a political resource.[32]

Unlike Western feminisms, African women's rights platforms tend to be 'intrinsically pro-natal and operate from shared assumptions that African women value marriage and motherhood' and are 'not fixate[d] on the female "body" ... [n]or question the value of marriage and motherhood'.[33] Indeed, Amadiume rejects the structural concept of the 'natural family' in favour of the 'basic kinship unit' of mother and child. She argues that 'European concepts of "natural family" ...

Afrocentric Theory', *Journal of Black Studies*, 28:5 (1998), 535-36.
[28] African womanism is a concept that has been shaped by the work of women such as Clenora Hudson-Weems, Ifi Amadiume and Mary E. Modupe Kolawole. See for overview, Dove, 'African Womanism', 535.
[29] Dove, 'African Womanism', 515.
[30] Amadiume, *Reinventing Africa*, 20–21.
[31] *Ibid.*, 21.
[32] Aili Mari Tripp, 'Women in Movement: Transformations in African Political Landscapes', *International Feminist Journal of Politics*, 5:2 (2003), 235.
[33] Gwendolyn Mikell, 'African Feminism: Toward a New Politics of Representation', *Feminist Studies*, 21:2 (2005), 411, 419.

[obscured] the matri-centric production unit ... [and were] therefore unable to see the very basic kinship unit of mother and child, or show its structural status'.[34] What Amadiume has called the 'moral force of matriarchy'[35] in fact invokes constraining and fickle rules that dictate the way women should behave both privately and publicly. The cultural capital of motherhood is also often eclipsed by the persistence of structural barriers to employment, education, and freedom from violence, all of which are materially damaging to women's health, wellbeing and prosperity. Not only are child rearing and education crippling expenses, motherhood also constrains education and employment prospects for mothers, which in turn severely limits mobility, maternal health, full-time employment and the ability to avoid or escape intimate partner violence.[36]

In my discussions with Kenyan women – almost all of whom have children – the foundational assumptions of the 'goods' of motherhood – that is, an elevation in status within the community and a corresponding increase in political power and authority – are also revealed to be problematic. Almost all the women interviewed for this study had multiple children. Many reported being very young mothers, and they often explained that they had given birth to more children than they had planned – and more children than they felt they could support and care for – often because of their partner's view that having many children is a sign of prestige. As one explained:

Kangemi woman: I'll just do whatever he [my partner] wants because he's the man. And I don't understand the term, 'love', all I know is that I'm grown up, I'm a full lady now, I need to get married, and also give birth like my mum, so I'll just go ... and do exactly what he wants.[37]

Women in Kangemi discussed the paradox of feeling compelled to become a woman through becoming a mother, and then having to live with the results of these choices, which they often made very early in their adulthood. They also explained the deep disconnect between their lives and those of their intimate partners. Several Kibera women reported that they secretly visited a city hospital while their husbands were away from the house so they could receive semi-permanent or permanent contraception (e.g., injectable contraceptives or Implanon, a contraceptive

---

[34] Amadiume, *Reinventing Africa*, 20.
[35] *Ibid.*, 22.
[36] The Kenya Demographic and Health Survey routinely asks questions regarding the acceptability of intimate partner violence (as discussed in Chapter 5).
[37] Kangemi Health Centre Women's Group, 4 August 2014, translator and facilitator Camilla Mwenda.

device implanted under the skin)[38] and would then feign ignorance with their partner as to why they could not conceive, explaining when questioned that the gift of children 'is in God's hands'. Many women reported that the father of their children was often financially, emotionally, and sometimes physically absent, and that when men came home, they were demanding of food, sex, and money. Women did not have high expectations of the quality or longevity of their intimate relationships; they understood that in their impoverished circumstances, a partner who was even a little financially supportive was more important than any emotional foundation for the union. As one woman described:

Kangemi woman: Ok you must start with love [for your husband/partner] but after giving birth to kids, and all the problems that come, the hardship of life, the man will forget about you and the kids, and you'll be perhaps fighting for love, but he don't want. He wants [to look for love/affection] somewhere else.

You'll be stressed in life, so something like love you just forget about it ... maybe there's no food in the house, and children they want to go to school, there's no money, so you can't be forcing love to come.[39]

In many situations, women reported that once a woman becomes pregnant, it is very difficult for her to extricate herself from her relationship, even when there has been serious physical, emotional, financial, or other abuse. Although women do often have the choice to report the bad behaviour of their partners to their parents or other cultural authorities, men are shamed by being brought before the village elders or their wife's family, and women reported that this is a strong deterrent for reporting abuse, because the women may incur further abuse as punishment for attempting to report it.

Woman 1: Women [have] problems, but because they have no way, *yaani* ['that is to say' or 'for instance'], they have just got pregnant, you know, they are just sitting there crying but she cannot go somewhere because, if she thinks that she can go to ... for example, if you have a problem with your husband, someone can just cry there, because [s]he says my husband says that they can't go. You know [because of] culture?

---

[38] Pillars of Kibera – Women's Group, Kisumu Ngogo, Focus Group Discussion, 11 October 2012, translator and facilitator Joseph Ochieng.
[39] Kangemi Health Centre Women's Group, Focus Group Discussion, 4 August 2014, translator and facilitator Camilla Mwenda.

Woman 2: They mean that if you have a husband, and you have married, it is not good to go to elders, to go with your husband ... and stand with them there [in front of the elders to complain about his treatment of you]. So they, you know, you find someone is just crying. Sometimes you don't have money to go ahead with those things. They are just crying, this is what I'm saying, mostly they are just struggling they are just there, crying.[40]

The women in the Kangemi interviews were dismissive of their partner's ability and motivation to assist and support the family that had been so important to create. The result of this abandonment, which is ongoing and burdensome, is that women feel that they are fulfilling their role as 'adult' women by having children, but their family is broken almost from the beginning. The abandonment these women feel cannot be resolved by looking to men as a group for support. Thus, motherhood, which is a central value of African womanism and the embodiment of the Maat (the feminine divine[41]) seriously limits the autonomy and life choices of many Kenyan women.

These Kangemi women also believed that Kenyan men were unable and unwilling to help each other to be better husbands. Rather than creating a supportive environment for their family, women reported that when men met in groups, they encouraged each other to behave badly. The results of men sitting together were further moral corruption, the pursuit of hedonism and shirking of responsibilities. Women felt that men would not consider coming together to share problems honestly and strategise to better support their family, as the women do:

Kangemi: Normally men don't like to sit [and discuss] – taking beer, you'll find them, not making other important decisions, unless it's a company.

Interviewer: But not community groups like this?

Kangemi: They can't agree.[42]

When asked whether there were groups like the women's Kangemi Health Centre group for men, the women were scathing:

---

[40] Bar Ober, Church at Bar Ober, focus group meeting, 10 September 2014, translator and facilitator Joan Ouma (Group 2 Session 1).
[41] Dove, 'African Womanism', 535.
[42] Kangemi Health Centre Women's Group, Focus Group Discussion, 4 August 2014, translator and facilitator Camilla Mwenda.

Kangemi: Also, they can't sit in a group talking [honestly] about what they do to their women, 'cause they know it's all their weakness, 'cause each one of them knows that 'this is what I do to my wife', and 'this is what I do when I find a lady'. So they all know what they do [when they mistreat women], so when they sit together, in fact they'll kind of [encourage each other. There is] peer pressure.[43]

The discontent with men's behaviour towards their family was an oft-repeated theme in my focus groups and informal conversations with women during my time in Kenya and has a long history. Women in all locations reported that men were not to be relied upon, used scarce resources selfishly and treated their partner (and often their children) poorly. They frequently reported criminal levels of abuse, mistreatment, sexual and physical assault, and financial and emotional abuse. Wipper noted that this view of Kenyan men was prevalent in the early postcolonial period and was attributed to women's enthusiasm for participating in government and civil institutions to redress the balance of power at all levels of the new Kenyan state – between state and citizens, and between citizens: 'In the attack on male superiority, men are accused of not performing their roles adequately ... accusations [include] drunkenness, adultery, and brutality. (Customarily, it was – and, often, still is – acceptable for husbands to beat their wives for misdemeanours.)'[44]

Women described having sex with men because they felt it was expected of them, that it was their role in the household and because they had no option. This lack of choice, combined with the pressure they felt to fulfil their adult roles and become 'real women', trapped the women in situations in which education and stable economic and social worlds were out of reach. In the Kangemi case, the women joined an HIV support group that provides information and knowledge about their illness, including how to prevent their children from contracting their disease through breastfeeding, and other information and support. In the context of women's groups, the women can discuss the issues that most affect them, although long-term solutions to many of these problems remain as out of reach as they were before, in large part due to the contradictory goals of early motherhood as a core identity as African women, as well as a lack of financial and emotional stability.

---

[43] *Ibid.*
[44] Audrey Wipper, 'Equal Rights for Women in Kenya?' *Journal of Modern African Studies,* 9:3 (1971), 436.

Colonial history of women's organisations and community groups

I return now to the colonial manifestations of women's organisations, through which the regime sought to centre and remake African womanhood in an attempt to control women's reproductive potential and labour migration. During the colonial encounter, women across the country resisted the regime and fought to protect their communities, cultural identities and languages. The 'women's movement', however, is grounded in different notions of the constituency of Kenyan women. The first movement, which comprised militant, informal associations of women, was motivated by resistance to colonial policies that were 'destroying local culture and economies, and replacing these with colonial structures and ideology'.[45] Notable instances of resistance include resisting demands to terrace farmland for soil conservation, planting trees and intercropping, which greatly increased women's already onerous workloads. The riots that began in the 1930s prompted a colonial commissioner to note that 'if left unchecked, [they] might have precipitated a landslide in government authority'.[46] A particularly notable instance occurred in the Muranga district in 1948, when women

> resisted soil conservation measures, and 2,500 women danced and sang and informed everyone that they had enough to do at home, without also doing soil conservation. When the DC [District Commissioner] ordered their arrest, they were freed by more women, brandishing sticks and shouting Amazon war cries.[47]

In contrast, the colonial establishment's promotion of women's organisations sought to remake gender roles and women's organising to achieve specific goals of the colonial government. The explicit ways in which colonial women sought to 'teach' local women how to make a home and care for their children suggests that these initiatives were completely foreign to Kenyan women, rather than being a natural development of precolonial women's organising. Modern women's organisations in Kenya continue to be explicitly tied to these colonial goals for women and the Kenyan nation. Women's organisations carry this history in their leadership group and their cultural and sexual politics. Rather than attempting a radical decolonisation of these official structures of the women's rights movement,[48] the move-

---

[45] Oduol and Kabira, 'The Mother of All Warriors', 194.
[46] *Ibid.*, 195.
[47] *Ibid.*, 107.
[48] As discussed, the 'women's rights movement' is a fraught term among Kenyan women because of its inheritance from internationalised discourses of gender rights and because of the debate among Kenyan women about the existence of such a movement – that is, whether women in Kenya who

ment locates the origins of women's collective organisation within an untroubled, precolonial past.

The relationship between home-making, nation-building and the colonial women's movement is explicit in the aims and programme of the Jeanes School at Kabete (in Kiambu County, north-west of Nairobi). The idea to set up a school to train supervising teachers and their wives was supported by a handsome bequest from the estate of U.S. Quaker and philanthropist Anna T. Jeanes following a report from the Phelps Stokes Commission in 1924.[49] The model was a blend of teacher training to deploy African teachers to rural areas and training teachers' wives in housekeeping, cleanliness and hygiene.[50] There is an irony in that the direct result of this education and training these women received was that they were taught a new kind of subservience that emphasised their roles as home-makers and helpmates rather than autonomous subjects with their own political and cultural agendas and identities.[51]

The evangelising mission of the project is explicit in the description of the programme, which describes the schools as 'a sort of parish, with particular attention to the schools and the people those schools served'.[52] Teachers were to help around their school area, 'with all the strength and impetus of the religious motive which alone can master the dead hand of sloth and tradition and fecklessness … The teacher would [go] about like a traveling evangelist of good things'.[53] Christopher Kirchgasler explains that the Jeanes School:

---

are fighting particular cultural, political and personal battles pertaining to gendered rights access consider themselves part of such a movement on its nationalist terms.

[49] T.G. Benson, 'The Jeanes School and the Education of the East African Native', *Journal of the Royal African Society,* 35:141 (1936), 421.

[50] Mary Ciambaka Mwiandi, 'The Jeanes School in Kenya: The Role of the Jeanes Teachers and their Wives in "Social Transformation" of Rural Colonial Kenya, 1925–1961' (PhD Thesis, Michigan State University, 2006), https://profiles.uonbi.ac.ke/mwiandi/files/the_jeanes_school_in_kenya.pdf; Thabo David Raphoto, 'The Jeanes School in Kenya, 1924–1964: A Social Experience to Train Teachers for Rural Education and Community Development' (PhD Thesis, unpublished, Syracuse University, 1984).

[51] Robertson, 'Putting the Political in Economy', 77.

[52] Benson, 'The Jeanes School', 421. Similarly, a Quaker boarding school in Western Kenya sought to spread the 'gospel of domesticity' with mixed results: see Samuel S. Thomas, 'Transforming the Gospel of Domesticity: Luhya Girls and the Friends of the Africa Mission, 1917–1926', *African Studies Review,* 43:2 (2000), 1–27.

[53] Benson, 'The Jeanes School', 421–22: 'This idea had been slowly evolved in Negro States, where amid the welter of decrepit schools light had been brought through the kindly and far-seeing provision of little Miss Jeanes [who gifted her entire estate to two men to support "little country" schools]'.

represented the efforts of British colonial administrators, U.S. social scientists, and transitional education reformers to intervene in modes of life in the colony's Native Reserves seen as socially unconscionable; Jeanes teachers were to live and work in the villages of the Reserves, identifying elements impeding progress, and acting as agents in the 'transformation of village life'.[54]

In order to achieve the social transformation of African communities, the Jeanes School at Kabete 'pathologised difference' based on U.S. racialised psychological and sociological frameworks, which were applied to understandings of the 'African',[55] for 'only the African can really know the African and how to get things done among them'.[56] Kirchgasler described the Jeanes programme as a 'living consciousness of the community's needs'[57] that provided a centre for 'homes, health, agriculture, handiness, recreation, religion ... for a centre is needed very sorely'.[58]

The teachers aimed to '[plant] seeds, of ideas, of fruitful lines of self-activity, habits of sturdy self-reliance and resourcefulness'.[59] Jeanes School teachers were to reimagine African womanhood as 'a singular attention to hearth, home, and the nurturing of one's children' and 'youth' as an elimination of 'degrading' dances and development of 'self-regulation'.[60] The subservience of African women that was encouraged in this refiguring of womanhood was reflected in the structure and content of the training:

> We want to train 'home-makers' ... they have been taught the value of cleanliness and take a pride in the cleanliness of their houses, their persons, their children ... We want to develop a sense of pride in a swept house, a clean table, a healthy child, and appeal to the mother's intense affection for her child and interest her in its progress, physical and moral ... They may not be able to do more than run their own homes well, but if they do that they are setting an example which other women in their neighborhood will follow, and, above all, they will be starting their children off on the right road.[61]

[54] Christopher Kirchgasler, 'The Limits of "Knowledge for All": Historicizing Transnational School Reforms in Kenya', *Knowledge Cultures*, 4:2 (2016), 75–76.
[55] 'As both a racial and sociological category, "Africans" contained colonial officials' hopes and fears of development and its perils' (Colony and Protectorate of Kenya Education Department, 'Education Department Annual Report, 1924'), 19, as referred to in Kirchgasler, 'The Limits of "Knowledge for All"', 79.
[56] Benson, 'The Jeanes School', 421.
[57] Kirchgasler, 'The Limits of "Knowledge for All"', 79–80.
[58] Benson, 'The Jeanes School', 421.
[59] *Ibid.*, 421.
[60] Kirchgasler, 'The Limits of "Knowledge for All"', 79–80; see also T.J. Jones, *Education in East Africa* (London: Edinburgh House Press, 1925), 28–29, 34.
[61] Benson, 'The Jeanes School', 428.

This presumed lack of proficiency in women ('they may not be able to do more than run their own homes well') also extended to their intelligence:

> The women in training have a weekly meeting something after the style of Mother's Union, and it is hoped they will develop the idea in their own villages where no such thing has yet started. A certain number have recently begun classes for Red Cross training, working with their husbands who help explain things to them.[62]

The re-organisation of African homes and education aligned with the Jeanes project's core aim of 'disciplin[ing] individual minds and bodies towards a more rational ideal'.[63] This implicit rejection of the previous community structures, values and practices portrayed Africans as disorganised, lazy and unappreciative of the benefits of hard work – work that the colony desperately needed to raise the onerous taxes levied against African families[64] and staff the extensive and fertile farmlands under the control of largely ineffectual white farmers.[65] An African teacher expounding the benefits of the programme observed that:

> We never realized before that it is up to us to make our own country prosperous by our own efforts. We are always talking about our needs and especially about the difficulties we have in keeping our schools going and so on ... The thing we have tended to despise, which is really the most valuable of all, is agriculture. We do cultivate, but I do not think we do it anything like enough to fulfil our wants. If we did twice as much we should not only get enough to supply ourselves with food, but we should be able to sell the surplus and earn money to supply our other needs ... the unhealthy person is no use at all.[66]

'Transformation' of the African was necessary to provide a ready workforce for the colony; however, literacy and mission education also brought the threat of revolution.[67] African demands for political representation were dismissed using racialised psychology – 'Africans' demands ... were "immature" owing to their "tribal consciousness" that had also inhibited the development of their "civilization"'.[68] The newly

---

[62] Ibid.
[63] Kirchgasler, 'The Limits of "Knowledge for All"', 84.
[64] Carl G. Rosberg and John Nottingham, *The Myth of Mau Mau: Nationalism in Kenya* (Nairobi: East African Publishing House, 1966), 21.
[65] Caroline Elkins, *Imperial Reckoning: The Untold Story of Britain's Gulag in Kenya* (New York: Henry Holt and Company, 2005), 10.
[66] Benson, 'The Jeanes School', 431.
[67] Derek R. Peterson, *Creative Writing: Translation, Bookkeeping and the Work of Imagination in Colonial Kenya* (Portsmouth: Heinemann, 2004).
[68] 'Consciousness' was henceforth made a gatekeeper of political participation and represented the necessary sensibilities, dispositions and behaviours associated with progress and civilization: Colony and Protectorate of Kenya

realised benefits of agricultural development and work came at a time when Africans were protesting the forced labour of women and the burdensome taxation of African workers. Here, African labour has been reframed to emphasise the utility of labour for the success of the colony, and to cynically conflate the economic and labour requirements of the colony with the needs of displaced and exploited Africans. It is noteworthy that Englishman Thomas Askwith migrated to the Kenya Colony in the mid-1930s to become both the Commissioner of the Community Development Department and the principal of the Jeanes School, where he promoted his belief in African advancement and was ostracised for his belief in racial equality.[69] Askwith's role was expanded during the Kenya Emergency to include community development and the rehabilitation of Mau Mau supporters.[70]

The Emergency was announced to address the Mau Mau Rebellion twenty years after the Jeanes School programme was established, and the colony experienced serious food shortages in many parts of the country, as well as significant pressure on the Gĩkũyũ labour forces that were vital to colonial crops such as rice, tea and coffee.[71] This productivity drive on behalf of the Jeanes School programme should also be read in the context of the colony's continuing reliance on increasingly reluctant African labour, as well as the increasingly severe food shortages experienced during the Emergency.

National, formally constituted women's organisations in Kenya began with the colonial government-affiliated Maendeleo ya Wanawake Organisation (Women's Progress, MYWO). The first and largest women's association in the country was established in 1952 by Commissioner Askwith and his rebranded Community Development and Rehabilitation Department on the cusp of the Emergency, announced the following year. The history of MYWO exposes the ways in which colonial authorities were involved in shaping the daily lives of Kenyan women and encouraging certain types of domesticity and gender identities.

The Organisation was staffed by upper-middle and upper-class British women associated with the colonial government[72] 'who sought to advance the status of women according to western values'.[73] These women:

Education Department, 1924, 19–20; Jones, *Education in East Africa*, 12–13); Kirchgasler, 'The Limits of "Knowledge for All"', 79. See also Jones, *Education in East Africa*, 24, 26.

[69] Elkins, *Imperial Reckoning*, 102–03.
[70] Ibid., 104–05.
[71] Tabitha Kanogo, *Squatters and the Roots of Mau Mau* (London: James Currey, 1987), 35–64.
[72] Elkins, *Imperial Reckoning*, 261–02.
[73] Oduol and Kabira, 'The Mother of All Warriors', 196.

As a group ... cultivated an aristocratic style of life that even in the early twentieth century was outdated in Europe. Freed from housework by servants, motivated by Christian values and the spirit of *noblesse oblige*, these women unstintingly gave their time to organizations they considered important. Dynamic, forceful and self-confident, they instilled in their protégés similar qualities, and some of them quietly supported women leaders even into the period of independence.[74]

These newly productive and civilised African women were also expected to be supportive of the failing and combative colonial regime. A critical goal of MYWO was to increase 'interaction between white and black women ... to diffuse the tensions that were [to culminate] in the liberation war'.[75] As it had little funding and was under the auspices of Askwith's Community Development and Rehabilitation Department, MYWO 'could not be separated from the colonial government's preeminent objective of punishing Mau Mau and rewarding loyalism'.[76] British women working with MYWO found the limits of their influence when they wrote to complain of the 'excessive use of women's communal labor ... as it causes great suffering'. Caroline Elkins summarised the government response: 'the villagers weren't dying from the combined effects of forced labor, torture and famine; they were sewing and weaving and learning the virtues of British hygiene'.[77] The food shortages were largely and deliberately ignored by the colonial government, which publicly blamed African parents for not making adequate food available to their children and claimed that 'intelligent Gĩkũyũ are adept at leaving Government to feed their children, and are also fully aware of the propaganda value of apparent malnutrition among the young'.[78] This tactic targeted women and children in the villages and illustrates the central concern of the colonial authorities in controlling women and households during the Emergency.

Throughout the Emergency, MYWO members were targeted by a series of government propaganda articles published in monthly papers in KiSwahili, Gĩkũyũ, KiKamba and DhoLuo.[79] The Organisation withheld food stamps and other critical aid to women in the Central Province who refused to renounce Mau Mau during the Emergency. Oathed Gĩkũyũ

---

[74] Wipper, 'Equal Rights for Women in Kenya?' 441.
[75] Oduol and Kabira, 'The Mother of All Warriors', 196.
[76] Elkins, *Imperial Reckoning*, 261.
[77] Ibid., 261.
[78] Ibid., 260.
[79] Myles Osborne, '"The Rooting Out of Mau Mau from the Minds of the Kikuyu is a Formidable Task": Propaganda and the Mau Mau War', *The Journal of African History*, 56 (2015), 93.

women watched their children starve and were unable to send food and supplies to the Mau Mau battalions in the forests outside village settlements. It was claimed that women who had forsworn Mau Mau could join MYWO. In reality, clubs often enforced a 'loyalist first policy ... regardless of a woman's level of cooperation, priority would always be given to those Gĩkũyũ who had remained faithful servants to the British Crown throughout the Emergency'.[80] Thus, for many in the Central Province in the 1950s and early 1960s, MYWO was synonymous with the colonial government and the loyalist home guards. This created tensions between Mau Mau supporters and members of MYWO.[81]

Through MYWO, Kenyan women were organised and trained to perform particular kinds of femininity and to become particular kinds of subjects. African women's identities across the Kenya Colony were also being remade from *African* women of particular ethnic communities to *Kenyan* women. The national organisation offered a unifying language of participation, development, civilisation and achievement. This imaginary of the 'constituency of women' has persisted throughout the independence period and is a factor in the continuing homogeneous approach to addressing women's marginalisation across the country. Although the reality of the heterogeneity of the lives and identities of Kenyan women has been characterised as a strength rather than a weakness, the diversity of ethnicity, class education, language and geography continue to limit consensus-building across engaged Kenyan women's rights activists and movements.[82]

Historian Audrey Wipper has described the establishment of MYWO as the origin of the women's movement in Kenya and MYWO was, for a time, the most influential women's organisation in the country.[83] By 1964,

[80] Elkins, *Imperial Reckoning*, 262.
[81] Ibid., 261–62; Kanogo, *Squatters and the Roots of Mau Mau*, 143–48.
[82] Shaw, *Colonial Inscriptions*, 14–15.
[83] Wipper, 'Equal Rights for Women in Kenya?' 432. Wipper developed a cogent analysis of both the reception and efficacy of MYWO and offered a critical and incisive assessment of the limitations of its leadership group. The Organisation is a longstanding public institution that is affiliated with powerful political families; therefore, robust published critiques of its aims and efficacy within Kenya have been scarce. Informally, many Kenyans working in the area of women's rights are frustrated at the lack of support MYWO lends to the wider women's movement in Kenya, as well as the conservatism of its politics. This phenomenon is also discussed in Anne Namatsi Lutomia *et al.*, 'Examining and Contextualising Kenya's Maendeleo ya Wanawake Organisation (NYWO) through an African Feminist Lens', in Christina Schwabenland *et al.* (eds), *Women's Emancipation and Civil Society Organisation: Challenging or Maintaining the Status Quo?* (Bristol: Policy Press, 2016), pp. 321–41. See, for example, a statement by the sitting president of MYWO, Rahab Mwikali, during the 2017 elections responding to a question about the state of domestic violence shelters and support for victims in the county: Nanjala Nyabola reports that surprising 'even

the organisation had more than 42,000 members and 1,120 clubs across Kenya and was quickly joined by other groups seeking a national reach.[84] Although its large membership numbers have been used as evidence of the national reach of the organisation and the relevance of MYWO to women's empowerment on a national scale, debate exists within the academy as to the actual reach and influence of MYWO.[85] Researchers, including the Kenyan gender and human rights advocate Maria Nzomo, have argued that MYWO has always been closely associated with the ruling class, with nominees for the leadership of MYWO approved by either the colonial regime or Jomo Kenyatta's party, the Kenya Africa National Union (KANU). MYWO was therefore unable (and perhaps unwilling) to effectively advocating for women against the prevailing regime.[86]

The organisation was established by the colonial government and only taken over by local Kenyan women after independence. As Wipper noted in 1971, 'although sponsorship of the colonial government initially caused it to be looked upon negatively by many Africans, it has by now become thoroughly indigenized'.[87] Following independence, MYWO quickly became the women's branch of KANU – the only political party of the de facto one-party state of the new republic. MYWO's close relationship with the ruling party has created tensions with other women's organisations and activists in the contemporary period; it remained formally affiliated with KANU until Daniel arap Moi left power in 2002.[88] The history of its explicit ties to the regime and mobilisation of women's allegiance and labour to the cause of the colonial government have continued to constrain the reach and aspirations of the organisation. Not only is the peak women's rights organisation in Kenya so constrained, Oduol and Kabira have argued that 'while the ruling party rewards and financially supports

---

the interviewer, Mwikali responded that while a woman should never accept, for example, a beating that lands her in hospital, she felt that women had taken the idea of empowerment too far. She insisted that her role as the leading women's rights activist ended at her doorstep. For her, men were created inherently superior to women, and women are required to recognise and submit to that dynamic. The chair argued that marriage was the best institution "created by god ... to be nurtured and protected ... and women who get beaten by men are probably asking to be beaten"': Nanjala Nyabola, 'Kenyan Feminisms in the Digital Age', *Women's Studies Quarterly*, 46:3&4 (2018), 269.

[84] *Ibid.*: including 'church groups, the Kenya National Council of Women, the Federation of University Women; the Kenya Women's Society, the Girl Guides, the Yong Women's Christian Association (YWCA) and the Red Cross'.

[85] Oduol and Kabira, 'The Mother of All Warriors', 198.

[86] Maria Nzomo, 'The Impact of the Women's Decade on Policies, Programs Empowerment of Women in Kenya', *Issue: A Journal of Opinion,* 17:2 (1989), 10–11.

[87] Wipper, 'Equal Rights for Women in Kenya?' 433.

[88] Tripp, 'Women in Movement', 238.

organizations such as MYWO that promote its interests, it harasses and heavily censures those organizations that challenge its oppressive patriarchal structure'.[89]

'We are tired of being told to sit in the kitchen': Women's organising under the new Republic

Kenyan women found that the independent government was even less receptive to their concerns than the colonial regime. Women's formal representation had also fared better under the colonial regime, in which women held one or two specially elected seats. When the opposition tried to introduce legislation to ensure this practice continued post-independence, it was defeated. Although twelve special seats were filled by appointment in 1965, it was only in 1969 that the first woman, Grace Onyango, was elected to the National Assembly.[90] The new African political order appeared to support women's branches of political parties merely to 'mobilise votes for male contestants', and post-independence institutions appeared to be designed to cater for men, whereas 'women are treated as an adjunct to, rather than an integral part of, the modernizing process'.[91] In 1962, Jael Mboga, who was then part of the Luo United Movement (later leader of MYWO) railed: 'We are tired of being told to sit in the kitchen. We have women and girls who are educated and can represent us better than men'.[92] The conservative stance of MYWO was reflected in the statement of its president, Jane Kiano, who claimed ten years later that 'women in this country do not need a liberation movement because all doors are open to us'.[93] In 1971, while Wipper assessed the representation of women in Kenya's new national government, two women attained the position of mayor in two major cities (one was Margaret Wambui Kenyatta, sister of Jomo Kenyatta, in Nairobi), but there were no women in high-ranking civil service roles or cabinet positions. Women had attained some seniority in positions that primarily concerned women.[94] Perhaps the best example of this attitude is that the organisation with the largest membership in Kenya in 2003 was confined to improving childcare, domestic care, hand-

[89] Oduol and Kabira, 'The Mother of All Warriors', 203: 'For example, under the strong leadership of Professor Wangari Maathai, the NCWK [National Council of Women of Kenya] was censored by KANU and the government for publicly challenging government policies that undermined women's progress and the promotion of human rights.'
[90] Wipper, 'Equal Rights for Women in Kenya?' 437.
[91] Ibid., 431.
[92] Ibid., 437.
[93] Tripp, 'Women in Movement', 235.
[94] Wipper, 'Equal Rights for Women in Kenya?' 437.

icrafts, agricultural techniques, literacy and engaging in sports,[95] rather than grooming women for national leadership positions and infiltrating patrilineal state power structures and funding.

As a result of this marginalisation:

> a militant women's equal rights movement has developed in Kenya. Led by urban, educated women, the movement rejects what is now seen as the traditionally inferior role of women. It wants for them an equal share in the responsibilities and opportunities of nationhood.[96]

This first group of Kenyan women leaders were well-educated urban elites who had rejected the inferior role of women that the big men of the new nation had envisioned and perhaps unconsciously relied upon. Thus, the movement's impetus was found in the 'gap between what the women expected and had been promised, and what they actually received, on the coming of independence'.[97] However, although strident in its demands for representation, this militancy did not extend to other cultural and social rights with which Kenyan women continue to struggle, including freedom from poverty, access to education and reproductive and sexual health.

The distinction between grassroots women's organising and formal, government-affiliated and approved women's organisations has persisted through the postcolonial period, as has the social and geographic separation of the women involved in these movements. The popularity of both types of groups was so marked that the 1988 annual report of the Women's Bureau estimated the total number of registered groups as 27,000, with more than one million members.[98] These groups were typically 'informal voluntary women's groups ... formed to engage in business enterprises, community projects, and revolving loan programs'.[99] Oduol and Kabira argue that women's development projects were 'carefully designed [and] ... implemented in attempts to improve women's status but without challenging fundamental gender relations'.[100] These women's groups remain fundamentally apolitical; they talk generally about women's rights but do not aspire to revolutionise or disrupt politics.

Women's rights suffered under the Moi dictatorship (1978–2002), as did civil society more broadly. Despite this oppressive political climate, there were concerted attempts to demand that Kenya and the world pay attention to the situation of Kenyan civil society and the situation of Kenyan women in particular. The Third World Women's Conference

[95] Tripp, 'Women in Movement', 235.
[96] Wipper, 'Equal Rights for Women in Kenya?' 429.
[97] *Ibid.*, 430–31.
[98] Oduol and Kabira, 'The Mother of All Warriors', 197.
[99] *Ibid.*, 197.
[100] *Ibid.*, 200.

was held in Nairobi in 1985,[101] just three years after a coup attempt had threatened the Moi government. Women at the conference demanded 50 per cent political representation, prompting demonstrations on the streets of Nairobi.[102] The famous women's and environmental rights campaigner and environmental activist Wangari Maathai protested alone, without the support of the women's movement, against Moi's plans to 'immortalise himself' by building a 60-storey skyscraper that would host media houses and be the headquarters of the ruling party. The plans would have taken over Uhuru Park in the heart of Nairobi city, which was (and has remained) public land and

> one of the few green spaces in the city where working class people can gather and relax. That protest was symbolic not just because of the environmental struggle, but also of the right to disagree and challenge presidential powers, and the right to freedom of expression when most political dissent was still underground.[103]

Although Maathai's protest attracted state-sanctioned violence (Maathai and her supporters were badly beaten by thugs while police looked on), she was successful in preventing the development and international funders pulled support for the project.[104]

Perhaps the women's protests remembered best by Kenyans are those that were not initiated or publicly supported by formal women's rights organisations. In February 1992, a group of more than fifty women, including Wangari Maathai and other 'rural, elderly, Gĩkũyũ women' who were mothers of unlawfully incarcerated democracy activists, began protesting the incarceration of their children by the Moi government. The women staged a hunger strike and three of the mothers stripped and performed the curse of *guturamira ng'ania* when they were attacked by police. Although Tibbetts argues that these women 'strategically employed motherhood to demand the release of their sons', she also claims that the women were not only motivated by the 'care ethic' but also made 'rights-oriented arguments and exhibited concern for abstract principles such as justice and freedom'.[105] The protest was an

---

[101] Karen Maters, 'The Nairobi World Conference', Supplement No. 24 to Women of Europe (Brussels: Commission of the European Communities, 1986), http://aei.pitt.edu/33993/1/A470.pdf.
[102] Muthoni Wanyeki, 'Women's Agency and the State: The Kenyan Experience', African Feminists Forum (African Women's Development Fund, 2006).
[103] *Ibid.*
[104] Gebisa Ejeta and Richard Strage, 'Obituary – Wangari Muta Maathai 1940–2011', *Food Security*, 3:4 (2011), 412.
[105] Alexandra Tibbetts, *Mamas Fighting for Freedom in Kenya* (Cambridge: Harvard University Press, 1993); 'Kenyan Women Clubbed at Protest: Police Attack Hunger Strikers, Supporters in Nairobi Park', *Globe and Mail* (Toronto, 4 March 1992) (subscriber archive).

important factor in the subsequent release of the prisoners. Significantly, in describing the protest Kenyan political scientist and human rights activist Muthoni Wanyeki argues that while the protest 'catalysed our second liberation struggle in earnest',[106] it was led by urban and rural women again without the support of the organised Kenyan women's movement, who watched in frozen silence, offering only the most discreet support through daily donation of food and water, as tensions mounted within the country.[107]

African independence governments continue to seek to co-opt women's movements by deploying 'divisive politics based on class, rural-urban, ethnic, and educational differences among women'.[108] These differences, as well as a lack of clear national direction and priority areas, have followed women's rights discourse into the present. Women's organisations were co-opted by post-independence regimes to support the new hierarchies and power structures of the government, while at the same time diminishing the power of women to advocate for their own interests against the government. Successive dominant political parties have sought to 'dilute the threat' of women refusing to support the government of the day, and the threat of united women posing a major threat to male superiority in Kenya by 'manipulat[ing] and shaping the direction of the [women's] movement to suit [their] purposes'.[109]

These explicit cultural, political and personal ties between the development of the Kenyan nation as a cohesive and viable whole and the development of the women's movement within this new nation can be seen in the personal histories of the women who led the early movement. Women were often tied to the political elite through family or marriage to the 'big' men of African politics. Women who were prominent in the international rights environment were often from moneyed families, who profited from the ways in which power and assets were distributed following independence. Women leading the more prominent national women's organisations were from a small social group that attended the same schools and were often related to powerful men in politics. In this way, women's organisations and projects were frequently co-opted by politicians and national political parties and frameworks that placed their own relatives, wives or other partisan women in strategic roles within prominent women's organisations to support their political aspirations and garner votes during election periods.[110]

---

[106] The first liberation was from colonialism and the second was from Moi's dictatorship.
[107] Wanyeki, 'Women's Agency and The State'.
[108] Oduol and Kabira, 'The Mother of All Warriors', 199.
[109] *Ibid.*, 199.
[110] *Ibid.*, 199–200; see also Tripp, 'Women in Movement', 238; Wipper, 'Equal Rights for Women in Kenya?' 439.

It is this fragmentation on the basis of class, geographic spread and lack of a unified goal in promoting the rights of women that troubled Oduol and Kabira when they were invited to write on the women's movement in Kenya in the mid-1980s. The authors mused, that while there was active participation by women in activities which were aimed at improving the status of women, the fragmentation and lack of coordination in response to specific and ongoing threats to women's wellbeing led many women to believe 'that the women's movement either does not exist or is insignificant':[111]

> [W]hen we were first approached about writing on the women's movement in Kenya, one question emerged in both of our minds: Is there a women's movement in Kenya? When we considered this, we simultaneously answered 'No'. After more reflection, we began to ask, 'if there is no women's movement, what is this intense activity going on around us of women's group meetings, workshops, seminars, and even individual women agitating for women's rights in the courts, in the media and on the streets?' ... Our conceptualization of a conventional definition of a movement, emphasizing a common objective, continuity, unity, and coordination, led to our initially negative reaction on the question of a women's movement in Kenya.[112]

Modern women's organisations have directly inherited the structures and organisations set up by the colonial administration. Colonial-era organisations, including Maendeleo ya Wanawake, remain influential voices in the public discourse on women's rights and are used as examples of the history of women organising for rights advocacy in Kenya. The leadership of these types of organisations continues to suffer from a lack of connection with poor women and women in rural and remote areas. Human rights practitioners in Kenya typically speak English, a dominant, internationalised human rights language of the elite. At a meeting to discuss civic education in the lead up to the 2013 elections, I was the only participant in a room full of Kenyan women's rights advocates and policy leaders to note that the Independent Elections and Boundaries Commission had not been able to provide education materials in languages other than English and KiSwahili (and the latter were not available at the time I requested education materials to deliver to women's groups I would be visiting in western Kenya). The combination of elitism and class, geographic distance, ethnic diversity and a lack of clear national direction and priority areas has followed women's rights discourse into the modern era.

---

[111] Oduol and Kabira, 'The Mother of All Warriors', 188–89.
[112] *Ibid.*, 187.

Troubling the myths of women's organising today

The history of women's organising in Kenya has been a fraught and often fragmented enterprise. The goals and modes of organising have adapted to meet the challenges that women have faced throughout the colonial and postcolonial periods, but they are not derived from precolonial, traditional practices. To better understand why Kenyan women organise in the modern period, I interviewed three informal women's groups at their regular meeting places. Although the groups face many similar challenges, each group's history demonstrates a range of motivations and they have had varying success in their aims. The interviews challenge assumptions about the efficacy, longevity and 'traditional' nature of women's organising in Kenya in both urban and rural areas. The interviews also demonstrate the inability of women to solve endemic challenges such as structural economic inequalities and serious family violence through organising. Knowledge of their constitutional and other legal rights is also found to be of little utility in the environments in which these women live.

I begin by introducing the origins and current structure of each group, and then present the women's views on a variety of issues that are pertinent to their quality of life, and that are also the focus of a great proportion of Kenyan NGOs, international donor funding and policy design. Membership in these groups offers potentially significant financial, emotional and community support. However, the groups also require at least a small amount of capital investment as well as time and money to allow participants to travel to meetings. I address two key myths of women's sorority here: first, that women have always organised collectively and naturally turn to each other for support and guidance; second, that women can affect their economic circumstances by participating in savings and other micro-lending activities run by women's informal support groups.

Rather than naturally forming associations and groups and relying on these networks for support and advice, the women I interviewed across all locations reported difficulties in forming and running the groups to which they belonged. Further, their group was often the first in their area and the first the women had joined. Thus, in the Kenyan case at least, the assumption of the organic and intergenerational nature of African women's organising needs to be re-examined.

In Bar Ober, 60km west of Kisumu city, the women I interviewed in 2014 had formed a group following a focus group I conducted with women members of the same church in that village in 2013. They reported that they could not think of any group to which their mothers or grandmothers had belonged, and they were not members of any other groups concurrently.[113] The myth that women have always successfully and organically organised in the face of economic and physical hardships was also challenged by the oral histories of the members of the Nyabende Human Rights Network:

Interviewer: I'm wondering what about your mothers, and your grandmothers? Do you know if they were members of women's groups, or church groups that had other projects, or table banking or merry-go-rounds, or anything like this?

Nyabende Human Rights Group: There was nothing.[114]

Forming women's groups – which is a favourite idea of the government and of neoliberal models of self-help and autonomous development, and an idea that is also grounded in reports of 'traditional' African cultural organisation – is not well received by husbands and partners, who are often suspicious of women meeting alone and organising for their own purposes. As women in Bar Ober explained:

Bar Ober women: There is another problem here – husbands and sons will not allow women to be in a group. [Sh]e's not allowed [by her husband] to be in a group.

Interviewer: Do they say why?

Bar Ober women: If you were in a group, they will teach you something that is not good, that you will be stubbornheaded, such things.[115]

The irony of this is that men often rely on women for material and financial support, to keep the house and provide food and clothing for the children and food for themselves. Men often *want* women who have money, or who might be able to make some money running a small business, and it is reported that they often harass their wife to give them the day's earnings. However, these women understand that men also prefer women who are quiet and subservient.

Rather than self-reporting feelings of solidarity among the groups – perhaps instinctively derived from the bonds of African womanism and

---

[113] Bar Ober, Church at Bar Ober, focus group meeting, 10 September 2014, translator and facilitator Joan Ouma.
[114] Ahero, Aweyo Canteen Focus Group, 14 September 2014, translator and facilitator Caren Omanga.
[115] Bar Ober, Church at Bar Ober, focus group meeting, 10 September 2014, translator and facilitator Joan Ouma (Group 2 Session 1).

the unifying force of the feminine divine – Kenyan women also reported that they often preferred to keep their problems to themselves rather than risk gossip in the village. Only in the new women's group did these women feel safe enough to share some problems with each other. The women in the Bar Ober group all trusted each other: 'in our groups here, they love each other, so maybe they trust them'.[116] However, this group is unusual in their area:

Bar Ober women: You know, there are certain people, if you have a problem, if you go to them, you will say your problem, and instead of helping you they will go outside to tell other[s]. You know that is bad. So that, I have seen other groups have that problem. For example, you have a problem with your husband, you have come to your brother or your sister, you have told her, instead of helping you with ideas, what you can do? He is going to ... [tell people] outside the group ... So ... she's like feeling bad with her problems but she don't want to say. But here, we can say, because we are in one church, some are in one area, so we trust each other, they can say your problems. And if you want it [the trust] to continue ... you must keep in your heart, you help [her] and you keep it, not to tell someone.[117]

Similarly, after a woman is married, if she hears that someone in the village is talking about her, she must not go and confront them because:

Bar Ober women: you will be shamed with noise. You just keep quiet, and your, you go to her politely, and just ask her politely, and not go with angriness when you ask [them] why they are saying these things about you and your household.[118]

The dominant emotions here involve fear of being publicly shamed, fear of others knowing their business and, literally, fear of being loud – 'shamed by noise'. As discussed in Chapter 4 in relation to strategies that women might use to combat crime and violence in their communi-

---

[116] Bar Ober, Church at Bar Ober, focus group meeting, 10 September 2014, translator and facilitator Joan Ouma (Group 2 Session 1).
[117] *Ibid.*
[118] *Ibid.*

ty, women are controlled through accusations of philandering or denigrated for speaking up.

The assumption of self-sufficiency underpins the establishment of these modern self-help groups in similar ways to the early colonial women's organisations, which had similar aspirational ideals of responsibility, financial security and independence. Although some of these goals are longstanding and obvious goals for poor women, they also reflect the capitalist, neoliberal foundations of these groups. Even when women can create income-generating activities, they face serious challenges in reaping the rewards of their savings and labour. They often cannot protect these meagre assets from theft, or they deposit the money into a saving and loan scheme, only to be paid out the money without interest.

Women in Bar Ober reported that even when they save money and open a stall or accrue goods for market, they are robbed so routinely that they feel as though there is little point in trying to participate in the activities that are recommended by the international rights movement because of a lack of material assistance and access to basic protection of property and livelihood by local authorities and police.

Bar Ober: We don't have faith in [the police], if you are trying to go to your business, you have got thieves, so you are just going back[wards].

Interviewer: So all your effort is wasted?

Bar Ober: You are wasting your ... *nini* [Sw. 'what?' (Colloquially, 'what do you call it?')]. The big problem here in Africa, security, it is very bad security.

Bar Ober: So it makes us think something bad of police – we think, how [are they behaving this way]?! These people know what is going on here, they know why you have a problem, and they are switching [off] the light. So you are afraid, those who have shops, you are afraid because you don't know at the end of the day, what can happen, if you are a woman who has business, you are afraid going earlier, because you don't know. You have money, two hundred shillings, you can be beaten, your phones [might be taken], and [then] you have [lost your] two hundred shillings, you see? So such things make life so lazy, you see, because you don't have [a] way forward. You work so hard, and someone steals everything you've made. Children [need] to eat ... [but there's] nothing, you try and you lose hope.[119]

Women reported that this profound lack of security and denial of any guarantee of physical safety makes them 'lazy'. These women had internalised the messages of the neoliberal development project, with its emphasis on the individual's responsibility to generate and accrue wealth through labour. Their 'failure' to do so is taken on by these women as *their own failure* to take up the responsibilities and opportunities of entrepreneurship. In truth, their projects failed primarily due to systemic state failures of basic physical security and the denial of basic state protection and supports, including education and primary health care.[120]

In order for these groups to make money to support their members, the members need disposable income to join groups that have particular financial support purposes. Women need to deposit into the savings of the group or contribute to the 'merry-go-round'[121] when called on. However, many members of Nyabende reported that they had been members of other saving and loan groups and other self-help groups, but those groups were not run well and they saw little, if any, return on their investments, which represented very small amounts of money but which were also the

---

[119] *Ibid*.

[120] The 'girl effect', 'the idea that investment in the skills and labour of young women is the key to stimulating economic growth and reducing poverty in the Global South[,] has recently become a key development strategy', but it shifts attention from more significant drivers of poverty and disadvantage; see Jason Hickel, 'The "Girl Effect": Liberalism, Empowerment and the Contradictions of Development', *Third World Quarterly,* 35:8 (2014), 1355–73.

[121] A 'merry-go-round' is a form of group saving in which each member of the group will contribute X shillings each payment period (usually fortnightly or monthly), and each member in turn will receive the total donation of the group. For a detailed examination of 'merry-go-round' systems (also referred to as 'Roscas'), see Mary Kay Gugerty, 'You Can't Save Alone: Commitment in Rotating Savings and Credit Associations in Kenya', *Economic Development and Cultural Change,* 55:2 (2007), 251–82. As an example: 'Meeting weekly, the 23 Msingi Bora members each contribute 50 shillings (60 US cents), which is pooled for members to take loans from. At each meeting, the members also contribute 20 shillings (26 US cents) each – to be given to one member in what they term their 'merry-go-round' as they draw lots to determine the order of receiving the money. Numbers are written on small pieces of paper and folded and each member picks one; the number you get determines your position in the order of receiving the merry-go-round money'. ('"Merry-go-round" Micro-finance Keeps Slum Residents Fed', *IRIN News Network* (23 April 2010), www.irinnews.org/feature/2010/04/13/merry-go-round-micro-finance-keeps-slum-residents-fed [accessed 23 November 2017]). As at May 2022, 50 shillings is equivalent to c. 40 US cents (c. 34 pence GBP) and 20 shillings to c. 17 US cents (c. 13 pence GBP).

total of their disposable incomes. Therefore, they had to be productive if the money was not going to be used for food or school fees.

The advice that these women received from the international aid/development community was that their mobilisation as a group would, through the act of coming together and pooling their resources, create opportunities to develop economic and social structures. Women are also much more likely to be able to access capital through these informal loan networks than through formal lending.[122] For instance, Helene Gayle, then president and chief executive officer of CARE USA, explained that 'CARE has found that the answer is not necessarily to bring banks or microfinance institutions to the poor, but instead enable and empower poor women to set up informal saving and loan groups'.[123] Yet this type of 'self-help' often does not address the situation of women who are at the bottom of the economic ladder and who have few external support systems and negligible family, material or in-kind support. The temptation to make money through these groups can also result in women believing that joining more than one group will be more beneficial, because they understand that members can reap the benefits of multiple payouts. However, as one woman in Ahero explained:

> In fact, you can be lured into joining so many groups because you think there is a lot of money, you think 'I take here, I take here, I take here', but at the end of the day now, she left one, she remained with two … They just shared out in that group, and they remained with nothing, and the school fees is still [due to be paid] … And they have shared out in the group and she has gotten nothing.[124]

Joining the groups also takes time and money away from the more immediate concerns of running the family and sustaining other sources of income. As one woman explained:

> I'm in two groups, I'm in Nyabende and also in the other one. And I think the other one shared out recently – last week, I'm very sorry that they didn't make any money for the sharing out. For one year, they have been doing nothing. They have been going for meetings. They go very early in the morning; I normally … go for a meeting at 7am in the morning … So they don't see the reason to go back to that group.[125]

---

[122] Ashley Francis et al., 'Are We Formal Yet? The Evolving Role of Informal Lending Mechanisms to Support Entrepreneurship and Poverty Alleviation in Central Kenya', *International Journal of Social Entrepreneurship and Innovation*, 2:2 (2013), 109–29.
[123] *IRIN News Network*, '"Merry-go-round"'.
[124] Ahero, Aweyo Canteen interview, 14 September 2014, translator and facilitator Caren Omanga.
[125] *Ibid*.

The fundamental need for capital investment for women to generate income for themselves is demonstrated through the donation of a sewing machine, overlocker and sewing materials to the Nyabende human rights groups through a fundraiser I ran in Australia after returning from field work. The machines allow all the members in the group to make reusable sanitary pads and other items with no start-up infrastructure costs to the group or the individual women. A woman explained that her colleague was:

> very happy you people have brought the machines, now she might be able to make some IGA [income-generating activities] to be able to get some little money to do saving in Nyabende and continue getting, you know. And you can earn some money, as you are making those bags, then you can be able to save in the group saving account, and make some money and take the girls back to school and to not be late [with school fees].[126]

Her participation in the saving group, which was supposed to provide a method of income generation and an emergency loan facility, was only possible through a donation of equipment using significant external capital. These types of external donations have been the history of women's organisations in Kenya, including MYWO. Even the largest and most prestigious organisations were never self-sustaining. However, the modern expectation is that 'grassroots' women should pool their resources to effect change in their own home and community. As one woman explained, if a woman borrows from the group bank to pay school fees, the money she has borrowed does not make money. This leaves the borrower with the interest debt and without any way to generate the money.

Nyabende woman I: What is coming out clearly is that to belong to these groups, you must be a bit stable, financially, [this is] why we encourage them, there must be something they are doing [to make money] for those groups to grow. You cannot go into these groups and not do anything [to generate income] ... And that's why we introduced table banking.[127]

Nyabende woman II: Most of our women [have] ... no source of income, and she has joined this group so that can she can be able [to] support herself ... maybe like I give her example, she is the mother of a son [who needs

---

[126] *Ibid.*
[127] A system in which each member of the group pays into a communal pot, which can be borrowed from at agreed rates of interest to fund income-generating projects or cover emergency costs.

school fees]. And she goes and borrows like 5,000 [shillings (about GBP £34, US $43 as at June 2022)] for school fees, and she takes [it] to school. And when she takes that money to school that she has borrowed, you know that is not money that is now going to bring income. That is money that has gone to sleep somewhere, it is gone. So when one month elapses, that money has some interest – 10 per cent interest. So every month 500 [shillings (about GBP £34.40, US $4.30 as at June 2022)], every month 500, so at the end of the day even her savings will be swallowed in that group because she will not able to [repay] this 5000 because she not working, and she does not know to, you know, maybe how to do business.[128]

Without a regular, sufficient income, this mother will never be able to access the benefits of the group. Ultimately, she will be financially crippled as a result of being a member of the organisation, although she is of the demographic whose quality of life would be most enhanced by her successful participation in the scheme.

The regulation of women through the colonial and postcolonial periods in Kenya has been, and continues to be, framed by the aspirations of the regulating authorities for African women's 'advancement' and 'development'. Scholarly and literary work has contributed to addressing and complicating the position of women within precolonial societies and the ways in which the violent transition to independence affected women's ability to participate in the new nation and take control of their post-independence lives. These narratives predominantly centre either men or women; they alternately draw attention to women as the keepers of cultural authority of the family, and to men in relation to the fragmentation of African political and intercommunity life.[129] At times, these works have attempted to reconstruct various styles of matriarchal authority to demonstrate the destructive influence of colonial regulation on African communities and culture; at others, writers have focused on the experiences of men.[130] One of the most pervasive strands of this argument posits that women have previously derived strength and support from women's age-sets and structures of matrilineal authority, and that these cul-

---

[128] Ahero, Aweyo Canteen interview, 14 September 2014, translator and facilitator Caren Omanga.
[129] See Ngũgĩ wa Thiong'o, *Weep Not Child* (London: Heinemann, 1964), which follows the fates of two brothers during the Emergency and the Mau Mau insurgency.
[130] Charles Mangua, *Son of Woman* (Nairobi: East African Publishers, 1971).

tural structures *should* and *can* be mobilised in the postcolonial period to empower women across the now-canonical areas of development of economic empowerment, bodily autonomy and reproductive health, and equitable political representation.[131]

Assumptions of the utility of women's organising in contemporary Kenya are uneven at best. Even the valorisation of motherhood – a most fundamental transformation of identity – is experienced by many Kenyan women as a necessary condition for womanhood and a logistically challenging endeavour. Kenyan women are encouraged to be mothers and form women's groups, but they see little return on these emotional and physical investments. This is not to suggest that children are unrewarding or that, where it exists, sorority is not valued, but these gains are frequently accompanied by poverty and violence rather than assisting women to alleviate some of their burdens.

In spite of the unpredictability of, and the serious structural and cultural barriers to, the success of these groups, the idea of gendered organisation lies at the heart of three apparently disparate discourses: colonial policy-making, the African postcolonial academy and the internationalised human rights discourse of the Global North. Critically, none of these iterations focuses on the ritual transformation that is central to the origins of African gendered organisation in the precolonial period – the process of initiation that transformed children into adults. In some ways, modern women's organisations seek to support cultural and communal goals, although the tools and structures are neoliberal and economic rather than trans-substantive. Rather than initiation, which transforms a girl into a woman, modern women's groups seek to transform impoverished women into contributing neoliberal citizens.

[131] The extent to which 'gender' as the primary lens through which women's empowerment can be achieved has also been criticised for not adequately engaging in wider social justice projects and goals; see, for instance, Andrea Cornwall and Althea-Maria Rivas, 'From "Gender Equality" and "Women's Empowerment" to Global Justice: Reclaiming a Transformative Agenda for Gender and Development', *Third World Quarterly,* 36:2 (2015), 396–415.

4

Everyday Violence: Violence against Women during Elections and Times of Peace

Following the contested result of the 2007 elections, tens of thousands of Kenyans were sexually and physically assaulted, driven from their homes and communities, and in some cases murdered by their fellow Kenyans and state security forces. Although this violence was unprecedented in scale, intercommunal and state violence has accompanied all of Kenya's post-independence elections. In addition, Kenyan women have been dealing with interpersonal violence and institutional failures of security and other state institutions for decades before the 2007 elections. I argue here that the catastrophic 2007 election violence needs to be understood within the context of the high levels of normalised interpersonal and institutional violence that many Kenyan women contend with throughout their lives.

Outside the election cycle, interviews I conducted with women in Bar Ober and Butere (60km north-west of Kisumu) illustrate the challenges women routinely face in dealing with intimate partner violence, theft, police corruption and denial of basic health care. These discussions present these women's own assessment of the utility of the strategies available to them to address these significant and ongoing challenges. I then examine the ways in which women's experiences of post-election violence are represented by the Kenyan national human rights sector and assess the utility of the recommendations made by these organisations. Although local human rights advocates and organisations are aware of the fundamental limitations of law enforcement, primary health care and other social welfare services, they continue to recommend that women employ strategies that the women themselves understand to be ineffective at best and which, at worst, may create new risks to the women's physical safety. By tracing the threat of violence in peacetime through to the violence experienced in times of national crisis, we can see that the memories, strategies and expectations of peacetime violence are imbricated in the violence of the crisis. This analysis also examines the aims and outcomes of the liberal peacebuilding process, which reinforce rather than problematise institutional and cultural power imbalances, including ethno-patriarchal and neocolonial power structures and constricting gender roles, as we have seen in previous chapters.

This chapter begins with the return to multiparty democracy in 1992 and an overview of the elections in the late-modern period (1992, 1997 and 2002), focusing on the treatment of women candidates and the minimal representation women achieved at these elections. Fundamentally, these elections demonstrate that an emphasis on democratic principles and processes alone does little to promote the rights and representation of women or minority populations.[1] The latter part of this chapter addresses the 2007 post-election violence, and the national and international responses to this violence. Through this analysis, I demonstrate that the demands that human rights practitioners and organisations make of Kenyan women in periods of crisis ask women to deftly negotiate several identities simultaneously, as well as to contend with deeply flawed national justice and security institutions. As Sally Engle Merry has argued, for many women, speaking to authorities or human rights organisations about their experiences accesses new cultural and regulatory spaces and is often an unfamiliar experience. In order to be heard and understood in these new spaces, victims and witnesses are required to adopt new subjectivities that are particular to transnational human rights culture and that most probably exist outside local cultural and social networks and identities,[2] most prominent among these being woman-as-victim. David Morris explains that 'suffering, in short, is not a raw datum, a natural phenomenon that we can identify and measure, but a social status that we extend or withhold'.[3] A woman's insistence that her suffering be made legible and visible through reporting therefore radically reframes her social status.

---

[1] The long view of democratising processes has been argued to have a democratising effect on emerging democratic countries, as argued in Staffan Lindburg (ed.), *Democratisation by Elections: A New Mode of Transition* (Baltimore: Johns Hopkins University Press, 2009). Its Chapter 6 shows that there are also onerous expectations of women who attain public office, including that they should focus on promoting the rights of women and children; see Douglas Kimemia, 'Case of Representation of Women in Kenya', *Current Politics and Economics of Africa*, 5:4 (2012), 451–72.
[2] Sally Engle Merry, 'Transnational Human Rights and Local Activism: Mapping the Middle', *American Anthropologist*, 108:1 (2006), 38–51.
[3] David B. Morris, 'About Suffering: Voice, Genre, and Moral Community', in Arthur Kleinman *et al.* (eds), *Social Suffering* (Berkeley: University of California Press, 1997), 40.

The end of Moi, the rise of Kibaki, and the promise of multiparty politics (1992–2007)

The return to multiparty democracy in 1992 – optimistically called the 'second liberation' – reanimated calls for restorative constitutional reform. The reintroduction of a multiparty system was expected to do the work of changing the political culture,[4] but it did nothing to alter the values or governance strategies of the incumbent administration. Thus, the flawed and frequently amended constitutional dispensation of the Moi era remained.[5] Exemplifying the limitations of only partial democratic reform, Moi was returned to office in the 1992 elections. His victory was the result of a deeply problematic vote and count (although 'there were far more complaints about the count than the voting' – a phenomenon that has marked all Kenyan general elections in the late-modern period).[6] Further illustrating the dangers of relying on the 'mere presence of multiparty democracy ... [as a] palliative for all of the problems that continue to plague Kenyan women',[7] only six of the 250 women who ran for office in the 1992 elections were elected to parliament, and none were appointed to cabinet positions.[8] Among these 250 women was the first woman to ever stand for president. Member of Parliament and ethnic Kamba woman Charity Ngilu ran with the support of 'an alliance of women's organisations, Kamba elites and radical intellectuals'.[9] In spite of these small material gains, the multiparty era opened new spaces for women to participate in electoral processes;[10] indeed, women had some success at the local level, doubling the previous number of women in these posts to fifty.

After the initially unfulfilled promise of multipartyism, the peaceful transition of power from Moi to Mwai Kibaki in the 2002 elections was heralded as the next and best moment of democratic rejuvenation. The 2002 elections were the first time Kenyans had voted against the ruling

---

[4] For instance, Charles Hornsby, *Kenya: A History Since Independence* (New York: Palgrave Macmillan, 2013), 596; Kenya Human Rights Commission, *Interim Suffrage Report* (Unpublished, 2013).
[5] Henry Amadi, 'Kenya's Grand Coalition Government: Another Obstacle to Urgent Constitutional Reform?' *Africa Spectrum,* 44:3 (2009), 151.
[6] See Hornsby, *Kenya: A History Since Independence,* 466–538.
[7] Bessie House-Midamba, 'Gender, Democratization, and Associational Life in Kenya', *Africa Today,* 43:3 (1996), 295.
[8] Wanyiri Kihoro, *Politics and Parliamentarians in Kenya, 1944–2007* (Nairobi: Centre for Multiparty Democracy, 2007); Kenya Parliamentary Chamber: National Assembly, 'Elections Held in 1992', http://archive.ipu.org/parline-e/reports/arc/2167_92.htm [accessed 12 October 2017]
[9] Hornsby, *Kenya: A History Since Independence,* 594.
[10] Jennifer Lawless and Richard Fox, 'Women Candidates in Kenya', *Women and Politics,* 20:4 (1999), 51.

KANU party. The outgoing Moi (who had finally agreed that he had reached his term limit) had selected Uhuru Kenyatta as his successor to the leadership of KANU, which had been in power since independence under Uhuru's father, Jomo Kenyatta. The 2002 elections were also the first time since independence that a national political alliance had brought together significant sections of the Gĩkũyũ, Luo, Luhya, Kamba and other ethnic communities under Kibaki's National Rainbow Coalition (NaRC).[11] The 2002 elections were well managed by the Electoral Commission of Kenya (ECK) compared with previous elections. However, a number of election petitions were lodged at the Supreme Court following the announcement of the election results, with some people raising allegations of irregularities such as the bribery of returning officers.[12] Nonetheless, the consensus at the time was that Kenya's systems of suffrage were beginning to mature, and that the country had turned the corner towards a more robust electoral democracy.[13]

Although some commentators have pointed to the peaceful change of government in 2002 as evidence of a weakening in the ethnic pattern of voting in Kenya,[14] in the wake of the 2007 elections Sebastian Elischer has argued that the peaceful handover in 2002 'constitut[ed] an exception rather than a new period in Kenyan political history'.[15] Indeed, more cynical commentators have argued that the only reason KANU conceded the 2002 elections to the NaRC was that the margin was too large to successfully manipulate.[16] Charles Hornsby has argued that NaRC's victory could be attributed to a combination of the superficial, but briefly momentous, advent of the cross-ethnic coalition that NaRC represented and the inability of KANU to claim legitimacy given the years of state violence and abuse of power. Hornsby concludes that although there was 'violence, bribery and government interference

[11] Kimani Njogu et al. (eds), *Ethnic Diversity in Eastern Africa: Opportunities and Challenges* (Nairobi: Twaweza Communications, 2010), 12.
[12] Hornsby, *Kenya: A History Since Independence*, 695.
[13] The Carter Center, *Observing the 2002 Kenya Elections* (Atlanta: The Carter Center, 2003), 30, www.cartercenter.org/documents/1355.pdf [accessed 20 August 2021].
[14] Michael Bratton and Mwangi S. Kimenyi, 'Voting in Kenya: Putting Ethnicity in Perspective', *Journal of Eastern African Studies*, 2:2 (2008), 272; For a discussion of the role that ethnicity plays in forming political identities in postcolonial Kenya, see Gabrielle Lynch, 'Negotiating Ethnicity: Identity Politics in Contemporary Kenya', *Review of African Political Economy*, 33:107 (2006), 49–65.
[15] Sebastian Elischer, 'Do African Parties Contribute to Democracy? Some Findings from Kenya, Ghana and Nigeria', *Africa Spectrum*, 43:2 (2008), 187.
[16] Tom Wolf – lead researcher with the polling organisation Ipsos Synovate and career commentator on Kenyan politics and opinion polls – has made such comments, noted in Elischer, 'Do African Parties Contribute to Democracy'.

in the election', the incumbent government did not cheat in a manner comprehensive enough to affect the result.[17]

Mumbi Ngugi argues that in the early 1980s Kenyan women began to politicise their identities and take a more 'transformative approach to gender' in which 'the woman is cast as occupying a new and wider socio-political space as demanding a new and dynamic gender contract with the state'.[18] The demand for wider sociopolitical space was driven by crises in local development and the interest of external and international donor agencies. This energy was focused by the United Nations Decade for Women (1975–1985), which culminated in the 1985 Women's Forum in Nairobi.[19] But in spite of this effort, by the mid-1990s little had changed. For Kenyan women candidates and their supporters, the elections of the late-modern period – 1992, 1997, 2002 and 2007 – were characterised by threats, serious physical and sexual violence and intimidation, as well as rallies that were violently disrupted by thugs affiliated with rival male candidates.[20] One of the most visible results of this concerted and violent campaign to repress women's participation in public life can be seen in the persistently low rates of women elected to parliament. Less than 10 per cent (9.8 per cent) of the parliament elected in 2007 were women, which was a slight increase from 7.3 per cent in 2002.[21] Men 'control Kenya's political machinery more thoroughly than elsewhere in Africa'.[22]

'They beat you very, very hard, so that you cannot raise your hand again': Living with everyday violence

In order to better understand the ways in which women dealt with the violence they experienced in the 2007 post-election period, I begin

[17] Hornsby, *Kenya: A History Since Independence*, 694–95.
[18] Mumbi Ngugi, *The Women's Rights Movement and Democratization in Kenya: A Preliminary Inquiry into the Green Formations of Civil Society* (Brighton: Eldis, 2000).
[19] Jean F. O'Barr *et al.*, 'Reflections on Forum '85 in Nairobi, Kenya: Voices from the International Women's Studies Community', *Signs: Journal of Women in Culture and Society,* 11:3 (1986), 584–608; Judith P. Zinsser, 'From Mexico to Copenhagen to Nairobi: The United Nations Decade for Women, 1975–1985', *Journal of World History*, 13:1 (2002), 139–68.
[20] Katy Migiro, 'Kenya Politics: Cash, Violence Limit Women', *Chicago Tribune*, 27 February 2013, Katherine Houreld, 'Women Candidates Face Curses and Worse in Kenyan Elections', *Reuters*, 4 August 2017, www.reuters.com/article/us-kenya-election-women-idUSKBN1AK1E1 [accessed 20 August 2021].
[21] Nduta J. Kweheria and Charles B.G. Ouma, *Achieving Gender Equality in National and Devolved Legislature without Amending Kenya's Constitution (2010)* (Nairobi: Kenya Human Rights Commission, 2012).
[22] Lawless and Fox, 'Women Candidates in Kenya', 50.

here with an examination of rural women's experiences of violence and criminal activity in periods of relative political stability. In Bar Ober[23] and Butere,[24] the women who participated in the focus groups explained the complex and dangerous living conditions they navigated as a matter of routine.

The combination of a corrupt and disinterested police force with husbands and intimate partners who were frequently violent meant that women were reluctant to report mistreatment and crime to authorities. They sometimes resorted to risky strategies outside cultural or institutional frameworks to try to protect themselves and their children. Excerpts from these conversations are presented below, followed by a close reading.

Interviewer: How do you feel about security and the police ... how do you feel about these things here?

Butere women: Corruption, they are so corrupt. These policemen, eh, [the women] are just saying the police men are corrupt, they consider to go to [arrest] these guys that are taking local [alcoholic] brew, [called] *chang'aa*, they will consider to go there to arrest the people that are drunkard, because they will get [paid] something small. That['s] corruption.

As compared to when *you* want the attention [of the police] – you have been mugged by some-

[23] In Bar Ober, I was assisted by translator Joseph Ochieng, who travelled with me from Nairobi, and Joan Ouma, a local woman who volunteered to assist us. Occasionally, the syntax of the transcription reflects the fact that one of the translators was explaining in English a point that a participant was making. For instance, where Bar Ober women are attributed as saying 'they are saying', this is where a translator was explaining what the group was discussing in KiSwahili or DhoLuo. I have tried to render the interviews as closely as possible to the original transcript to ensure that the women's voices are at the forefront of these discussions, and to honour the time and effort they contributed to this project.

[24] Butere women's group, focus group discussion, 3 December 2012, interpreter Joseph Ochieng and interviewer Christina Kenny. This focus group was conducted in four languages: DhoLuo, KiLuyha, KiSwahili and English. Interpreter Ochieng was fluent in English, KiSwahili and DhoLuo. Women who preferred speaking in Luyha were assisted by their fellow participants. After the women spoke, their statements were translated from KiLuyha to KiSwahili, and then Ochieng translated them to English. This process is why the transcription reads as it does: Ochieng explained the women's thoughts as they were expressed to him. As I wanted to avoid altering the transcription as much as possible, there are some syntax issues and points at which Ochieng prefaced statements with 'they are saying'. Occasionally, when Ochieng mentioned something that was not a translation of what the women were saying, I have noted this as an 'interpreter aside'.

body, and ... you have an urgent need [for] their support. They'll not consider that one, [but] they'll consider the *chang'aa*.

When you have an urgent thing to maybe to do with the police, they will ask you for fuel [money, a bribe], to fuel the van, the car, to take them to that place, and if you don't have something they will just assume what has happened [rather than investigate].

Butere women: It's a concern that ... when you report the issues of ... sexual or gender-based violence, they'll take advantage of [you], insulting you, [saying] that you are 'a stupid woman', [they say] 'I think ... you are the cause of the problem', they'll not attend to you. Because they'll say you're like a failure, [that] you are the cause of the problem in the family, maybe you have some injuries ... you've been beaten, your husband or boyfriend from the family, and then they'll not attend to you.

Interviewer: Do women report sexual and gender-based violence? Do they try to report?

Butere women: Women they don't necessarily report the cases because of one thing. When they report, the officer they don't take the issues very, very serious. They have [medical] clinic questions, *maswali* (questions). Stupid questions.

Interviewer: Oh, like?

Butere women: You've been battered, and then someone is asking you, have you been beaten? And they think [there needs to be] ... something that shows you've been beaten. Are you sick? And yet you are at the clinic, you *are* sick. So [these women] feel like women they are not open to report.

At the same time, there is the issue of corruption when you report the case, for the case to be followed up, you must give something small [cash], if there is not something small or something big, it's like they will not do anything to that case.

So, it's like the issue of ... cattle rustlers, when somebody steals your cattle, um, you find out, and you maybe you catch the person, and they are carting your cow, and then you report to the police.

	The police will take ... the cow to the police station, and then you be forced to give something small to get the cow back.
Interviewer:	To get the cow back!?
Butere women:	And if you don't, the thief will come, will give something small [to the police officer] and will be given your cow. They just say, you'll be looking at eh, somebody taking your property, your cow and they're like [dismissive utterance] because they don't have something to give.
Interviewer:	That's awful. I'm sorry to hear that, it sounds like you have a very hard time here, it sounds like you have very little help from the police at all.
Butere women:	The cows are there! They also take the milk as well [wry laugh from group]. The police! And if you decide not to give something small ... the cows will be crowded there [at the police station], they will start selling the cows.

For these women, police corruption, theft and intimate partner violence are interrelated. The discussion moved from their lack of trust in the police to using examples of bribery and corruption to explain why they believe that reporting interpersonal violence is not a useful strategy. Police corruption is defined here as the combination of a failure to investigate unless a bribe is paid and an eagerness to investigate crimes only where is a potential benefit for the officers, and in a manner that benefits the police officer at the expense of the victim (here, either *chang'aa*, cows or cow's milk). This materially affects how safe women feel to report the violence they experience at home. The conspicuousness of police corruption and criminality reinforces the impunity with which police in these locations operate. Visible injuries that the women sustained at home at the hands of their partner are similarly ignored, dismissed and belittled. 'Extreme suffering', Elizabeth Pfeiffer reminds us, 'is not always the result of direct, physical assaults. It is also produced through an insidious and covert process that can inflict unrelenting harm ... manifest physically or through attacks on dignity and self-respect.'[25] The experience of these women is that all physical

---

[25] Elizabeth Pfeiffer, '"The Post-Election Violence Has Brought Shame on This Place": Narratives, Place and Moral Violence in Western Kenya', *African Studies Review*, 61:2 (2018), 185.

evidence is ignored – the evidence of their broken and bruised bodies is dismissed by medical and police officers, and they are blamed for their assaults. They understand that their physical pain is not worthy of consideration, and that they will waste their time if they try to demand assistance or acknowledgement of their suffering.

Women in the rural town of Bar Ober recounted similar experiences of abandonment by police, who left the villagers to the mercy of armed thieves:

Bar Ober women: For example, thieves are in the area, you have run to the police station, to tell them 'there are thieves!' There is such a time [that] we had thieves in the area, so someone ran to the police [station] and when they went to the police, [they] switch[ed] off the [station] light. And we worried, why [would they pretend the station was not occupied]? Security *iko wapi*? (where is it?) Someone has come for help, you have switched [off] the phone; and thieves are cutting people, slash[ing] us with pangas [machetes], with pistols: we have no security, security is bad! And the police was just there in their office, they just lock their doors and are in the office ... they come out when the problem is over – [the police ask] 'thieves also have pistols?' and they just stay [in the station. Meanwhile] the thieves are cutting people.

In all aspects of their lives, the lack of an effective police presence pervades the women's sense of insecurity. In the face of such egregious violations of physical autonomy, I asked what strategies the women had used to try to counter this pervasive violence. In international human rights discourse in recent years, much has been made of the culturally embedded conflict-resolution strategies that are available to women. Disputes between married couples are often referred to village elders or the parents of one of the couple for mediation and resolution, or they may apply to the village chief or elders for conciliation of a dispute or to seek redress for an 'unjustified' beating.[26] The tension between protecting cultural life while also protecting human rights lies at the heart of critiques of human rights-based policy interventions – particularly in non-

---

[26] In all the focus groups, women reported that as a group they lived with high levels of sexual and physical violence. Some women also reported acquiescing to unwanted and often aggressive sex acts, including anal sex, as the safest strategy. The lack of qualitative data on these kinds of interactions is noted in Annabel S. Erulkar, 'The Experience of Sexual Coercion among Young People in Kenya', *International Family Planning Perspectives,* 30:4 (2004), 182–89.

Western contexts. This tension has also produced the distinctions between cultures, 'cultural values' and 'cultural practices' in commentary on the UN Convention on the Elimination of Discrimination Against Women (CEDAW). These distinctions theoretically allow human rights practitioners to preserve the 'fundamentals of a culture while chipping away at targeted anti-human rights aspects'.[27] Thornberry has noted that this strategy is 'broadly reflected in human rights practice'.[28] Although these distinctions have some utility, in practice it is often incredibly difficult to offer a solution which separates values and practices. As Thornberry has observed, practices that are 'bound up intimately with a language, view of the world, creation myth, religious observance and social practice ... cannot be easily "detached" or "severed" from the body politic'.[29] Indeed, in the interviews conducted for this study, the local culturally embedded strategies so favoured by the international community[30] were reported to be rarely effective and failed to address the severe and ongoing physical, emotional and financial abuses that the women routinely experienced. The promise that international rights mechanisms and values will 'fashion ... new, liberating remed[ies]'[31] which will address endemic intimate partner violence seems fanciful in this context.

[27] Patrick Thornberry, *Indigenous Peoples and Human Rights* (Manchester: Manchester University Press, 2002), 424.
[28] *Ibid.*
[29] *Ibid.*
[30] *Ibid.*, 423–24. Many studies and reports have emphasised the utility of local, culturally embedded dispute-resolution mechanisms to support rights claims, but they have also frequently reported that progress is perennially slow or just beginning; for example, in the Nyanza province in Kenya, 'at least 20 women who were evicted from their matrimonial homes by relatives were reinstated ... and their homes re-constructed. [Despite this small number of reported successes, the document states,] there is now an appreciable level of understanding of the detriments of widow inheritance and local people are beginning to appreciate the nature and applicability of human rights': Government of Kenya, *The 7th Periodic Report of the Government of the Republic of Kenya on Implementation of the International Convention on the Elimination of All Forms of Discrimination Against Women (CEDAW)*, 2004–2009, 11–12, www2.ohchr.org/english/bodies/cedaw/docs/AdvanceVersions/CEDAW.C.KEN.7.pdf [accessed 11 June 2022]; Julie Freccero et al., 'Responding to Sexual Violence: Community Approaches', Working Paper (Berkeley: Human Rights Center, University of California, 2011), 25: 'while countries that impose stricter punishments for sexual violence have seen rates of intimate partner and sexual violence decline, researchers have been unable to attribute the decline to the criminalization of the act, and not to other factors like economic development, increase in women's agency and rights, or other social and cultural shifts'.
[31] Jean G. Zorn, 'Translating and Internalising International Human Rights Law: The Courts of Melanesia Confront Gendered Violence', in Aletta Biersack et al. (eds), *Gender Justice and Human Rights: Seeking Justice in Fiji, Papua New*

Given the failures of the Kenyan police and NGOs to support these women, when I asked women what the alternatives were, the options were stark.

Interviewer: So ... since the police are not helpful, what should women do when you have a problem? What do you do when you have a problem at home, or your cow has been stolen, are there any other ways that you help each other, or there's some other way you can find help?

Butere women: That is why men nowadays, are being beaten by women.[32]

Interviewer: So if you hit me, I hit you?

Interpreter (aside): I think I cannot stay in this place, I will be beaten!

Butere women: So it's like, they are just saying like because of frustration, they don't get any help from these officers, it's like they have come with their own, they invent their own form of responding to these issues. When you beat me, I beat you. They beat you very, very hard, so that you cannot raise your hand again. And they can also kill, so that next time, you take away that problem. So, that's ... some of the things people do, when they are being frustrated.

They have another option of doing it, you can go to the village elders, and then you settle everything as a family, as a clan, with the village elder ... Also, they have the last one [option], [group laugh] – you just keep quiet, and you relax, and you just wait for what will come. Because it's normal, it's something normal. Yeah, ok.

Guinea and Vanuatu (Canberra: ANU Press, 2016), pp. 229–70.

[32] There is a persistent counter-discourse – particularly in popular news outlets – around the violence that Kenyan men experience at the hands of women; for instance, Paul Wafula, 'Western, Nairobi Men Frequently Beaten by Their Wives', *Standard Digital Newspaper*, 15 January 2016, www.standardmedia.co.ke/article/2000188171/western-nairobi-men-frequently-beaten-by-their-wives [accessed 18 October 2017]; Eunice Kilonzo and Ng'ang'a Mbugua, 'One in 10 Men Beaten by Wives', *Daily Nation*, 8 April 2015, www.nation.co.ke/news/1056-2679830-l80dhoz/index.html [accessed 18 October 2017]; Catherine Karongo, '400,000 Kenyan Men Battered Yearly', *Capital News*, 16 February 2012, www.capitalfm.co.ke/news/2012/02/400000-kenyan-men-battered-yearly [accessed 18 October 2017]; Julius Gathogo, 'Men Battering as the New Form of Domestic Violence? A Pastoral Care Perspective from the Kenyan Context', *Hervormde Teologiese Studies,* 71:3 (2015), 1–9.

Interpreter (aside): I think that one is now the bad one. Otherwise you'll be at the village elder *kila siku, kila siku* [every day, every day]. It's not effective, because you continue with, you keep on going there with the same-same problem [collective agreement]. So the man will just look at this woman [and see she] is causing a lot of trouble.

Interviewer: Ok. So it becomes more trouble to go?

Bar Ober women: Our village elders [are all men]. It's difficult to go to the village elder each and every time, because it reaches a point that they, say blame with the man [they take the man's side] or the men, so you'll be left alone.

Interviewer: The village elders men as well? So there are no women elders here? Did you know that in Taita there are women elders?

Butere women: Here it is not good. Maybe one day. They are saying maybe one day it will happen. But now, [it's all] the men.

This reliance on the fact that perhaps future women elders may be more empathetic to the struggles of local women is a common reason given for promoting women's leadership more broadly in Kenyan public life. The women in the Bar Ober focus group discussed at length how to address problems in their household. They believed that women should pray and then seek out church elders and members to assist them to solve problems within their households, who 'can help her through praying, advices, consoling.'[33] Should the church assistance fail, then a woman has the option of going home to her parents and explaining that 'she is staying badly with her husband'.[34] Initially, the women agreed that these were the acceptable options for redress, and no one offered an alternative or suggested that the options were insufficient for the resolution of serious domestic problems. After almost forty minutes of discussion of the strategies of going to the church elders and then parents, and having moved on to an oral history of women's groups and self-help associations in the area, I paused to ask if anyone had any questions before I moved on to the next topic, to which a woman responded:

---

[33] Bar Ober, Church focus group meeting, 10 September 2014, translator and facilitator Joan Ouma (Group 2 Session 1)
[34] *Ibid.*

Bar Ober women:	She is asking, where do we take our problems? Because let's say you have a problem with your husband, you will go ... the problem does not end in the house. If you go to the ... let's say you go to the chief, the husband feels bad that you have taken him to the chief.
Interviewer:	I see.
Bar Ober women:	Which is also bringing more problems [interjection from the group – 'it's culture']. Feeling[s] of the husband. He feels 'how can my wife take me to the chief?' But the problem is not ending, you go to church, the church you will tell them, maybe they pray, but the problem will not end [interjection from the group – 'it's still there'].
Interviewer:	I see, ok.
Bar Ober women:	That is what she is asking.[35]

Circling back to the initial question I had asked an hour earlier, 'she is asking – where do we take our problems?', the women perhaps felt more comfortable in interrogating their own earlier answers. Where a woman seeks help through local, apparently culturally sanctioned channels – such as at the Chief's house or with her family – her husband feels bad, which actually exacerbates the problems in her home rather than alleviating them. The barriers to accessing support or changing their situation are always described as complex and intersectional.

Bar Ober women:	Because it is what I tell you, you don't have, you are struggling, you don't have education you don't have money, *yaani* you are just there, you don't have business. Let me just live. That's the problem. Because you are, sometimes you have children, you don't have money, children are here also to eat. So I am thinking, if I take this person there, how can he treat my children.
Interviewer:	Because you also have to stay with him?
Bar Ober women:	So, you are just there, you are feeling bad, but you are just there. *Lakini* [but], you just live, there's nothing you can do.[36]

[35] Bar Ober Group 1, Session 1, September 2014.
[36] Bar Ober, Church Group 2, Session 1, September 2014.

This shows that while culture is often used to argue that Kenyan women and communities have their own methods of dispute resolution, these women found no relief in them. The women had no trust in the police or government authorities and received no support from their church, family or elders; therefore, they continued to live with partners who were abusive and unsupportive of the family unit.

Bar Ober women: I'm just trying to say that [with] most of these things it depends, because women don't know their rights, they never know their rights. That's the problem. If you know your rights, and you know if my husband beat me badly, I can take action. There [was] a case [where a] woman [was] ... beaten by her husband. You can [find] the leg is broken.

Interviewer: A man will beat his wife? It's a crime.

Bar Ober women: But you don't know your rights. You have no power.[37]

Rather than needing more human rights education, these women 'know' their rights in the sense of being able to understand what their rights *should* be. They described several strategies they have used or considered, such as going to the police, but they understand the futility of this option. Women could return to their parents, but that usually makes the situation worse. The Kenyan poet Shailja Patel vividly captures this multivalent silencing in her poem, 'How This Works'.[38]

---

[37] Bar Ober, Church Group 1, session 1, September 2014. The Kenya Demographic and Health Survey reported in 2014 that 42 per cent of women believed that wife-beating is justified under particular circumstances, including neglecting children, arguing with their spouse, refusing sex and burning food. Men also reported high rates of acceptance of wife-beating, although they were less likely to report that wife-beating is justified than women: 'Acceptance of wife beating decreases with increases in education and wealth. By region, the proportion of men who justify wife beating ranges from 25 percent in Western to 52 percent in North Eastern.' Acceptance also decreased from the previous survey. In 2008–2009, 53 per cent of women and 44 per cent of men agreed with wife-beating for at least one of the specified reasons, compared with 42 per cent of women and 36 per cent of men in 2014. Kenya National Bureau of Statistics, *Kenya Demographic and Health Survey 2014* (Nairobi: Government Printer, 2014), 284–85, https://dhsprogram.com/pubs/pdf/fr308/fr308.pdf, 285.

[38] Shailja Patel, 'Three Poems by Shailja Patel', *The Johannesburg Review of Books*, 5 February 2018, https://johannesburgreviewofbooks.com/2018/02/05/three-poems-by-shailja-patel [accessed 21 August 2021]. Reproduced by permission of Shailja Patel.

> First they said
>
> If it really happened, report it to the police. Don't you know how serious such allegations are? You can't just come to the community without official charges.
>
> Then they said
>
> Why did you have to go to the police? Don't you know how trivial such allegations are? You should have come to the community instead of filing charges.
>
> You said
> what community?
> They said
> shut up bitch shutup bitch shutupjustshutthefuckup

During the interviews in Nairobi and in rural areas across all communities I visited, I constantly heard the English phrase 'women need to know their rights'. This phrase carries many meanings for the women in these communities. It refers to knowledge dissemination and training, as well as the human rights education projects taking place across the country, such as access to contraceptive and reproductive health services, access to primary and secondary education for girls and women, and access to civic education. However, 'women need to know their rights' may also refer both to the fact that some women do not understand that what is happening to them is a crime and the fact that that most women in Kenya do not *experience*, and therefore cannot access, their rights. Currently, women cannot *know* their rights because, in their experience, there is no avenue through which these rights can be provided. Understanding (knowing) that something *should not* happen is not the same as experiencing (knowing) support to recover, escape and prevent the circumstances and actors that impinge on their rights. This expansive reading of 'know' echoes Murray-Brown's interpretation of Kenyatta's speech rejecting Mau Mau, which was discussed in Chapter 2 and is repeated here for completeness: 'the Gĩkũyũ idiom Kenyatta employed ... apparently had greater force to it than its English translation as "know" implies. Kenyatta was saying, rather, that "we do not want" or "recognise" or "approve of" Mau Mau.'[39]

Thus, the refrain 'women must know their rights' may be heard rather as a demand for women's rights to be recognised, both by the women themselves, their governments and their communities. The women are caught between a failing cultural system and a failing and corrupt regulatory and political environment. There is no recourse in any direction. I suggested that if a woman is taken to the hospital with a broken

---

[39] Jeremy Murray-Brown, *Kenyatta* (London: George Allen and Unwin, 1972), 244.

leg because her husband beat her, the women in the group could go to the chief and demand that he take care of the rights of the women in his area. The Bar Ober women responded:

Bar Ober women: So I'm telling them, in this area of ours, it is hard, it is hard. It is good to do that, but ... But it is hard. Why? They say, me, going to somebody's office, let's say chief, or who, trying to do whatever you are saying, people outside there will start judging you with words. They say, nowadays that is your man, she is moving with that man [having a sexual relationship], every sort of things they call you. It is hard. You will want to do it, but if you look how they are going to judge you outside there. Yes [it is hard!].

The social controls of gossip and shaming of women who speak up for even walking into public spaces and seeking audiences with people of authority are powerful. The reality of the likely negative outcomes of such risky behaviour, combined with the serious cultural and social repercussions of their choice to speak out in any of these fora, make the likelihood of women electing these pathways extremely unlikely and probably fruitless.

The barriers to accessing support and social welfare services are not only financial and logistical. Women in Bar Ober reported that people travel to the police station or government office and ask to be served, but they cannot speak good English. The officer pretends not to understand the person who has travelled some distance to lodge a complaint. When their fellow tribespeople will not speak their language at work, Kenyans are reminded – often at times when they are feeling most vulnerable – of the supremacy of English as a tool of control and the explicit promotion of a neocolonial hierarchy of language.

Bar Ober women: Education is important. Because if you went to someone and you don't know English, *halafu [then]*, Africans they have such a habit, you can go somewhere at the office, and that person is a Luo tribe, if you go there, because he goes to school, he don't want [to] talk to you [in] your language. He cannot help you.

Interviewer: He refuses to speak Luo?

Bar Ober women: He refuses! I'm just talking English, English, English, and it is a Luo. *Yaani*, there is something there in discrimination, you will find someone talking outside [that's in] your language, but he will

	not talk DhoLuo[40] with you, and he is your person [also a Luo]. Such things bring problems, if you go there with a problem.
Interviewer:	It just makes it worse?
Bar Ober women:	Yeah you have no effort, because your idea, who can understand your idea? Now, nothing you can do now, because he is a Luo he can help you, but he is just talking English. You go in the hospitals, just English ... and that one is a Luo. So you are *unashanga* [you wonder] what's wrong? If you are not going to school you are just useless to others, because you don't know.
Interviewer:	You can't speak English?
Bar Ober women:	You don't hear anything, you can just sit here and you are going in there for a case, and they are just talking.
Interviewer:	They are just talking around you?
Bar Ober women:	And you are not hearing. So you can just go.

Recalling David Morris's observation that 'suffering tends to make people inarticulate', here it is not women who are inarticulate but people in positions of authority, who are deliberately refusing to hear these women's suffering. To understand that you are linguistically locked out of processes of justice is to appreciate that your suffering does not matter: 'you don't hear anything. .... So you can just go'. 'Structural violence', Pfeiffer tells us, 'is structured and structuring. It constricts the agency of its victims ... it is a lived experience that normalises petty brutalities.'[41] The police and other government employees, including staff at medical centres and hospitals, are not only deliberately ignorant of the threats facing their community but are seemingly callous in their disregard for the problems faced by the community in reporting such crimes or calls for assistance. As a result of police deliberately ignoring physical evidence (e.g., the stolen cows penned at the police station, waiting for a bribe) and dismissing the severity of injuries sustained in incidents of intimate partner violence, the women understand deeply that their testimony is not valued. Perhaps the most egregious manifestation of their voices being silenced is the literal denial of lan-

---

[40] The language spoken by members of the Luo ethnic group.
[41] Pfeiffer, '"The Post-Election Violence Has Brought Shame on This Place"', 186.

guage in cases in which medical staff, security personnel and government officials refuse to speak the local language and insist on 'English, English, English'; literally silencing victims in this way excludes these women from support services and the processes of justice.

If testimony lies at the heart of the human rights project, these women are symbolically and literally excluded from the human rights community by the petty brutalities of administrative injustice. Human rights discourse encourages these women to speak up; however, the systems upon which they rely – state security forces and medical facilities – explicitly refuse to acknowledge their personhood and their citizenship. The fact that these women are physically incapable of communicating their experiences is also counter to the most basic advice from human rights policy and practitioners, which is to always try to report the violence against you, thereby validating and testing the systems of justice so that they will strengthen. This chapter will return to these themes later in relation to analysing women's coping strategies and the recommendations of NGOs dealing with the massive increase in reports of sexual and gender-based violence in the wake of the 2007 elections.

The 2007 elections

Although more women made it through the competitive political party nomination process to stand for elective office than ever before, this increased visibility was accompanied by the increased targeting of female candidates.[42] Some women candidates were attacked and beaten, while others were threatened with physical and sexual violence, and their rallies were aggressively disrupted. One candidate was shot dead.[43] In an interview with Kathambi Kinoti, Wangari Kinoti, from the Education Centre for Women in Democracy, reported an unprecedented surge in violence against women candidates for political office. Kinoti explained that the patriarchal view that women should not hold public office, combined with a violent political culture,

---

[42] Lynne Muthoni Wanyeki, 'Lessons from Kenya: Women and the Post-Election Violence', *Feminist Africa*, 10 (2008), 91.
[43] Kathambi Kinoti, 'Kenya's Elections: How Did Women Fare? Interview with Wangari Kinoti', *Association for Women in Development*, 12 February 2008; Wangui Kanina, 'Kenyan Women Bear the Brunt of Election Violence', *Reuters*, 22 December 2007, www.reuters.com/article/us-kenya-election-women/kenyan-women-bear-brunt-of-election-violence-idUSL2127700220071221 [accessed 20 August 2021]; Kwamboka Oyaro, 'A Call to Arm Women Candidates with More Than Speeches', *IPS News*, 21 December 2007, www.ipsnews.net/2007/12/politics-kenya-a-call-to-arm-women-candidates-with-more-than-speeches [accessed 20 August 2021].

'translated into violent opposition to women's leadership'.[44] Although Kinoti expressed the view that the visibility of women aspirants is an important step towards better representation of women in elected positions, others have argued that many of the women who ran in the 2007 elections ran with periphery parties that had little chance of success, and therefore little effect on the real representation figures for women.[45] However, increased visibility draws negative attention to women aspirants and, as Kinoti argued, 'there is also the factor that women have become a real threat to reckon with and therefore all means of intimidation are used against them'.[46] A harrowing example of this attitude towards women candidates was the experience of Martha Kibwana, who ran for the position of councillor in Taveta Town, Taita-Taveta County. I interviewed Kibwana on a field work trip to Taita with the Kenya Human Rights Commission in August 2012, and her experiences are presented below.

Interviewer: Your daughter mentioned you ran for election [in 2007] ... How did that go?[47]

MK: They hit me. You see what they did [shows me long scars on her face, and under her chin]. Pangas [machetes], knives.

Returning from work one afternoon in the lead up to the elections, Kibwana's daughter-in-law noticed people peering through the gate into her property, whom she recognised from their clothing. Later that evening, as Kibwana returned from a local store, she was brutally attacked outside the gate to her house by several assailants. Kibwana believed that the store clerk alerted the thugs that she was on her way home. Outside her front gate, she was beaten with metal pipes and stabbed repeatedly in the face and head with pangas. Kibwana's jaw was caved in by blows to her head, and she sustained stab wounds that penetrated her mouth and sinus cavity. She was left for dead and fell against the gate – the noise of which alerted her daughter-in-law inside. Once the alarm had been raised, Kibwana recalled, 'neighbours asked, "why are they trying to kill Mama Africa"? ... Mama Africa, it's [what they call] me'. Kibwana's daughter explained:

---

[44] Kinoti, 'Kenya's Elections'.
[45] Kwamboka Oyaro, 'Kenya: 87 Percent of Female Candidates are Peripheral to Race', (New York: Global Information Network and Inter Press Service, 22/24 December 2007).
[46] Kinoti, 'Kenya's Elections', paragraph 12.
[47] Interview with Martha Muili Kibwana, candidate for Taita Taveta, 2007 General Elections. Taveta Town, Taita Taveta, 6 August 2012, translator Monica Karethi (programmes officer, KHRC).

Interviewer:	Does [Martha] know who the [perpetrators] were?
WO:	Yah, she knows all of them.
Interviewer:	And she lives with them, still?
WO:	Yes, but she can't do anything. And nothing has been done by the police. Because the people who did that are the rich men in this society. *Yaani*, so you can't. There's nothing you can do. Yeah, you can't defeat them because they use money, and you don't use money. *Yaani*, our policemen, so long as you are the one who has higher pay. They consider you according to what you get.
Interviewer:	I see. So they don't treat everybody the same?
WO:	Yeah. Even in the case of, let's say just a fight – we fight, we all reach the police station at the same time, we call write our statements at the same time, we are all given P3s [the Police Medical Report Form which records physical evidence of a violent act]. So, when we come back, we are told, it's a fair game, and the case is closed. After a while, the other person, because he's rich or something, he comes and pays, if he pays, the other person will be taken, he will be jailed, because you never had money, and you were told the case is closed, but now it's reopened and you'll be jailed. That's our policemen in Taveta.

Four months of surgery and rehabilitation followed Kibwana's attack, and she has metal plates in her jaw to stabilise the shattered bone. Faced with this lethal violence, I asked Kibwana what she thought about women running for election.

Interviewer:	What do you think about women running for election? Do you think they can?
MK:	Yeah, they can.
Interviewer:	It sounds very difficult here?
MK:	It's difficult, but they can. You know women, they are jealous. Women they are jealous. They don't want to let the others [succeed] … So, women are the largest population, they are the ones who have the most power, especially when it comes to voting

	[if they voted as a block], yet they are the ones who are so jealous of each other, they can't progress.
Interviewer:	How do you feel about the police in Taveta?
MK:	The police in Taveta don't do anything. They only get bribe.
Interviewer:	So they didn't help you?
MK:	They don't help [with] anything, unless you go with money ... When [I] was attacked, and [I] left [for hospital], [my] house was broken into, and everything was stolen. [But] when [I] came back to report it, the police didn't even show up at the premises to investigate.
Interviewer:	Ok. Do you think, is that because you didn't have money?
MK:	Yeah, because I don't have money. They need those who have money.
Interviewer:	Ok, so it's not because you were running for office, it's because you didn't pay?
MK:	Yes because they knew she was poor. [My] neighbour was robbed, similar circumstances, so they went to see the neighbour, cause the neighbour is from Somalia, he's a Somali man and of course, Somali men have a lot of money. So when they were leaving his house is when they happened to make a courtesy call to [my] house and ask [me] what [I] said [to follow up the report of her robbery], and [I] said, 'you know what, I don't want to you guys to "help" me any more'.[48]

Although Kibwana's experience was a result of her vying for office, the narrative structure of her story is similar to that of the women's focus groups examined earlier. All the women have noted the relationship between their lack of safety and police corruption, the local relationships between police and violent criminals and the pervasive power of money to manipulate situations in favour of the richer party.

These stories of violence and institutional failure have similar narrative structures. They move from personal experience of trauma to

---

[48] Martha Kibwana, interview translated by Monica Kariethi, KHRC field trip, 6 September 2012.

explaining endemic corruption and types of corruption used by police and why women choose not to report the crimes they experience. Women are often physically and financially exposed to violence and have developed their own strategies and resources for dealing with this reality. These strategies include a dark aspiration to beat men who assault women, although the efficacy of such an approach seems marginal at best. Other options are to 'just keep quiet, to relax, and you just wait for what will come. Because it's normal' or, like Kibwana, to tell the police 'not to help [her] any more'.

Post-election violence and (re)building a liberal peace

Polling day in 2007 was generally peaceful, but a significant delay in announcing the successful presidential candidate raised doubts about the overall conduct of the election. Violence against women aspirants is rarely mentioned in commentary on the overall quality of peacefulness associated with an election; however, it was a recurring theme among employees of human and women's rights NGOs in Nairobi and an assumed reality when speaking to local women. Matthew Carotenuto and Brett Shadle capture the characteristic pre-election optimism of the scholarly and donor communities when they say that in the lead up to the elections in December 2007, 'Kenya seemed pointed to cement its image as one of Africa's most "mature" democracies' and that Kenyans anticipated 'the most free and fair elections in their history.'[49] A report by the Kriegler Commission investigated the post-election violence and found that electoral fraud had saturated every element of the voting process. The malfeasance was so great that it was 'impossible to reconstruct from the formal record who in fact won the presidential contest'.[50] Despite growing concerns among international and domestic observers, as well as obvious inconsistencies in local and central electoral records, the ECK announced that incumbent Kibaki (Party of National Unity [PNU]) had won the presidential race by a mere 230,000 votes of a total of more than ten million cast.[51] Although opposition

[49] Matthew Carotenuto and Brett Shadle, 'Introduction: Toward a History of Violence in Colonial Kenya', *International Journal of African Historical Studies*, 45:1 (2012), 1.
[50] Judge Johan Kriegler *et al.*, 'Report of the Independent Review Commission on the General Elections Held in Kenya on 27th December, 2007' (Nairobi: Government Printer, Government of Kenya, 2008); Department for International Development, 'Elections in Kenya 2007', www.dfid.gov.uk/Documents/publications1/elections/elections-ke-2007.pdf [accessed 22 February 2013].
[51] Guled Mohamed, 'Kenyan Police Fight Protesters, 2 Dead', *ReliefWeb*, 16 January 2008, http://reliefweb.int/node/254523 [accessed 25 September 2011]; Wanyeki, 'Lessons from Kenya'.

candidate Raila Odinga rejected the result outright, 'celebrations began in Central Province, Kibaki's stronghold. The rest of the country – with the exception of Eastern Province, home to the third but insignificant presidential candidate, and North East Province – erupted in rage'.[52] Samuel Kivuitu, who was then chair of the ECK, subsequently stated that he made the announcement of Kibaki's win 'under duress'.[53]

Kibaki announced his new cabinet days later, but the opposition considered this action inflammatory because the election results were still in dispute. Riots that erupted across the country were dominated by violence targeting Gĩkũyũs, who were thought to have benefited from the fraudulent results.[54] The Kenya Police Force and the General Service Unit – a national government paramilitary force – were deployed throughout Nairobi. Police engaged in extrajudicial executions and fired tear gas and live rounds into unarmed protestors.[55] Bans were imposed on live broadcasting and public demonstrations, and shops and residences in areas supporting Odinga's Orange Democratic Movement (ODM) were burnt and looted. The Nairobi Women's Hospital, in collaboration with the Psychological Association of Kenya, opened counselling centres in the slum areas of Mathare, Huruma and Kibera, which were the areas most affected by violence in the capital.[56] The Nairobi Women's Hospital reported that their sexual violence case load had tripled.[57] More than a thousand people were killed by police, as well as by criminal gangs and militia groups that were often motivated by ethnic affiliations.[58]

[52] Wanyeki, 'Lessons from Kenya', 94.
[53] Isaac Ongiri, 'I Acted Under Pressure, Says Kivuitu', *The Standard Newspaper Online*, 2 January 2008, http://allafrica.com/stories/200801010051.html [accessed 5 January 2012].
[54] For a detailed explanation of the escalation of violence and its inter-ethnic nature, see Wanyeki, 'Lessons from Kenya', and Kriegler *et al.*, 'Report of the Independent Review Commission on the General Elections'.
[55] Dialogue Africa Foundation, 'Kriegler and Waki Reports: Summarized Version' (Konrad Adenauer Stiftung, 2009); IRIN News Network, 'Police Under Fire Over Live Rounds', *IRIN*, 17 January 2008, www.irinnews.org/report.aspx?reportid=76297 [accessed 5 January 2012]: 'between late December and early January 44 people had died of bullet wounds in Kisumu alone'.
[56] IRIN News Network, 'Kenya: Health Workers Grappling with Conflict-related Sexual Violence', *IRIN*, 28 January 2008, www.irinnews.org/report.aspx?ReportId=76247 [accessed 6 January 2012]: '[other areas severely affected by the violence in other parts of the country were areas in the Rift Valley] Eldoret, Timboroa, Nakuru, Burnt Forest and Limuru and the cities of Kisumu and Mombasa'.
[57] Wanyeki, 'Lessons from Kenya', 94; Human Rights Watch, *'I Just Sit and Wait to Die': Reparations for Survivors of Kenya's Post-election Sexual Violence*, 15 February 2016, www.hrw.org/report/2016/02/15/i-just-sit-and-wait-die/reparations-survivors-kenyas-2007-2008-post-election [accessed 24 April 2022]
[58] Dialogue Africa Foundation, 'Kriegler and Waki Reports: Summarized Version'.

Fleeing the violence in their home areas, women were also at risk of assault after reaching the internally displaced person (IDP) camps that were set up to deal with victims of the violence. By the time a transitional government was formed in April 2008, up to 660,000 people had been internally displaced across the country.[59] Women's vulnerability to sexual victimisation was exacerbated by makeshift sleeping arrangements in which men and women slept in the same tent or out in the open, as well as a lack of basic infrastructure such as lighting, water and sanitation facilities, and the availability of firewood.[60] Although some women went to hospitals and support services for assistance and treatment, most victims living in slums and IDP camps did not seek medical attention or report incidents to authorities for fear of stigmatisation and because of a lack of security.[61] Significantly, sexual violence was not only an opportunistic by-product of the collapse in social order during the post-election period; women also reported that it was being used as a tool to 'terrorise individuals and families and precipitate their expulsion from the communities in which they live'.[62] Sexual violence was also reported against men; for example, Luo men, who traditionally do not circumcise, were forcibly 'circumcised', and in some cases castrated, during this period, although there continues to be debate around the motivation and agents behind these acts.[63]

[59] International Crisis Group, *Kenya's 2013 Elections*, Africa Report No. 197 (Brussels: International Crisis Group, 2013); International Crisis Group, *Kenya in Crisis*, Africa Report No. 137 (Brussels: International Crisis Group, 2008), 44; Human Rights Watch, Turning Pebbles: Kenya National Dialogue and Reconciliation (KNDR) Monitoring Project: Draft Review Report, 2011, http://katibainstitute.org/Archives/images/KNDR%20Review%20Report%202011.pdf [accessed 22 April 2022]. Reported numbers of displaced persons vary considerably. For instance, the UK Department for International Development estimated that 350,000 persons were displaced as a result of the post-election violence: Department for International Development, 'Elections in Kenya in 2007' (2017), www.dfid.gov.uk/Documents/publications1/elections/elections-ke-2007.pdf [accessed 22 February 2013].
[60] IRIN News Network, 'Kenya: Displaced Women "Still Facing Threat of Sexual Violence"', *IRIN* 10 March 2008, www.unhcr.org/refworld/docid/47d658ee5.html [accessed 11 January 2012].
[61] Philip N. Waki, *Report of the Commission of Inquiry into Post-Election Violence (CIPEV)* (Nairobi: Government Printer, 2008), https://reliefweb.int/attachments/d6939d3c-0869-373d-8612-6a38cb141f16/15A00F569813F4D-549257607001F459D-Full_Report.pdf [accessed 25 May 2022].
[62] Office of the United Nations Humanitarian Coordinator in Kenya, 'Humanitarian Update', 21–28 January 2008, www.icc-cpi.int/RelatedRecords/CR2009_08681.PDF [accessed 13 May 2017].
[63] For a discussion of the implication of the Gĩkũyũ cult the Mungiki in the castration and circumcision of Luo men, see Beth Ahlberg *et al.*, '"We Cannot Be Led by a Child": Forced Male Circumcision during the Post-election Violence in Kenya', Paper presented at the Fourth European Conference on African Studies, Uppsala,

In keeping with the post-Cold War response of the international community to situations of intranational conflict, national, regional and international rights organisations mobilised to repair the damage to Kenya's democratic institutions and to provide some measure of accountability for the violence.[64] The African Union Panel of Eminent African Personalities, led by Kofi Annan, facilitated both the negotiation between the two political parties contesting the election results and the formation of a power-sharing government.[65] Subsequently, President Kibaki announced a new cabinet to cement a power-sharing deal with Prime Minister Odinga. Cabinet positions were divided equally between ODM (Odinga) and the PNU (Kibaki), and the parliament would work on framing a new constitution and 'tackle long-standing grievances over land, wealth and power'.[66] In spite of an

---

15–18 June 2011, www.nai.uu.se/ecas-4/panels/41-60/panel-44/Ahlberg-Njoroge-Olsson-Full-paper.pdf [accessed 5 January 2011]; Caroline Wanjiku Kihato, '"Go Back and Tell Them Who the Real Men Are!" Gendering Our Understanding of Kibera's Post-Election Violence', *International Journal of Conflict and Violence*, 9:1 (2015), 13–24. Kihato has argued that, although women experienced pervasive sexual and physical violence during this period, they were also involved in constructing notions of manhood that compelled men to participate in conflict when they may not have chosen to do so otherwise, explaining that 'notions of masculinity and femininity modified the character of Kibera's conflict. Acts of gender-based violence, gang rapes, and forced circumcisions became intensely entwined with ethno-political performances to annihilate opposing groups. The battle for political power was also a battle of masculinities'.

[64] Edward Newman et al. (eds), *New Perspectives on Liberal Peacebuilding* (New York: United Nations University Press, 2009), 10–23; Oliver P. Richmond and Jason Franks, *Liberal Peace Transitions: Between Statebuilding and Peacebuilding* (Edinburgh: Edinburgh University Press, 2009), 9; Valeri Oosterveld, 'Sexual Violence Directed at Men and Boys in Armed Conflict or Mass Atrocity', *Journal of International Law and International Relations*, 10 (2014), 107–28: Oosterveld also discussed the ways in which violence experienced by men was characterised by prosecutors at the International Criminal Court as 'sexual violence' rather than 'inhumane acts' in an attempt to 'broaden the Pre-Trial Chamber's understanding of how men and boys were targeted for various forms of sexual violence, pointing out that they not only suffered forced circumcision and penile amputation, they also suffered rape, forced nudity and/or sexual mutilation. In other words, the overarching context of the forced circumcision and penile amputation was one where other forms of sexual violence also occurred.'

[65] Annan, together with Condoleezza Rice (U.S. diplomat), Graça Machel (former South African and Mozambican First Lady), Benjamin Mkapa (former Tanzanian President) and Jakaya Kikwete (African Union Chairman and then Tanzanian President) helped negotiate a power-sharing deal between Oginga and Kibaki. Kenya National Commission on Human Rights, *On the Brink of the Precipice: A Human Rights Account of Kenya's Post-2007 Election Violence – Final Report*, 2008, 34, www.knchr.org/portals/0/reports/knchr_report_on_the_brink_of_the_precipe.pdf [accessed 1 March 2015].

[66] BBC, 'Deal to End Kenyan Crisis Agreed' (*BBC News*, 12 April 2008), http://

agreement signed in February, power-sharing talks were suspended in April and violent clashes resumed – particularly between rival ethnic groups.[67] However, by mid-April, the grand coalition government was sworn in, and by 24 April, Kibaki and Odinga were touring Rift Valley 'trouble spots' together.[68]

Liberal peacebuilding projects are frequently grounded in and guided by international or regional values and goals, rather than prioritising vernacular modes of community regeneration.[69] Not only has peacebuilding become part of the 'official political and global governance discourse', but it has also come to represent 'the new imaginary of peace in the minds of policymakers'.[70] To analyse the key characteristics, goals and forms of external interventions deployed to address the post-election violence in Kenya, I draw here on the analysis of Oliver Richmond and Jason Franks and their critique of internationally driven transitional justice processes. The international response to the post-election violence in Kenya is emblematic of what Richmond and Franks identify as the 'orthodox model' in their schema of international peacebuilding strategies. The orthodox model focuses on statebuilding and liberal institutions, while also attempting to be sensitive to local ownership.[71] However, the strategies designed to achieve these outcomes are shaped by privileging the 'initial provision of security' and the 'normative universality' of the goals of the liberal peace over local ideas of positive peace, governance preferences and styles of conflict resolution.[72] Richards and Franks argue that even if desires for self-government, human rights, rule of law and prosperity *were* universal, 'such claims mask much dissensus about their detail, contextuality and the mechanism[s] of governance' that will support these goals.[73] This dissensus is frequently elided by the urgent need for cessation of hostilities, which is often thought to be best achieved through statebuilding and the support and regeneration of state institutions. This concurrent investment in peacebuilding and statebuilding assumes that stable governments and economic systems are necessary foundations for peace.

---

news.bbc.co.uk/2/hi/africa/7344816.stm.
[67] Human Rights Watch, *Ballots to Bullets* (New York: Human Rights Watch, 2008).
[68] Christina Kenny, '"She Grows to Be Just a Woman, Not a Leader": Gendered Citizenship and the 2007 General Election in Kenya', *Intersections: Gender and Sexuality in Asia and the Pacific,* 33 (2013); Human Rights Watch, *Turning Pebbles.*
[69] Richmond and Franks, *Liberal Peace Transitions,* 5.
[70] Oliver P. Richmond, *Peace in International Relations* (London: Routledge, 2008), 22.
[71] Richmond and Franks, *Liberal Peace Transitions,* 8.
[72] *Ibid.*
[73] *Ibid.,* 16.

The International Peace Institute described Kenya before the 2007 post-election violence as 'an island of political and economic stability and as an essential hub for international activity', and it was in this context – explicitly focused on state and regional stability – that the post-election violence was 'a crisis the world could not afford to ignore'.[74] The agenda and timetable developed by the Panel of Eminent African Personalities to guide the programme of the Kenyan National Dialogue and Reconciliation reproduces this hierarchy. Presented in four chronological stages, the first three agenda items deal with restoring a minimal, negative peace[75] – noting that 'the short term objective [was to find] a resolution to the immediate crisis':[76]

- immediate action to stop violence and restore fundamental rights and liberties
- immediate measures to address the humanitarian crisis, promote reconciliation, healing and restoration
- how to overcome the current political crisis.[77]

Agenda Item Four, 'Long term issues and solutions', included:

- undertaking constitutional reform
- tackling poverty and inequality as well as combating regional development imbalances
- tackling unemployment, particularly among the youth
- consolidating national cohesion and unity
- undertaking land reform
- addressing transparency and accountability.[78]

---

[74] Elizabeth Lindenmayer and Josie Lianna Kaye, *A Choice for Peace? The Story of Forty-One Days of Mediation in Kenya* (New York: International Peace Institute, 2009), 1.

[75] 'Negative peace' is the absence of physical violence and 'positive peace' includes the absence of structural injustices, as discussed in Kora Andrieu, 'Political Liberalism After Mass Violence: John Rawls and a "Theory" of Transitional Justice', in Susanne Buckley-Zistel et al. (eds), *Transitional Justice Theories* (New York: Routledge, 2014), 88; Johann Galtung, 'Cultural Violence', *Journal of Peace Research,* 27:3 (1990), 291–305.

[76] Kenya National Dialogue and Reconciliation, 'Annotated Agenda and Timetable', 1 February 2008, as referenced in Meredith Preston McGhie and E. Njoki Wamai, *Beyond the Numbers: Women's Participation in the Kenya National Dialogue and Reconciliation* (Geneva: Centre for Humanitarian Dialogue, 2011), 16.

[77] Kenya National Dialogue and Reconciliation, 'Through the Mediation of H.E. Kofi Annan and the Panel of Eminent African Personalities on the Resolution of the Political Crisis – Annotated Agenda and Timetable', 1–2, http://peacemaker.un.org/sites/peacemaker.un.org/files/KE_080101_Annotated%20Agenda%20for%20the%20Kenya%20Dialogue%20and%20Reconciliation.pdf.

[78] McGhie and Wamai, *Beyond the Numbers,* 16.

The initial desire to halt the violence and to restore rights to life, security and freedom of expression and peaceful assembly, among others, is not contentious. However, as is increasingly the case with liberal peacebuilding processes, the Kenyan process explicitly emphasised statebuilding as a 'necessary and logical step in the peace process'.[79] But statebuilding is intrinsically a conservative endeavour that focuses on *restoring*, rather than *remaking*, state institutional structures. Without deeply engaging with the nature and quality of governance before the 2007 post-election violence, the transitional justice process uncritically reinforced the patriarchal and autocratic structures that had contributed to the crisis. The focus was on 'bringing the two parties to agree a political resolution to the impasse which had engulfed the country'.[80] Therefore, the process of mediation validated the centrality of the two political parties and their leadership cohort.

The African Union mediation supported the retention of Kibaki as president and created the position of prime minister for his opponent, Odinga, both of whom were implicated in the funding and assembly of the ethnic militias that perpetrated much of the post-election violence.[81] The men at the centre of the transitional justice process – whether characterised as remade heroes of the peace process (e.g., outgoing President Kibaki and opposition leader Odinga) or perpetrators of violence (e.g., Uhuru Kenyatta and William Ruto)[82] – belonged to families that had been at the centre of Kenyan politics since before independence.[83] Thus, from its inception, the programme of transitional justice was uncritically engaged in the process of explicitly and deliberately remaking Kenya's democratic institutions *as they were* and reinforcing the patriarchal power structures that had been the source of decades of political violence, dispossession of tribal lands and endemic corruption at every level of government. These choices demonstrate not only the limits of peacebuilding initiatives that privilege state stability, but also that 'some aspects of the contemporary statebuilding agenda, in

---

[79] Joanne Wallis, 'Building a Liberal-Local Hybrid Peace and State in Bougainville', *The Pacific Review,* 25:5 (2012), 613.
[80] McGhie and Wamai, *Beyond the Numbers,* 18.
[81] Human Rights Watch, 'Ballots to Bullets'.
[82] See the cases brought (and subsequently contentiously dropped due to insufficient evidence) at the International Criminal Court as a result of investigations into the 2007 post-election violence against, among others, William Samoei Ruto, Joshua Arap Sang and Uhuru Kenyatta: *The Prosecutor v. William Samoei Ruto and Joshua Arap Sang,* ICC-01/09-01/11, www.icc-cpi.int/kenya/rutosang; *The Prosecutor v. Uhuru Muigai Kenyatta,* ICC-01/09-02/11, www.icc-cpi.int/kenya/kenyatta [both accessed 10 September 2018].
[83] Mwai Kibaki began his political career in 1960 with Uhuru Kenyatta's father and first President of the Kenyan republic, Jomo Kenyatta, and Raila's father, Jaramogi Oginga Odinga, leader of the opposition party at Independence.

fact, *do not support peace* … or at least anything more than a very crude and negative peace'.[84] The nature and immediate goals of the mediation also significantly limited any serious engagement with the historical and systemic roots of political and intercultural violence in Kenya.

One of the few deliberate attempts to disrupt these power structures was the Panel of Eminent African Personalities' focus on women's representation within the negotiation team and around the negotiating table. The most senior woman involved in the mediation, former First Lady Graça Machel, pushed the participation and representation of women at all levels of the process, including insisting that each political party's mediation team included a woman.[85] The Centre for Humanitarian Dialogue's report on the involvement of women in the mediation stated that the Women's Representatives and civil society were 'critically important' in shaping Agenda 4, which called for mechanisms to address the underlying causes of the 2007 post-election violence.[86] However, rather than introducing an enduring and longitudinal focus on the gendered nature of Kenyan politics and the transitional justice process itself, the requirement in fact illustrated the expectations of and constraints on women in politics.

Women representatives for each party – Martha Karua (PNU, led by Kibaki) and Sally Kosgey (ODM, led by Odinga) – were each chosen for their 'party loyalty, strength of character and negotiating abilities', and both 'advocated strongly and consistently on behalf of their respective parties'.[87] Civil society representatives expected the women to push the centrality of women's rights, post-conflict needs and continued involvement in peacebuilding (represented in Agenda 4 items); however, each woman reportedly advocated strongly for her party's interests. This created tension between Karua, Kosgey and the women's civil society representatives.[88] Kosgey chose to wear traditional Kenyan fabrics and modest, matronly, loose-fitting clothes, which reminded the negotiators (almost all of whom were men) that she was to be trusted and relied upon to negotiate fairly. In stark contrast, Karua chose to wear her signature business skirt suit. This was much more in the style of successful, authoritative Western women and was read by the men as cold, officious and difficult. Anecdotally, Kosgey was thought to extract more concessions for her side, in part because of her choice of attire.[89]

---

[84] Richmond and Franks, *Liberal Peace Transitions*, 13. Emphasis added.
[85] McGhie and Wamai, *Beyond the Numbers*, 17.
[86] Ibid., 18.
[87] Ibid.
[88] Ibid.
[89] John Rabuogi Ahere, personal communication, 1 October 2017.

Although the team of women who represented civil society and were involved in drafting Agenda 4 were understandably frustrated at Karua and Kosgey's apparent lack of support for the critical task of gendered responses to the structural fragility of Kenya's democracy, it should not be surprising that women carry multiple representational mandates. Deniz Kandiyoti describes this phenomenon as a 'patriarchal bargain' that requires women to 'strategise within a set of concrete constraints … which may exhibit variations according to class, caste, and ethnicity'.[90] These bargains 'act as implicit scripts that define, limit and inflect their market and domestic options'.[91] As McGhie and Wamai's analysis of the role of women in the transitional justice process has noted, representatives from women's civil society are also assumed to have particular political interests and preferences that will influence their position in negotiations and the reception of their involvement by political parties.[92]

The focus on ending communal violence, combined with a lack of interest in helping women to access health care, rebuild homes and market businesses post-violence, illustrates the legacy of what Magdelena Zolkos terms the 'feminization of trauma', which identifies particular types of distress within clinical notions of trauma such as warfare and exposure to violence. This circumscription of trauma results in the exclusion 'of other aspects of mass violence … such as indirect and socio-material stressors'.[93] Zolkos also notes that these definitions include women and children as gendered subjects of trauma 'in cases of direct physical violence, but not, for example, in cases of socio-material hardship. These manifestations of the conflict violence remain 'absent from redressive politics'.[94] The lack of motivation to implement Agenda 4 themes in the years following the peace negotiations is also evidence of the 'international legalist paradigm' that 'focuses on generating elite and mass compliance with international humanitarian norms',[95] often while underrating 'the gendered and socioeconomic ramifications of violent conflict, which may include HIV/AIDS, widowhood and poverty'.[96] While the process of statebuilding offers the opportunity to 'address engrained gender inequalities and develop a state that is accountable to women', these opportunities are often

---

[90] Deniz Kandiyoti, 'Bargaining with Patriarchy', *Gender and Society*, 2:3 (1988), 275.
[91] Kandiyoti, 'Bargaining with Patriarchy', 285.
[92] McGhie and Wamai, *Beyond the Numbers*, 8.
[93] Magdelena Zolkos, 'Redressive Politics and the Nexus of Trauma, Transitional Justice and Reconciliation', in Susanne Buckley-Zistel *et al.* (eds), *Transitional Justice Theories* (New York: Routledge, 2014), 176.
[94] *Ibid.*, 176–77.
[95] Rosemary Nagy, 'Transitional Justice as a Global Project: Critical Reflections', *Third World Quarterly*, 29:2 (2008), 278.
[96] *Ibid.*, 278.

lost in processes that are gender blind.[97] Some of the most egregious failures in terms of recognising the centrality of gender in the period immediately following the cessation of violence in early 2008 are the continuing internal displacement of women and children years after the initial violence,[98] as well as elevated rates of post-traumatic stress disorder, depression and suicidal ideation among women.[99]

National human rights community response

In the aftermath of the 2007–2008 post-election violence, Kenya was dealing with an extraordinary humanitarian crisis that finally, if perhaps belatedly, troubled the international fiction that Kenya was a stable democracy. Amid the shock and incredulity of Kenya's urban elite in the face of such apparently well-organised atrocities reaching the heart of major urban and regional centres, the human rights community working in Kenya was formulating its response to the crisis. The most fulsome of these reports is the *Waki Report*, published in October 2008. The *Waki Report* was produced by the Commission of Inquiry into Post-Election Violence (CIPEV) and named for the Chair of the Commission, Justice Philip Waki. The Commission was established as one of three commissions as part of the Kofi Annan-negotiated power-sharing agreement between Odinga and Kibaki. The CIPEV was tasked with 'investigating the facts and circumstances surrounding the violence, the conduct of security agencies in their handling of it, and to make recommendations concerning these and other matters'.[100] Several reports were also published by NGOs, detailing the experiences of victims of the violence, which contributed to the demand for a national inquiry.

Two reports provided complementary accounts of the crisis, which will be examined in some detail here: *On the Brink of the Precipice: A Human Rights Account of Kenya's Post-2007 Election Violence*, produced by the Kenya National Commission on Human Rights (KNCHR), and *Women Paid the Price!*, produced by the women's rights NGO the Centre

---

[97] Clare Castillejo, 'Gender, Fragility and the Politics of Statebuilding', Norwegian Peacebuilding Resource Centre, 2012, http://genderandsecurity.org:8080/sites/default/files/Castillejo_-_G_Fragility_Statebuild.pdf [accessed 6 January 2017].
[98] Human Rights Watch, *Turning Pebbles*.
[99] Kirsten Johnson *et al.*, 'A National Population-based Assessment of 2007–2008 Election-related Violence in Kenya', *Conflict and Health*, 8:2 (2014), https://conflictandhealth.biomedcentral.com/articles/10.1186/1752-1505-8-2 [accessed 6 January 2017].
[100] Waki, *Report of the Commission of Inquiry into Post-Election Violence*' (also referred to as the *Waki Report*), vii.

for Rights Education and Awareness (CREAW). The KNCHR's report addressed the experiences of violence and displacement of all victims across the country, explicitly from the position of a national human rights institution. The CREAW report dealt with the experiences of women and was a contributing report to the *Waki Report* mentioned above.[101] Reflecting its national mandate and international obligations,[102] the KNCHR report offers national coverage and examines a range of categories of violence experienced in each province. Further, it hypothesises about the culpability of the Kenyan government and its security forces in domestic and international criminal jurisdictions, as well as their obligations under human rights law. In contrast, the CREAW, which is a Nairobi-based NGO with fewer resources, dealt with the treatment and experiences of women living in five of the worst affected areas of Kenya. As a result of its smaller geographic area of interest and focus on one subset of victims – women – the CREAW report could present more self-narration as testimony. In contrast, while the KNCHR conducted more than a thousand interviews with a variety of victims and witnesses, very few extended quotes or individual perspectives from these sources appear in the final report. As David Morris observes, 'voice matters precisely because suffering remains, to some degree, inaccessible. Voice is what gets silenced, repressed, pre-empted, denied.'[103] Despite the imperative to bear witness, the strength of many voices in aggregate paradoxically weakens the narrative force of the report and moves away from foregrounding the pain and hardship endured by these witnesses and survivors.

As both reports are explicitly bounded by national legal rights and international human rights frameworks, the texts are used here to explore the limitations of the transnational discourse of human rights, insofar as the expectations and demands of this framework require certain kinds of bounded subjectivities and are predisposed to particular types of solutions. This study examines the ways in which these

[101] The CREAW was invited to contribute to gathering evidence of sexual violence during the post-election violence by the Kenya National Human Rights Commission which was considered in the *Waki Report* along with reports by the Catholic Diocese of Nakuru, CARE Kenya and FIDA Kenya. *Waki Report*, 261, http://reliefweb.int.sites/reliefweb.int/files/resources/15A00F569813F4D-549257607001F459D-Full_Report.pdf [accessed 22 April 2022].
[102] Kenya National Commission on Human Rights, The Kenya National Commission on Human Rights Act, No. 14 2011 (KNHCR/National Council for Law Reporting, 2011/2012), www.kenyalaw.org/kl/fileadmin/pdfdownloads/Acts/KenyaNationalCommissiononHumanRights_Act_No14of2011.pdf [accessed 10 September 2018]; Office of the High Commissioner for Human Rights, *Principles Relating to the Status of National Institutions (The Paris Principles)*, GA Resolution 48/134, 1993, www.ohchr.org/EN/ProfessionalInterest/Pages/StatusOfNationalInstitutions.aspx [accessed 30 August 2021].
[103] Morris, 'About Suffering: Voice, Genre, and Moral Community', 29.

reports contextualise their findings and represent the interviewees, as well as the types of expectations the authors have of their subjects.

The Kenya National Human Rights Commission Report

Kenya's first National Commission on Human Rights (KNCHR) was established by statute in 2002.[104] The constituting Act of the KNCHR empowered the Commission to investigate 'any human rights violation', 'ensure that the government complies with its human rights obligations' and 'cooperate with various institutions for the promotion and protection of human rights'.[105] Unsurprisingly, the KNCHR report entirely relied on international human rights frameworks and investigative structures. The KNCHR also contextualised the post-election violence within an uncritical, linear history of electoral violence, endemic disadvantage experienced by particular communities, unequal resource allocation and ethno-political power structures that were in place before independence and consolidated under Jomo Kenyatta. However, as I have illustrated in earlier chapters, political, gendered and ethnic violence were features of the colonial period and a preferred governance strategy of the colonial government. Therefore, any attempt to examine the 2007 post-election violence must trace the roots – tangled as they are – at least as far back as the colonial epoch, when public violence was employed to assert social and political authority, and take up the challenge of Carotenuto and Shadle, as they implore us to move Kenyan historiography beyond the usual discussions of violence as anticolonial resistance to 'challenge the broader portrayal of violence in histories of colonial Africa'.[106] Instead of seeking a more complex truth, the human rights discourse reproduced in these reports combines with the repetition of a well-accepted, unexamined history of violence to give an impression of violence as a recurring and unsurprising element of Kenya's postcolonial democracy to be reported on in the aftermath, but with no real commitment or aspiration to effectively prevent its recurrence.

Following the post-election violence, the KNCHR undertook 'an investigation on the character and scope of human rights violations ... [and] document[ed] the post-election violence to ensure that there would be a comprehensive record of the violations committed during that period as a basis for enabling redress'.[107] Its investigative teams conducted thirty-six missions across 136 constituencies in Kenya and Uganda. The

---

[104] Kenya National Commission on Human Rights, 'About Us', n.d. www.knchr.org/About-Us/Establishment [accessed 10 February 2022]. The current Kenya National Commission on Human Rights (KNCHR) was established under s59 of the 2010 Constitution. Both the Constitution and the KNCHR are products of the internationally brokered peace deal following the 2007 poll.
[105] Kenya National Commission on Human Rights, *On the Brink of the Precipice*.
[106] Carotenuto and Shadle, 'Introduction'.
[107] Kenya National Commission on Human Rights, *On the Brink of the Precipice*, 10.

missions collected more than 1,200 statements from victims of violence, secondary materials from newspaper reports, and international and local NGO reporting.[108] The title – *On the Brink of the Precipice: A Human Rights Account of Kenya's Post-2007 Election Violence* – is evocative. It immediately directs the reader to the structural fragility of the post-independence Kenyan state and situates the KNCHR as an authoritative narrator of the 'human rights account'. When the report was published in August 2008, Kenya was, in fact, *still* on the brink. The African Union-brokered unity government was only six months old, and thousands of IDPs languished in poorly resourced camps in Nairobi and regional centres around the country.[109] In 2014, the African Union team of Annan, Machel and Mkapa declared that the crisis had passed.[110]

The structure, hypotheses and findings of the KNCHR report are directed and framed by the imperatives of international human rights law and culture, which use testimony as the primary evidence of rights violations. The domination of human rights culture can be seen in the KNCHR's moral indictment of the Kenyan government during the violence, which refers first to international law and culture rather than locally resonant law or messaging:

> at a point when Kenyans required the most protection, the Government of Kenya retrogressed [sic.] in the fulfilment of its obligations under various human rights conventions, including the International Covenant on Civil and Political Rights (ICCPR), the International Covenant on Economic, Social and Cultural Rights, the International Convention on Elimination of Racial Discrimination (ICERD), [the] Convention on the Rights of the Child (CRC) and [the] Convention on Elimination of Discrimination Against Women (CEDAW).[111]

The first two aims of the KNCHR report are 'to assess the treaty-founded human rights obligations of Kenya as a state' and 'analyse the criminal responsibility of alleged perpetrators within frameworks of international criminal law and domestic criminal law'.[112] The report profiled the types of violence experienced by Kenyans by geographic location, situating the violence within the long history of violent contests over elections and resources, which can be traced back to the colonial period. The report began by listing the three key concerns of the investigation into the post-election violence:

---

[108] *Ibid.*, 12.
[109] Human Rights Watch, 'Ballots to Bullets'.
[110] Kofi Annan, Graça Machel and Benjamin Mkapa, *Back from the Brink: The 2008 Mediation Process and Reforms in Kenya* (Geneva: African Union Commission, 2008)
[111] Kenya National Commission on Human Rights, *On the Brink of the Precipice*, 7.
[112] *Ibid.*

- to assess the treaty-founded human rights obligations of Kenya as a state as well as the obligations of various non-state actors whose actions or omissions contributed to the violations ... and recommend accountability measures to effectively redress these violations and to deter future violations
- to analyse the criminal responsibility of alleged perpetrators within the frameworks of international criminal law and domestic criminal law, to enable [the KNCHR] to make ... determination[s] of culpability and enforcement of sanctions against perpetrators
- to make other general recommendations on governance issues that would enable Kenya to undertake an effective truth, justice and reconciliation process.[113]

In keeping with this emphasis on international human rights and state responsibility, the recommendations fall into several categories that pertain to criminal culpability: domestic and international criminal liability; findings of whether the crimes of genocide and crimes against humanity were committed; and findings 'in respect of Kenya's human rights obligations'.[114]

Thus, a discourse based exclusively on international human rights law frames and narrows the scope of any investigation. Further, the report almost exclusively examined perpetrator behaviour, accountability and motivation. The focus on criminality drew attention to perpetrator groups, motives and actions rather than victim groups or witnesses. Further, the imperative to find the culprits and identify the rights violated did not prompt the authors to seek diverse causes, and it does not foreground, or even seek to represent, victims as embodied witnesses and stakeholders in the transitional justice process.

Although the investigation was exclusively concerned with the violence surrounding the 2007 general election, the report situated the violence within the broader history of postcolonial Kenyan politics. Chapter 2, 'Triggers, fuellers [sic.] and root causes of post-election violence', situated the latest, and one of the most serious, national humanitarian crises within a familiar post-independence narrative. Kenyans and academics who are interested in politics and public life in Kenya cannot escape the narrative of the triumphant, but increasingly authoritarian, Jomo Kenyatta and his uninterrupted fifteen-year reign, the institution of ethno-politics, land grabbing and resource inequity that has stunted Kenya's economic and human development. The report identified the canonical drivers of 'radical inequality' in Kenya, which we saw develop in Chapter 2 – 'ethnic-based political organisation ...

[113] *Ibid.*, 6.
[114] *Ibid.*, 8–9.

contending citizenship narratives, [the construction of] outsider-indigenous [dichotomies and] unresolved historical grievances, especially with regard to land allocation.'[115]

Finally, the KNCHR reprised the 'long train of violence and impunity', noting that the Rift Valley, which was the 'epicentre' of violence at the 2007 general election, was also the site of mass evictions and killings during the push for the reinstatement of multiparty politics in 1991. The KNCHR report structured the statements of victims into a familiar and unchanging world in which ethno-politics and structural disadvantage are the ever-present, unquestioned drivers of rights violations.

The combination of the predominantly legal narrative and the reproduction of the canonical history of politically driven violence does not allow for other voices or for speaking in other registers. Even the categories of suffering are limited to certain predetermined symptoms 'privileging particular types of distressing situation as proto-typical of traumatic events [which] ... excludes from its realm other aspects of mass violence, for example those that visually do not correspond to the ideas and images of traumatization'.[116] As Ian Patel argues, in the pursuit of evidence of violations, 'individual self-narration is often made to serve a collective or community function'.[117] The imperatives of the international human rights framework and the mission of the report have far-reaching implications for the design of any research that follows, as well as the characterisation of the findings. The legal framework of conventions and national and international criminal liability consume the report.

An abiding conundrum of international human rights law is that the responsibility to protect individuals lies with states, which are frequent violators of human rights. The unquestioning reproduction of these orthodox histories reinforces traditional power structures. Indeed, KNCHR's report demanded restorative justice from the government it condemned. This focus on state responsibility directs the analysis and recommendations of human rights reporting – often accusing the government of perpetrating human rights violations while also demanding more government services. The intention of much narrative-based research is to 'emphasise the ability of self-narration to undermine the authoritative discourses of those in power',[118] but the increasingly painful irony of this work is that self-narration can reinforce hegemonic power structures and entrench disadvantage by presenting the

---

[115] *Ibid.*
[116] Zolkos, 'Redressive Politics', 176.
[117] Ian Patel, 'The Role of Testimony and Testimonial Analysis in Human Rights Advocacy and Research', *State Crime: Journal of the International State Crime Initiative*, 1.2 (2012), 237.
[118] *Ibid.*, 240.

violence as inevitable. This disempowers victims and activists who are seeking to avoid future violence. As Patel argues, in the field of human rights, 'testimony is often presented as ratifying an existing normative discourse about human rights. This process in effect disenfranchises original narratives of their own terms of reference in favour of normative international discourses on human rights.'[119]

Although the plight of victims of the post-election violence is at the centre of the human rights violations investigated by the KNCHR, their needs as individuals and communities are rarely mentioned. The KNCHR report noted its travelling investigative teams offered some ad hoc assistance to IDP communities because they had occasional opportunities to do so:

> As we travelled the country to speak with people who have suffered during the post-election violence, we witnessed first hand the enormous humanitarian crisis caused by the violence. We, therefore, made it part of our work to liaise with organisations that have the mandate to provide humanitarian needs, to ensure that the plight of the people with whom we spoke was not overlooked and to help move Kenya as quickly as possible towards a better future for all of her people.[120]

But, in spite of the extensive gathering of victims' stories of violence, no attention was given to the victims' priorities in the aftermath. Although KNCHR staff reported that they assisted in enrolling orphaned children in schools and introduced victims to support services where this was possible, these acts were the ad hoc facilitations of concerned individuals rather than part of a strategy of post-conflict rehabilitation. Further, the self-identified needs of victims were not represented in the report. Witnesses and victims were invited to recount their experiences of violence, displacement and loss. However, if they discussed their future plans or how they would prefer assistance to be provided, these insights were not presented in the final report. As this was not 'solely dependent on empirically verifiable standards', the testimonies were a malleable commodity that had the flexibility to allow the KNCHR to 'direct [it] as it pleases' towards 'ends rooted in ... real political goods'.[121]

The limitations of the uses of testimony are indicative of the constraints that human rights processes can place on witness and victim statements, as well as the complexity of their narratives.[122] Patel argues

[119] *Ibid.*, 236.
[120] Kenya National Commission on Human Rights, *On the Brink of the Precipice*, 16.
[121] Patel, 'The Role of Testimony and Testimonial', 244.
[122] For a discussion of alternative, more complex narratives of the 2007 post-election violence, see Catherine Muhoma, *Versions of Truth and Collective Memory: The Quest for Forgiveness and Healing in the Context of Kenya's Post-election Violence*, 2012, *Research in African Literatures*, 43:1 (2013), 166–73, which

that testimony evidence 'is presented as an end in itself, as something that bears inherent use-value', but that also accrues an exchange value in which testimony – 'thick rivers of fact' – is used to promote political movements or support future legal mechanisms.[123] The uses of testimony prescribe the choice of speakers and dictate the narrative forms that can be heard and are acceptable – recalling here the experiences of women in Bar Ober who were *literally* not being heard by institutions when they spoke DhoLuo.

Centre for Rights Education and Awareness

The Centre for Rights Education and Awareness (CREAW) is a Kenyan NGO that was registered in 1999. It was established by women lawyers 'who had common goals and a shared purpose to confront the low awareness of women's real needs and rights in Kenya'.[124] The CREAW developed its mandate 'from established international, regional and local human rights principles, customs and practices'.[125] Its report, *Women Paid the Price!*,[126] collated evidence of women's experiences of post-election violence in five of the most seriously affected regional centres. It used focus group discussions, questionnaires, in-depth interviews and case studies to present the experiences of women in Nairobi, Naivasha, Nakuru, Burnt Forest and Eldoret. Further, it used statistical information on rates of sexual and other violence experienced by women, as reported by major medical facilities. The report relied on extensive interviews with women and girls and used their experiences to ground the analysis.

Women Paid the Price! began by outlining Kenya's international obligations under the African Charter on Human and People's Rights, the ICCPR, the Convention against Torture (CAT), the CEDAW and the Convention on the Rights of the Child (CRC). The CREAW also noted the government's obligations under national law – particularly the Kenyan Constitution and the *Sexual Offences Act 2006*.[127] The NGO stated that its motivation in conducting the study was to 'examine, understand and

---

examines the publication of the Kenyan literary series *Kwani?* and its special double edition and responds to the violence by publishing poetry, fiction, non-fiction and visual submissions; Billy Kahora (ed.), *Kwani?* 05 'Hung'arisha Haswa!' (2008).
[123] Patel, 'The Role of Testimony and Testimonial', 237.
[124] Centre for Rights Education and Awareness (CREAW), 'Mission, Vision and Values', 2014, http://creawkenya.org/ke/mision-vision-values [accessed 28 February 2015]; this is no longer accessible, and Information on the CREAW can now be found at https://home.creaw.org.
[125] *Ibid.*
[126] Centre for Rights Education and Awareness (CREAW), *Women Paid the Price!* (Nairobi: CREAW, 2008).
[127] *Ibid.*

document the nature and extent of gender-based and sexual violence experienced by the IDPs following the 2007 post-elections violence'. Further, it sought to understand the 'main causes and consequences' and the 'basic trends and patterns of sexual violence' reported by women in the post-election period. In addition, the authors sought to document the experiences of women who had survived sexual and gender-based violence, as well as their interpretations of the problem. Significantly, the report closed with 'legal and policy interventions for addressing the problem of sexual and gender-based violence against vulnerable women and young girls particularly in conflict situations'.[128] The move from international obligations and national and regional concerns to the 'temporal and circumstantial specificities of individual self-narration' is a 'familiar hermeneutic' for those working in the industry of human rights.[129]

Here, I explore the tensions between the transnational discourse of human rights, which was foregrounded in the CREAW report, and the voices and priorities of the women interviewed. There is a shadow between the narrative structure of the report writers and the narrative of the women at the centre of the interviews. The two images that emerge are contradictory – one requires women to report more, access more services, demand rights and speak out, while the other constructs women as being ignorant and physically and economically vulnerable, and as prioritising their dependents' needs above their own. Rather than presenting complex individual agents, the report sought a bounded narrative for the victims that reinforced the goals of the organisation of rights protection, promotion and education. Further, it illustrated the necessity of the organisation, given the women's demonstrable need for education.

Women who were (and in many cases, remain) living in IDP camps reported an inadequate police presence and inadequate food and shelter. Insecure sleeping arrangements, in which men and women slept in mixed groups outside or in mixed-sex tents, increased women's vulnerability to assault. Women and girls who could not earn an income in the camps reported exchanging sex for money, food and other essential items. The vulnerability of women in these camps may have encouraged them to stay in, or form, unsafe relationships to access male protection. Although it is reasonable to assume that rates of intimate partner violence were higher than usual, it is difficult to determine the rates because women were reluctant to report their breadwinner and protector to police. Critically, the CREAW lamented that:

> 82 per cent of survivors of sexual violence interviewed did not formally report the incidents to the police ... the high level of non-reporting of sexual violence can be attributed to lack of awareness of

[128] *Ibid.*
[129] Patel, 'The Role of Testimony and Testimonial', 244.

the law and or minimal understanding of human rights. In addition gender discrimination, lack of sensitivity and understanding of the nature of sexual crimes all contribute to minimal confidence in the way police handle sexual violence cases, the manner in which trials are conducted and concluded. The absence of protection for victims and witnesses is another factor impeding justice for SGBV [sexual and gender-based violence] survivors.[130]

Faced with these kinds of obstacles, and keeping in mind the experiences of women with police and health professionals in relative peacetime, it is unsurprising that most women chose not to report the violence they experienced. A mother interviewed by the CREAW explained her reasons for not reporting the rape of her daughter to police:

> [M]y daughter was molested in this camp ... when she had left to visit the toilets. There was no one who came to her rescue and I don't think there was any police around. When I came home, I was informed about the incident and I took her to the hospital. We got an ambulance and went to the Referral Hospital where she was treated. I however, did not make any further reports. The reason why I didn't report is because firstly I was thankful to God that my daughter didn't suffer a worse fate. Also, we have so many problems and I don't think I can handle further processes from the police.[131]

Paradoxically, these women are often ignorant of human rights and Kenyan national law, and the report implied that if women were willing to assume a human rights subjectivity and actively pursue their rights, they would receive real benefits. However, while the CREAW acknowledged that these women would have faced significant barriers to rights access, it did not address the structural barriers to service provision and institutional care in its response to the violence the interviewees experienced. Further, it did not note the woeful state of these services outside periods of crisis. Ideally, of course, women would have access to competent police who record and investigate their complaints and, where possible, prosecute the perpetrators. However, with a non-report rate of more than 80 per cent, the women instead chose to report their experiences to family or NGOs: 'high percentages of victims report their attacks to immediate family members, friends and the Church while the lowest scores constitute reports to the police, local administration and husbands'.[132] The CREAW's frustration was palpable:

> [D]espite the fact that [several of the women interviewed] could remember and even identify their attackers, most of them had not sought medical attention or legal redress for the crimes against them.

---

[130] CREAW, *Women Paid the Price!*
[131] *Ibid.*
[132] *Ibid.*

> The women all missed the 72 hour window during which they could receive medical protection from HIV and sexually transmitted diseases, and have medical evidence gathered for legal prosecution of rapists.[133]

Reading the CREAW report 'against the grain'[134] allows us to relocate the female subjects who are at the heart, and simultaneously at the margins, of these narratives. The human rights system requires a reframing of the narrative structure of the women's stories to fit them to the expectations of human rights discourse, which ironically so often silences the subjects of its inquiry. The report is evidence that women felt that recording their experiences was important. Instead of focusing almost solely on the lack of formal reporting and the related states' failures to make mechanisms for formal reporting and prosecution available, an examination of the informal and non-legal strategies and networks developed and used by these women would be instructive.

'The vulnerable, hard-won, confessional human voice': The limits of human rights subjectivity

The discourse of international human rights seeks out, and often creates, particular kinds of subjects and represents only the testimony that is pertinent to the goals of the rights project. The irony of this new subjectivity demanded by the human rights culture is that it deliberately limits the identities and voices of victims to prove human rights abuses. Victims' speech is reduced to its instrumentality – how well an account supports the larger aims of an NGO – or the investigative international committee becomes a primary concern of the interview. The imperative to speak and the centrality of witnessing to the human rights project have elevated the speech elicited in human rights contexts to what Patel describes as 'a species of sociological and legal evidence',[135] in which the experiential reality – 'the always irreducibly singular, subjective and corporeal lives'[136] of these victims and witnesses – is lost. This loss has profound implications for policy and the programme delivery of human rights projects. If the complexity of testimony is reduced to the one-dimensional requirements of transna-

---

[133] *Ibid.*
[134] Pamela Scully, *Liberating the Family? Gender and British Slave Emancipation in the Rural Western Cape, South Africa, 1823–1853* (Cape Town: David Philip, 1998). As Lalu notes, there are a number of strategies to read 'against the grain' that produce their own 'tactical implication[s]': Premesh Lalu, 'The Grammar of Domination and the Subjection of Agency: Colonial Texts and Modes of Evidence', *History and Theory*, 39:4 (2000), 68.
[135] Patel, 'The Role of Testimony and Testimonial', 236.
[136] Zolkos, 'Redressive Politics', 176.

tional human rights, how can programmes and policy be developed to reflect and accommodate local infrastructural, social and cultural priorities? Therefore, the final frustration of the process of human rights reporting is that even where human rights subjectivity is realised by individual speakers and they report their experiences, the agency and ownership of their speech is undermined by the human rights culture that first encouraged them to come forward.

Human rights culture requires victims and witnesses to speak out about their experiences for many reasons, such as to access the material and social benefits accorded to those who have experienced trauma, to prove their membership of a persecuted group and to provide evidence of the atrocities that occurred. Patel examines the dominance of narrative-based research in human rights research and advocacy and takes 'issue with ... [its] reliance and promotion of self-narration'.[137] He argues that although the imperative of first-person evidence *should* drive human rights work, the epistemological foundations, assumptions and uses of such testimony have remained largely unexamined. In part, Patel attributes this uncritical acceptance of the testimony of survivors and witnesses by the human rights industry to an understandable desire to respect those whose stories had previously been violently silenced. He observes that critiquing the framework and use of survivor speech risks, 'the criticism that in doing so one represses the voice of those who have suffered oppression'.[138] Further, he claims that victims and witnesses who self-narrate[139] often derive a significant 'use-value' from telling their story – the value of public acknowledgement of suffering – which has the potential to promote victim-centred justice programmes. For Patel, the central epistemological assumption underwriting testimony evidence has its basis in a notion of liberal self-determination:

> I am free to give an account of myself and in so doing proclaim the value of my life. As the sign of those rights I am born into, I am free to vindicate, reflect on, or celebrate my lived experiences, this narrative acting as a testimony which in itself can be seen as a form of legal, moral, and political standing.[140]

This 'humble, vulnerable, hard-won, confessional human voice'[141] is a critical element of another related academic inquiry. The responsibility to speak is not the only burden that victims must accept; it is coupled

[137] Patel, 'The Role of Testimony and Testimonial', 236.
[138] *Ibid.*,
[139] *Ibid.*: Patel used the term 'self-narration to refer to narratives told in the first person by a narrator who recounts the extreme experiences of conflict situations'.
[140] *Ibid.*, 253, emphasis in original.
[141] *Ibid.*

with the imperative to adopt what Merry terms a 'human rights subjectivity', in which the act of reporting one's experience of rights violation animates this double subjectivity. By reporting their experience to state authorities or a member of a human rights organisation, victims and witnesses adopt a subjectivity that is tied to a culture outside local community norms. Victims of harm who adopt a human rights framework to seek redress for the way their kinsmen have treated them assume 'a double subjectivity as rights-bearers and as injured kinsmen and survivors'.[142] Thus, Patel's formulation of 'self-narration as testimony' – a speech-act that is central to the human rights project – is a primary constitutive element of Merry's human rights subjectivity. However, as shown in the experiences of the Bar Ober and Butere focus groups, there is an absence of functioning formal and cultural support structures that can offer material assistance. They are often ostracised by people whose primary job is to support social justice outcomes in health and criminal justice. As these mechanisms have comprehensively failed these women in peacetime, why do human rights practitioners demand that they adopt risky new subjectivities during periods of great existential stress? Kenyan women often *know* their rights. They also understand that their rights are completely out of reach.

---

[142] Sally Engle Merry, *Human Rights and Gender Violence: Translating International Law into Local Justice* (Chicago: Chicago University Press, 2006), 180–81.

5

Gendered Citizenship, Politics and Public Space: Women's Participation in Government

'There's this belief that they can't lead, that's why they didn't stand up.'[1]

Following the 2007 post-election violence, this chapter examines the effects one of the important products of the transitional justice process, the (albeit protracted) promulgation of the 2010 Constitution and its extensive Bill of Rights; and the reception and effects of the constitutionally enshrined Two-Thirds Gender Principle at the 2013 elections, the first to be held under the new dispensation. As we have seen, the 2010 Constitution is heir to Kenyan political and cultural memory steeped in decades of resistance to autocracy, and multiple movements for constitutional reform. The history of demands from Kenyan civil society for constitutional reform is inextricably linked to demands for a return to pluralist politics, and for tangible improvements in service delivery and social justice outcomes. The drafting of this Constitution was the latest moment in the dominant, cyclical narrative of Kenya's always imminent democratic rebirth.

The persistent post-independence calls for a new constitution encompass demands relating not only to the primacy and integrity of the text of the Constitution itself, but also to the realisation of *constitutionalism*, a system of values that includes the separation of powers, the rule of law, the protection of fundamental rights and freedoms, and the promotion and protection of institutions that support democracy.[2] Indeed, Murunga, Okello and Sjögren characterise the postcolonial struggle as one driven by a rejection of the 'African experience of diluted constitutionalism ... justified and practised by ... African leadership as a trade-off between democracy and development'.[3] As previous constitutional renewal processes in Kenya have shown, however, the mere fact of constitutional reform alone is not sufficient to guar-

---

[1] Participants in the KHRC focus group explained why so few women contested positions in the elections, 'Focus Group Discussion Analysis II' (Nairobi: Kenya Human Rights Commission, 2013).
[2] Godwin R. Murunga *et al.* (eds), *Kenya: The Struggle for a New Constitutional Order* (London: Zed Books, 2014), 36.
[3] *Ibid.*, 3.

antee governance reform.⁴ Although it inherited the work of years of local activism around constitutional reform throughout the late colonial, and postcolonial periods, the 2010 Constitution was primarily developed and deployed as a direct response to the 2007 post-election violence and is, consequently, a product and keystone of the liberal peacebuilding project in Kenya – a process, as I argued in Chapter 4, that privileges security and state stability over building an organic and vernacular positive peace.

The explicit focus of the new Bill of Rights on gender and minority rights sits incongruously beside the local history of politically expedient colonial and post-independence constitutional reform detailed in Chapter 2. Although perhaps unexpectedly similar in form, the 2010 Constitution shares a focus on promoting minority and under-represented groups with the late colonial attempts to assuage rebellion by offering token representation of African and Indian communities in the colonial government. The emphasis on women's rights was so prominent in the public discourse around the 2010 Constitution that William 'Willie' Mutunga, the then Chief Justice of the Supreme Court and a well-known human rights activist before he joined the court, described it as 'Wanjiku's Constitution' – remembering that, as described in the Introduction to this book, the Chief Justice was known to keep a sculpture of Wanjiku on display in his chambers because 'Wanjiku is the boss'.⁵

While the need to address women's marginalisation in public life finds formal acknowledgement in the 2010 Constitution, these gains on paper have not been reflected in women's representation in public office or in access to prevention and redress for rights violations they experience. This chapter explores the reception of women in political and public spaces in Kenya by exploring the experiences of two of the first African women to occupy political office in Kenya, and by examining an August 2013 incident in which the inaugural Women's Representative for Nairobi County, Rachel Shebesh, was slapped by the Governor of Nairobi, Evans Kidero – an incident recorded on video by journalists at the scene and widely circulated and discussed. These events sit here in dialogue with the views of Kenyan women gathered through focus group interviews and informal discussions with women living in low-income and slum areas of Nairobi, and women living in rural areas of Kisumu County in western Kenya. These conversations raise foun-

---

⁴ For further discussion of African constitutionalism – particularly in East Africa – see H.W.O. Okoth-Ogendo, 'The Politics of Constitutional Change in Kenya Since Independence', *African Affairs*, 71:282 (1972), 9–34; Daniel Branch and Nicholas Cheeseman, 'The Politics of Control in Kenya: Understanding the Bureaucratic-Executive State, 1952–78', *Review of African Political Economy*, 33:107 (2006), 11–31.
⁵ Wambui Mwangi, 'Silence is a Woman' *The New Inquiry*, 4 June 2013, http://thenewinquiry.com/essays/silence-is-a-woman [accessed 16 August 2021].

dational questions about the ability of the liberal peace framework, and the human rights imaginary more broadly, to challenge both Kenya's ethno-patriarchal politics and Kenyan women's own ambivalent relationships with their citizenship rights.

I examine the risks and benefits of participating in this remade constitutional democracy for women at the margins of the economic and political nation. Further, I explore the reasoning of women themselves in choosing to inhabit particular kinds of gendered bodies and to perform (or to be *read* as performing) certain kinds of identities in public spaces as rights-bearing subjects, as citizens, voters and politicians. Rather than uncritically encouraging women to take up identities as rights-bearing, autonomous individuals, as human rights practitioners we must also ask ourselves, knowing the serious and pervasive risk of violence and harassment facing women who take on these contested subject positions, how can we in good conscience as a human rights community ask these women to take up such risky identities, where we have been fundamentally incapable of protecting them from the potentially catastrophic physical and emotional damage their assertion of a human rights subjectivity may invite?

'Honourable and gracious' ladies

There has been no period of Kenyan history in which women were a visible, numerically significant or powerful decision-making constituency. This invisibility has been exacerbated by the fact that, prior to the 1990s, the few women who *have* managed to hold positions in colonial or post-independence governments have received little scholarly attention and have been almost completely overlooked in the independence history of Kenya, in both primary and secondary sources.[6] This phenomenon has produced what Susan Geiger terms an 'accumulation of androcentric bias' in the understanding of Kenyan history; as a result, little is known about the early experiences of Kenyan women in public political life.[7] In fact, until Phoebe Musandu published her 2019 paper, 'Tokenism or Representation? The Political Careers of the First African Women in Kenya's Legislative Council', there had been little of substance written in English about the first two African women to join the government of the Colony of Kenya when they were nominated to the Legislative Council of Kenya (LegCo).

---

[6] Phoebe Musandu, 'Tokenism or Representation? The Political Careers of the First African Women in Kenya's Legislative Council (LEGCO), 1958–1962', *Women's History Review,* 28:4 (2019), 589.
[7] Susan Geiger, *TANU Women: Gender and Culture in the Making of Tanganyikan Nationalism, 1955–1965* (Portsmouth: Heinemann, 1997), 9. As quoted in Musandu, 'Tokenism or Representation?' 589.

Predating the 2010 Constitution and the provisions for women's representation under the Two-Thirds Gender Principle by over fifty years, women's representation in the LegCo began the in the same way that African men's representation was first achieved – through nominated positions. Jemima Gecaga was nominated by the Governor under the 1957 Lennox-Boyd Constitution. This power was preserved in the pre-independence 1961 Lancaster House Constitution, which is how Priscilla Abwao was able to be nominated to the LegCo that year by Governor Patrick Renison. Both Gecaga and Abwao were products of the missionary education system which sought to prepare Kenyan women to fulfil their roles as part of the 'civilising mission', their nomination influenced by forces of social change across the continent where the demand for women's engagement in public politics was becoming more urgent and visible.[8]

The women themselves were very different, and offer a stark contrast in motivations, effectiveness and longevity in the Legislative Council. Jemima Gecaga was a well-connected, but seemingly not politically inclined, woman 'whose privileged background and gender served the political imaging interests of the colonial state instead of African women'.[9] Musandu argues persuasively that if Gecaga's nomination was designed to offer African women a representative in the Legislative Council, 'then it failed and not simply because she did not advocate for women'.[10] Like the myriad policy interventions in the years since Kenya's independence, Gecaga's nomination served only 'the state's cosmetic effort to portray itself as gender conscious without actually launching a more comprehensive effort to address the country's structural gender imbalances'.[11] As her nomination was disconnected from the world of women's organising that was taking place outside the government, this nominated position for one African woman was always going to be an ineffective gesture.[12] In the time Gecaga served in the Legislative Council (1958–1962), she rose to speak only once – to note that, while women who did not otherwise qualify to vote could do so based on their husband's income, she worried that men with more than one wife might struggle to show income for each extra wife. This was an exceptionally narrow advocacy position that, while nominally concerned with women's capacity to vote, failed to identify the crux of the problem or agitate for a meaningful solution.[13]

[8] Musandu, 'Tokenism or Representation?' 588.
[9] *Ibid.*, 591.
[10] *Ibid.*, 593.
[11] *Ibid.*
[12] *Ibid.*, 594.
[13] *Ibid.*, 592.

In stark contrast, Priscilla Abwao was a determined and vocal advocate and rose to speak in the legislature on many occasions. She was a fierce advocate for African women, making many key arguments in support of expanded women's education and opportunities in the early 1960s that remain depressingly familiar to women's rights advocates working in Kenya today. Abwao argued that 'the delivery of quality education to girls was not only of benefit to [the girls themselves] but to the country as well'; equal access to education was a factor without which 'no country can progress', and the provision of more educational facilities for girls would enable them to become 'better citizens'.[14] Her potentially revolutionary contribution was, however, gravely hampered by the manner of her nomination, her gender and the causes for which she fought. She was often characterised as a 'female African MLC [Member of Legislative Council] representing a gender with concerns that were implicitly apolitical and easy to resolve within a clearly defined, private female sphere' and was received as such.[15] When she organised a delegation of women to visit to Jomo Kenyatta – who, at the time, was being detained in Maralal – it was described as 'a delegation of social visitors who will discuss with him social problems affecting the women of Kenya'. Abwao, like the national women's organisation of which she was a member, Maendeleo ya Wanawake, was expected to avoid political issues.[16]

These slights and dismissals, and the characterisations of women's concerns as 'social' or outside the interest of 'real' politics, although frustrating, are predictable and are representative of a struggle for recognition in Kenyan public life that women have waged since the days of the early colony. More subtly, though no less galling for students of the history of women's political representation in Kenya, is the rejection of Abwao's contribution on the basis of her nomination (rather than election) to the Legislative Council. Strategically forgetting that African men had first entered the legislature via a single, nominated position only seventeen years before Priscilla Abwao was nominated, the now majority-African Legislative Council took the position that her nomination was undemocratic and, therefore, illegitimate. Opposition spokesperson P.D. Marrian (KANU) argued that 'that only those who had emerged victors at the ballot' had the mandate to weigh in on legislative matters, insisting that 'if in today's debate the Government is kept alive only by the force of its Nominated Members, it will have sacrificed the moral right to its position'.[17] Prominent politician and Mau Mau lawyer (and the first Kenyan to be admitted to the London

14 Ibid., 597.
15 Ibid., 596.
16 Ibid., 596.
17 Ibid., 599.

bar)[18] Arwings Kodhek repeatedly accused Abwao of being a colonial government stooge and a 'paper MLC', arguing:

> [S]urely if others have to fight it out like the hon. Minister looking at me now, to represent people in any democratic government and we understand that there is a democratic union government here, surely there should be no privilege for any particular person to come into the Legislative Council without having to fight it through and having gone through its stages at elections.'[19]

Abwao retorted that

> the Government was forced to nominate a woman, and my introduction in this house is not my fault, it is the hon. Members', especially the African Elected Members' fault. They should have been generous, Mr Speaker, I would not have come in this way.[20]

Abwao was never able to operate as a member of the Legislative Council unfettered by her gender, her nominated status and her unapologetically political agenda, and she resigned her position shortly after this exchange.[21]

Under the 2010 Constitution, women and other groups traditionally locked out of representative politics are provided with quotas in order to increase diversity in Kenyan political life and create space for different issues and leadership styles. But, as Marie Berry *et al.* note, '*how* women get included in politics matters'[22] and women elected to 'women-only' positions have experienced criticism and harassment frustratingly similar to that Abwao endured during her term in the early 1960s. Women occupying nominated seats in the 2017 Kenyan parliament have also reported intimidation by their own parties. Characterised as 'flower girls', spokesmen for major parties speak openly of the narrow roles they expect nominated members to perform. The power struggle between women MPs – and women elected to Women's Representative positions in particular – and patriarchal party hierarchies remains public and relentless. When pushing for disciplinary action against nominated MPs, Senate majority whip Irungu Kangata explained that, when MPs – especially nominated MPs – defy the leader or the party position, 'the essence of democracy is killed ... Whereas this duty falls on those elected, it is more pronounced for nominated lead-

---

[18] Sammy Wambua, 'Argwings Kodhek: A Native Upstart Who Dared Marry a White Woman', *The Standard Newspaper*, 27 January, 2019.
[19] Musandu, 'Tokenism or Representation?' 602
[20] *Ibid.*, 601
[21] *Ibid.*, 599
[22] Marie E. Berry *et al.*, 'Implementing Inclusion: Gender Quotas, Inequality, and Backlash in Kenya', *Politics & Gender,* 17:4 (2020), 20. Emphasis in original.

ers.'[23] Frustrated at the constant attempts of male powerbrokers to derail agendas developed by the then inaugural women MPs following the 2013 election, Kiambu County Women's Representative Ann Nyokabi shot back, 'they have been branding us and treating us like flower girls in Parliament but we are elected women who represent counties. We are not flower girls. The MPs want to control everything and we shall not allow them.'[24] This pattern of intimidation and bullying has continued unabated, and in late 2020 women MPs spoke out to reject the roles thrust upon them. In a fight to have funding allocated to Women's Representatives so that they could run their own programmes and deliver policy promises to their constituents as other MPs could, Naomi Waqo declared that 'even if I'm nominated, I will not allow anybody to intimidate me ... When we say something, we are told "Remember you're nominated." I will not be intimidated because my future is in God's hands.'[25]

The Two-Thirds Gender Principle 'down there at the grassroots'

In addition to a set of safeguards protecting all Kenyans against discrimination across a range of grounds, including age, sex, disability and marital status,[26] the 2010 Constitution attempted to address the systemic under-representation of women in public office in innovative ways. The most significant of these was the introduction of the 'Two-Thirds Gender Principle' (The Gender Principle) under Articles 27 and 81(b) of the Bill of Rights, which sought to guarantee that not more than two-thirds of public office positions in Kenya will be occupied by one gender. Further, the Constitution allocates a number of seats exclusively for women representatives at Senate (Art 98(1)(b), (c)) and county levels (Art 177(1)(b), 197(1)).[27] Following the 2007–2008 period of catastrophic violence and displacement, Kenyan women finally had the attention of the nation – their chronic under-representation in public office, as well as the mistreatment and negative perception of women

---

[23] Samwel Owino and Ibrahim Oruko, 'Why it's No Walk in the Park for Nominated MPs', *The Nation*, 10 September 2020, https://nation.africa/kenya/news/politics/why-it-s-no-walk-in-the-park-for-nominated-mps-1936494 [accessed 20 August 2021].
[24] Njenga Gicheha, 'Kenya: We Are Not Flower Girls – Women's Rep', *The Star*, 9 October, 2013, https://allafrica.com/stories/201310091422.html [accessed 16 August 2021].
[25] Owino and Oruko 'Why it's No Walk in the Park for Nominated MPs'.
[26] Article 27(4), *Constitution of Kenya*, 2010.
[27] Kenya Human Rights Commission, 'Achieving Gender Equity in National and Devolved Legislature without Amending Kenya's Constitution (2010)' (Nairobi: KHRC, 2012), 5.

vying for office and of women voters, had found new prominence in this moment of Kenya's democratic renewal.[28]

On paper, the Gender Principle offered a radical mechanism to boost women's representation within a rejuvenated democracy. But realisation of the principle was fatally impeded by institutional and socio-cultural factors with which the peacebuilding agenda had failed to adequately engage. The burden placed on grassroots women to understand the new Constitution and the ways in which it ostensibly supports their rights, as well as the requirement of women themselves to fight for their rights, failed to understand gender as a foundational source of marginalisation. Mired, as women so often are, in the 'everyday ecology of fear, mistrust, and anxiety'[29] of the ethno-patriarchal state, inhabiting the identity of an autonomous, human rights-bearing subject is frequently impossible.

Almost immediately the Gender Principle and its promise to empower women through parliamentary representation hit an impasse. The provisions protecting and promoting women's representation in public office had not included an implementation strategy. As failure to successfully implement the rule in time for the 2013 elections would threaten the constitutionality of parliament, government and civil society scrambled to propose solutions.[30] The Attorney General requested an advisory opinion of the Supreme Court of Kenya, which was delivered in December 2012,[31] and held that the Gender Principle was to be achieved 'progressively' rather than immediately, setting the parliament the deadline of 27 August 2015 to resolve the issue. As of the time of writing, there have been more than ten attempts to pass legislation that would enliven the Gender Principle. Notably, and perhaps not accidentally, several attempts were stymied by a lack of quorum at the debate stage.[32] Court rulings holding that parliament was unconstitutional and should be dissolved have been fruitless. Although a court ruling in 2012 provided some cover for the otherwise unconstitutional composition of the 2013 parliament (by requiring parliament to

---

[28] Ibid.
[29] Veena Das and Arthur Kleinman 'Introduction', in Veena Das et al. (eds), *Violence and Subjectivity* (Berkeley: University of California Press, 2000), 6.
[30] Nduta J. Kweheria, *Achieving Gender Equality in Elective Public Office in Kenya by March 2013*, KHRC Internal Briefing Paper (Nairobi: Kenya Human Rights Commission, 2012).
[31] Rose Wachuka and Samuel Ngure, 'Advisory Opinion of the Supreme Court in the Matter of the Principle Gender Representation in the National Assembly and the Senate', *KLR e-Newsletter*, 48 (2012), http://kenyalaw.org/kl/index.php?id=3660 [accessed 19 August 2021].
[32] David Mwere, 'Kenya: Two-Thirds Gender Rule Still Elusive after 10 Attempts', *The Nation Newspaper*, 22 December 2020, https://allafrica.com/stories/202012220134.html [accessed 19 August 2021].

pass legislation to provide for the realisation of the Gender Principle by August 2015), no such protection is available for the parliament as it is currently constituted.[33] That the Kenyan parliament had repeatedly failed (or refused) to enact constitutionally required legislation at the direction of the court is, as Marilyn Kamaru argues, 'a perfect example of defilement of democratic institutions and norms by democratically elected leaders'.[34] 'Defilement' is a pertinent choice of phrasing here, a legal idiom that recalls the bodily violation of children – a phenomenon all too familiar to women's rights activists in Kenya – thus figuring the Constitution, and democratic institutions more broadly, as bodies susceptible to violence and requiring protection and advocacy, as urgently as women and children themselves.

One of the most enduring challenges of the Gender Principle is that it requires women to be available to contest and win positions in open democratic contests for the rule to be effective. This places the responsibility for finding women to run for office in the hands of political parties and pre-selectors. Thus, the mechanism designed to promote women's participation pushes women into systems and contests which had previously deliberately engineered their political marginalisation. Moreover, it failed to engage with the existing views held by political parties, and many voters of regardless of gender, that women were 'weaker' candidates than men.[35] The combination of a lack of eligible women – unable to gather the funding and political backing, community support, and time away from work and family obligations needed to run for office – and the creation of elected positions which only women could contest encouraged the strongest female candidates to vie for women-only positions. De facto, the remaining seats became almost exclusively for male aspirants. The overwhelming disinterest among political parties, and voters, in supporting and promoting women candidates was evidenced in the 2013 election outcomes – less than 19 per cent of elected representatives were women; less than 10 per cent of members of parliament are women; and no women were elected to positions in the Senate outside the forty-seven designated women-only seats.[36] Following the 2017 elections, women held 20 per cent of elected positions and, significantly, were elected as governors and senators for the first time. Following the 2017 elections, women held more seats that at any other time in Kenya's history – 172 of the 1,883 total seats. But

[33] Marilyn Muthoni Kamaru, 'The Missing Piece: The Legislature, Gender Parity and Constitutional Legitimacy in Kenya', in Nanjala Nyabola and Marie-Emmanuelle Pommerolle (eds), *Where Women Are: Tracing Kenyan Women's Involvement in Elections and Political Leadership from 1963–2002* (Nairobi: Africae, 2018), 194–97.
[34] Kamaru, 'The Missing Piece', 199.
[35] Kweheria, *Achieving Gender Equality in Elective Public Office*, 19.
[36] *Ibid.*, 63.

without the Women's Representative seats, women's representation falls to 7 per cent – lower than their representation in 2002.[37]

In addition to monopolising the time and resources of Kenyan civil society, the Gender Principle roadblock also drew attention away from the other critical areas of civil and political rights access – the right to hold an official identity card, access to voter registration, civic education and literacy, all fundamental to the success of the fragile democracy. Women's voter registration was low across the country, attributable partly to apathy[38] and women's inability to take time off work to register. For instance, the Kenya Human Rights Commission (KHRC) reported that women working in domestic and industrial farms would arrive at voter registration booths late in the evening, as the booths were closing.[39]

The confusion and indecision around how the Gender Principle could be implemented was not limited to the lawyers and policy advocates in Kenyan government and civil society organisations. Sitting with groups of women in empty market stalls, and on battered wooden chairs in school classrooms with beaten dirt floors, we explored their understandings of the Two-Thirds Gender Principle, and the creation of special elected positions for which only women could vie. Many of the women belonging to human rights networks (HuRiNets) set up by the KHRC held long-term links to human rights education programmes, identified as human rights advocates in their communities, and had been advocates addressing a number of human rights concerns prior to being involved in the HuRiNets programme. Many women interviewed believed in the symbolic power of the new Constitution, and its almost talismanic power to effect change. Interviewees often anticipated that the new Constitution would materially affect them, specifically by increasing the number of women represented in public office and, more broadly, in helping to reduce the physical insecurity and violence which continues to be such a part of their everyday experience. One woman explained that 'the Constitution has really tried to empower women by supporting women in leadership and in [government appointed and elected] positions'.[40]

While the women interviewed represented a broad spectrum of civil and political engagement and knowledge of human rights issues and advocacy practices, very few women could articulate the complexities of the new Constitution as it pertained to their civil and political rights.

[37] Musandu, 'Tokenism or Representation?' 602–03.
[38] Kenya Human Rights Commission, 'The Democratic Paradox: A Report on Kenya's 2013 General Elections' (Nairobi: KHRC, 2013), 29.
[39] Kweheria, *Achieving Gender Equality in Elective Public Office*, 43.
[40] Focus Group, KHRC HuRiNets in Ahero town, Nyando, 3 October 2012 (interview conducted around KHRC field work in English).

Most did not have a good understanding of the laws which are designed to protect women's rights, and although the Constitution had been in place for almost two years, many of the women interviewed could only talk vaguely about the content of their constitutional rights. It is relatively unsurprising that Kenyan women were not familiar with their new Constitution – for instance, the same is true of many Australians (in 2015, only 65 per cent of Australian survey respondents had heard of the Australian Constitution).[41] Much more problematic is the popular understanding that knowledge of rights leads linearly to 'empowerment' – a foundational assumption of neoliberal peacemaking. The pernicious discourse of 'empowerment' places the responsibility to access these rights on those most marginalised – the women themselves.

In response to the question 'Can you think of any laws in Kenya which protect women?' members of a women's support group in Kibera mentioned the Constitution as a source of protection for women's rights, but could not explain exactly how the provisions would assist them.[42]

Interviewer: Can you think of any laws in Kenya which protect women? ...

Pillars of Kibera Women's Group: In [the] Constitution we have laws that are protecting women.

Interviewer: What does it say?

Pillars of Kibera Women's Group: I don't know, but there is that protecting women. You have to vote for a woman, despite what. If she has come out to be elected, she has to. For example, the Constitution of now, you have to be voted, as a woman.

Interviewer: Yes there are some seats that are reserved for women that's true – in the counties.

Pillars of Kibera Women's Group: There is also that equality, everything is 50–50 now.

---

[41] 'Results for Australia', *Magna Carta International Public Opinion*, research study conducted for Magna Carta 800th Anniversary Committee Ipsos MORI, http://magnacarta800th.com/projects/international-poll/; for Australian results, see http://magnacarta800th.com/wp-content/uploads/2015/02/MC-International-Survey-Australia-Results1.pptx [accessed 26 January 2017].
[42] Pillars of Kibera – Women's Group, Kisumu Ndogo, Focus Group Discussion, 11 October 2012, translator and facilitator Joseph Ochieng.

Interviewer:	Where is that? In the Constitution?
Pillars of Kibera Women's Group:	No, I can't remember, but I think that's so.
Interviewer:	... So how effective do you think these laws are? Do you think they work?
Pillars of Kibera Women's Group:	Somehow. It has started to. So, we think it will work, if we follow the Constitution, according to what it say[s], it has to be the way it is. Unless women don't stand firm. Unless women don't stand firm, you should know your rights. Women have to fight for your rights. To stand firm.

In addition to needing to understand the content and importance of women's representation, these women in Kibera understood that it is their responsibility as citizens, and women, to take up the opportunities presented by this new constitutional dispensation. It is the women themselves who must 'know their rights', and 'stand firm' in order to bring the constitutional provisions into effect. This expectation women place on themselves is a direct product of the discourse of the liberal peacebuilding project. The empowerment of citizens through constitutional reform is marketed as a necessary and sufficient condition to boost women's representation in public office. Although critical of almost all aspects of Kenyans' preparation for the 2013 election, from the unavailability of women to stand for office to inadequate voter registration and education strategies, the KHRC 'call[ed] upon women to turn up in large numbers to register and vote as this is the only way they can participate in influencing the governance of the country'.[43] The KHRC reported that the responsibility for civic education placed an 'immense' burden on state and non-state actors responsible for conducting civic and voter education, as the 'goal went beyond the dissemination of information to the re-education of the public, [in order] to transform their interaction with governance structures and processes'.[44] Women living in Kibera were better able to access information and Nairobi-based NGO women's support services. But women in Butere, for example – a small town north of Lake Victoria in Kakamega County over 400km north-west of Nairobi, far from urban centres and unable to access any international or national NGO support – found it difficult to name any laws or policies which help women and, in our discussions,

---

[43] Kweheria, *Achieving Gender Equality in Elective Public Office*, 44.
[44] Ibid., 1.

did not mention the Constitution as a source of rights or protections. The only rights these women had heard about were those of women to inherit their husband's property, and to own property of their own.[45]

In Taveta, 300km south of Nairobi on the Kenya–Tanzania border, two constitutional provisions which were known to some women members of the local HuRiNet in Taveta were the Gender Principle and the nominated Senate seats reserved for women. However, when asked to explain the content of these provisions, these women were confused about how the provisions would function and how the ratio of one-third of women in elected positions would be achieved. Although the Constitution had been in place for two years, in the months leading up to the March 2013 elections the women interviewed could only talk vaguely about the content of their constitutional rights. For example, two women in Taveta explained:

Interviewee A: [I]n the new Constitution, there is the two-thirds *nani* the two-thirds gender equality. No, two-thirds women, *sindio*?[46]

Interviewee B: Two-thirds, something like that.

Interviewee A: *Halafu,*[47] there is a third. If there are ten people, amongst them there should be three women, *sindio*? Yeah, something like that ... ok in the seats, the higher seats, women should also be given chances there ... They shouldn't be discriminated due to their ... whatever.

Others described confusion about the process of voting for women-only positions, reporting a commonly held view in their community that only women voted for Women's Representative candidates. For instance in Nyando, Kisumu County, 300km from Nairobi, women explained that:

Nyando
HuriNets group: Some men believe that those who are [vying for Women's Rep. seats] will be voted by women only – so that men can't vote for women – they think that is what is happening. They have to be educated.

---

[45] Ochieng and Kenny interview with Butere Community Focus Group, 2012.
[46] *Nani* (Sw., 'what') is a filled pause often used when interviewees are thinking of the right word or how best to frame their thoughts. *Sindio* is a rhetorical question used to affirm a point. It translates to 'isn't it?' or 'right?' These phrases indicate that women were searching for words to explain the principle, while in other areas of the interview they spoke fluently and with clarity.
[47] *Halafu:* Sw., 'then'.

> There is Governor and Senator, most of them don't know the meaning of Governor, and Senator, and what is their intention. So there is a lot more work to be done.[48]

Civic education was identified as a major barrier for women, for a variety of reasons. Some respondents explained many voters were confused about the role of Women's Representatives, understanding that only women voted for Women's Representative candidates. Others noted that few voters understood the new Constitution, and the provisions protecting women's civil and political rights.

Nyabende Human Rights Network Focus Group II: Right now our Constitution is talking about the two-thirds, and the two-thirds, but nobody is understanding there is a post for women. So maybe women down at the grassroot level, now my fellow woman is going to vie for this seat, they think they are only going to vote for women not for men, and men will only vote for men. So that civic education is very vital.[49]

Women in the Ahero HuRiNet in Kisumu County, about 30km outside Kisumu town, explained that few voters understood the new Constitution, and the provisions protecting women's civil and political rights.

Ahero HuRiNet Focus Group: Even there is a verse in the Constitution that talks about equal representation of women and men, you see our people don't understand it. It's very complicated – so you see getting women to go to parliament is very difficult because they don't understand it. So they should be encourage[d], by telling them what it means, and [to] even vie for those seats.[50]

---

[48] Kenny, with group founder Caren Omanga and Nyando HuriNets group members, 2012.
[49] Focus Group II – Nyabende Human Rights Network conducted as part of a collaborative field trip with the Kenya Human Rights Commission, Ahero, Nyanza, 3 October 2012 (interview conducted in English after consultation with the interviewees).
[50] Focus Group, KHRC HuRiNet in Ahero town, Nyando, 3 October 2012 (interview conducted during KHRC research and advocacy trip and conducted by Kenny in English).

Shifting the responsibility of learning about and accessing their rights to women themselves fails to identify gender as a root cause of marginalisation. The human rights discourse these women have internalised focuses on the formal recognition of marginalisation but offers no tools to deconstruct the gendered assumptions and modes of governance which perpetuate their marginalisation. Even on its own terms, the constitutional solution to women's representation fails to address critical barriers to women's civic participation.

These women identified other fundamental impediments to their citizenship rights, reporting that they knew of women who did not hold official government identification, making it impossible to register to vote. Millions of Kenyans are without official identification documents for a number of reasons, including ethnic Somali Kenyans denied documentation as a result of corrupt and/or discriminatory government treatment.[51] In addition to this systemic disenfranchisement, Kenyan women from a variety of locations reported that many women's ID cards were held by their husbands, and were only given back on voting day with a promise to vote 'for [her] husband's people'.[52] The ways in which intimate partner violence affects civil and political rights access speak to the ways in which women experience trauma outside gender neutral understandings of violence – and the need to acknowledge 'indirect and socio-material stressors' as well as 'socio-material hardship' as forms of trauma requiring redress.[53]

Members of grassroots human rights networks I interviewed, themselves struggling to earn stable wages and support their families in villages far removed from the centres of political and financial capital, lamented that while they themselves were aware of the Constitution and its protection of women's rights, other women 'down there at the grassroots' were not able to access this knowledge, or the power these constitutional provisions promised. Even women adept at navigating the myriad challenges of living in the Kibera slum felt their peers were not able to vote for the candidate they would prefer. Interviewees recognised that these barriers to civic participation had been internalised

---

[51] Hervé Maupeu and Rachel Robertson, 'Kenya's Ethnic Somalis and Access to Identity Papers: Citizenship and Nation-Building in North-East Kenya', in Séverine Awenengo Dalberto and Richard Banégas (eds), *Identification and Citizenship in Africa: Biometrics, the Documentary State and Bureaucratic Writings of the Self* (London: Routledge, 2021), pp. 166–85; Kenya Human Rights Commission, 'Foreigners at Home – The Dilemma of Citizenship in Northern Kenya' (Nairobi: KHRC, 2008).

[52] Kibera, Pillars of Kibera Women's Group focus group meeting, 11 October 2012, translator and facilitator Joseph Ochieng.

[53] Magdelena Zolkos, 'Redressive Politics and the Nexus of Trauma, Transitional Justice and Reconciliation', in Susanne Buckley-Zistel *et al.* (eds), *Transitional Justice Theories* (New York: Routledge, 2014), pp. 176–77.

by many women, in the behaviour and attitudes towards voting they observed in other women.[54]

Pillars of Kibera
Women's Group: I think there are some problem[s] – another challenge is they are weak. They are easily bribed.

Interviewer: But aren't men also bribed?

Pillars of Kibera
Women's Group: For example, here a man comes with these *leso*s, you know you give women, you can't give men; *ai* she doesn't have many. Maybe she doesn't have that *kanga*. You see, I'll say, this man has given me a *kanga*, I'll vote for this man. But a man, will be given, but will say I want to vote for someone else. So, women, their minds are weak, they can be confused easily.[55]

Interviewer: Why do you think that is?

Pillars of Kibera
Women's Group: Illiteracy. They need to be educated …

Pillars of Kibera
Women's Group: They say voting is secret. [But w]e've agreed to be ruled, I think. We've agreed to be ruled. It's a culture. So women are not there to say, 'This is what we want'.

Compounding the confusion around the process of electing women to parliament, Kenyan women who claim public space when campaigning and protesting, as well as those who occupy public office, must navigate a complex web of conflicting perceptions about their capacities and fitness to lead. Women who do vie for office, or resist injustice within their local communities as part of grassroots collectives, are often characterised as masculine, aggressive, uncontrolled and uncontrollable. The imposition and perpetuation of these gendered cultural norms excludes many women from positions of leadership and strictly

---

[54] Kibera, Pillars of Kibera Women's Group focus group meeting, 11 October 2012, translator and facilitator Joseph Ochieng.
[55] *Kanga* (Sw.), also *leso*, refers to multipurpose fabric sheets that are usually 1 m x 1.5 m and often used by women to tie babies to their backs while working or travelling, and to protect their clothes from wear while working. *Kanga* can also refer to the pattern printed on a *leso*.

regulates their behaviour in public spaces, and can physically and psychologically push women out of these spaces entirely.

In response to these experiences, women have developed expectations of women politicians who, they hope, will defend against the most egregious violations. But, like many strategies born in environments of deep patriarchy, they place the burden on women who choose to run to comport themselves in a manner that is beyond reproach. Members of the HuRiNet in Ahero town, Kisumu County, explained to me the ways they thought women should behave when vying for office:[56]

Group member A: They should be gentle, they should be women of high dignity, of high passion, women of respect, and they should be role models from the community where they come to contest, that means they should be women of high integrity.

Group member B: They also have to behave before the men. The new Constitution allows the women to contest, better than other years. So this time, the women come, they say, the Constitution allows us and some of them behave badly, but we encourage them to behave well.

Group member C: So that they may not be boastful; now, let's say, I'm the coordinator of Nyando constituency, if I am boastful, they will talk to their fellow men, and the women will side with the men because they don't like you.

From the most fundamental denials of citizenship rights by their intimate partners, to rejection by established political parties, women who enter politics – or women who merely take an interest in politics as campaigners or public supporters of particular candidates – are faced at every stage with often insurmountable challenges to their participation. As Zimbabwean Hope Chigudu, a veteran women's rights defender, once explained: 'Women politicians will always be mauled and mangled in their homes, [on the] street, or [in] parliament.'[57] These barriers are exacerbated by the real threat of physical violence which accompanies any decision to occupy public space. While men build physical and cultural spaces which protect and nurture their interests, women are often unsafe in places where men feel safe – political assem-

---

[56] Focus Group, KHRC HuRiNets in Ahero town, Nyando, 3 October 2012 (interview conducted around KHRC field work in English).
[57] Quoted in Mona Lena Krook, 'Violence against Women in Politics', *Journal of Democracy,* 28:1 (2017), 77.

blies, party meetings and their own offices and homes.[58] Women who brave these obstacles are then faced with a foundational challenge to their participation – that politics itself is unwomanly and that through participating in politics, women lose the very dignity and respectability upon which they had based their candidacy.

Members of a HuRiNet group set up by the KHRC in Ahero explained that women who campaign for office and their supporters are vulnerable to physical attack and to having their rallies disrupted by men supporting other candidates.

Group member A: It is hard for women to be in public places.

Group member B: A man has youths to support you. The men can beat your ladies and rape them. As a woman, you need youths and men to support you.

Group member C: They [women] also need men's votes.

Group member B: You must create your space. You must come out and fight for it [space] ... That's why I was talking about the youths. Men can talk to the boys. Your supporters are like your bodyguards, how can you remain with only girls? The boys will take a girl and rape them. A boy is stronger than three girls.[59]

As we saw in Chapter 4, focus groups in all locations felt that police were not helpful and often exacerbated marginalisation and victimisation of their communities by participating in criminal activity, or ignoring or condoning the criminal acts of others. Frequently, participants would explain that there was no point in reporting violence or other offences if one did not have 'fuel money' to give officers. Martha Kibwana, nearly fatally assaulted outside her home for daring to vie for office in Taveta, was also scathing of the police but believed the Constitution will have some impact on their behaviour.

MK: when you try to go for help to the police or anything ... when you want to ask for your rights, the police will tell you that women don't have any rights, so you don't have a right to report whatever it is you are reporting. So, if you were at home and you said that want to go complain about property you would be told property belongs to your husband, property belongs to a man, no property belongs to a woman.

---

[58] *Ibid.*
[59] Focus Group, KHRC HuRiNets in Ahero town, Nyando, 3 October 2012 (interview conducted around KHRC field work, in English).

Interviewer: Was that here in Taveta?

MK: It was, and even now it is.

Interviewer: I see. But you think it's changing? Is it changing?

MK: I think it's going to change now …Concerning this *nini*, constitutions. It will change.[60]

'At the court of gender advocates and mob justice' – The slapping of Rachel Shebesh

On 6 September 2013, Rachel Shebesh, a woman well known for her outspoken political style and the newly appointed Women's Representative for Nairobi, marched to the offices of the Governor of Nairobi, Evans Kidero, to draw attention to the ongoing strike by Nairobi County employees protesting their unpaid salaries. In a video of the altercation that followed (which quickly went viral), Shebesh is seen to approach the office door of Kidero flanked by dozens of men, assumed to be striking county workers, filling the vestibule to capacity. Kidero opens the door to his office to speak with Shebesh and, only moments into the exchange, Kidero slaps Shebesh across her face, apparently without provocation. She yells, 'Kidero, you have slapped me! You have slapped me, Kidero!' and she is then hustled out of the vestibule by several of her supporters.[61]

Kidero's first response was to give a public statement in which he denied the event had happened: 'as far as I can recollect I was in my office and do not remember slapping anybody'.[62] The video of him clearly slapping Shebesh was swiftly and widely circulated on social media, however, and he soon apologised but explained he acted out of anger, reacting to Shebesh grabbing his genitals. In a newspaper article titled, 'What was she doing around my lower abdomen?', Kidero explained: 'I found the act embarrassing, disgusting and highly disrespectful … I

---

[60] Interview with Martha Kibwana, 6 August 2012, Taveta town, Taita-Taveta County; digital recording (in English and KiSwahili., with KHRC staff member as interpreter).

[61] 'Nairobi Governor Evans Kidero and Rachel Shebesh's Slapping Saga', *KTN News Kenya*, 7 September, 2013, www.youtube.com/watch?v=BY287dKPZkQ [accessed 20 August 2021].

[62] Moses Michira, 'Governor Evans Kidero Slaps Rachel Shebesh, Then Quickly Forgets', *Standard Digital*, 7 September 2013, www.standard-media.co.ke/article/2000092952/governor-evans-kidero-slaps-rachel-shebesh-then-quickly-forgets [accessed 13 August, 2021].

wish to regard what happened ... as a despicable act of aggression on my personal integrity and that of the office of the Governor.[63]

As it was not possible to see from the video whether Shebesh had, in fact, touched Kidero, and the footage had clearly captured Kidero slapping Shebesh, this left Kidero, as one popular online newspaper noted, 'at the court of gender advocates and mob justice'.[64] As Kidero counter-claimed he was also assaulted, both Shebesh and Kidero were charged with assault.

The criticism of Shebesh following this incident was voluminous, with one entertainment and gossip paper reporting that:

> one of Kidero's bodyguards confirmed that #Shebesh hit Kidero's balls with her knees. This is BAAD!! Don't even try hitting a man's strongholds ... The governor only reacted in self defence *if at all he did slap the fat 49 year old woman* ... the majority of Kenyans feel nothing for hon Shebesh as she is known for her goonish character, she has had a rough past with prominent personalities, she has no decorum.[65]

This framing of the event of the slap as questionable or contentious, although the story was built on the video footage of the event, creates a new reality. Here, Shebesh's exclamation 'Kidero, you have slapped me!' is discursively contested; even a video recording of the event is not enough to support her statement, but an unquoted account of an unnamed bodyguard is reported as fact. Many Kenyans also found the footage amusing.[66] Comments across a range of social media and popular entertainment news sites included, 'decent women don't hit below the belt ... you get a reflex jab. The brain is never consulted on reflex'; 'This line of "you don't hit a woman no matter what" is for sex-starved men or serial male whores.' 'Don't storm my office', '#ShebeshSlapped'; and 'Shebesh "behaves" like a man Kidero slaps her'[67] were accompanied by assertions that her Luhya husband was an embarrassment to the Luhya

---

[63] Abigael Sum and Ngari Gichuki, 'Evans Kidero: What Was She Doing around My Lower Abdomen?' *The Standard Digital*, 8 September 2013, www.standardmedia.co.ke/?articleID=2000093029&story_title=evans-kidero-what-was-she-doing-around-my-lower-abdomen&pageNo=1 [accessed 15 August 2021].

[64] *Kenya Today*, 'Nairobi Governor Evans Kidero Women Representative Rachel Shebesh Charged with Fighting', 9 November 2013.

[65] 'SHOCK: Shebesh Hit Kidero Under the Belt Before The Alleged SLAP', *Kenya Today*, 7 September 2013, www.kenya-today.com/politics/nairobi-governor-evans-kidero-slaps-rachel-shebesh [accessed 16 August]. Emphasis added.

[66] See, for instance, 'Dr Evans Kidero – Rachel Shebesh Social Media Reaction', *The Standard*, 2013, www.sde.co.ke/article/2000113556/dr-evans-kidero-rachel-shebesh-social-media-reaction [accessed 4 August 2021].

[67] Sue Watiri, 'Kenyan Celebrities React to Shebesh Getting Slapped!' *Ghafla!* 6 September 2013, www.ghafla.com/kenyan-celebrities-react-to-shebesh-getting-slapped-video [accessed 16 August 2021].

Figure 3 *I didn't slap her and I have evidence to defend my case*, cartoon by Gado, 8 September 2013 (reproduced by permission of Gado Cartoons/bunimedia.com).

community for his failure to control his wife and for not punishing her for grabbing the genitals of other men. Other commentators suggested that Shebesh enjoyed the feeling of so many men touching her body as she was hustled out of vestibule.

My own reading of the slap itself is that it was a gesture familiar to Kidero – and honestly expressed his feelings. Rather than shock or embarrassment, which perhaps would have been expressed through pushing her away, trying to move her hand away from his body or stepping back into his office to create some distance between them, Kidero's instinctive response is punitive. His slap was a gesture – both visual and kinaesthetic – a ritualistic and immediately recognisable act which compelled Shebesh's retreat from public space and reasserted his control over his body, and his office. She is then manhandled out of the room. Shebesh has demonstrated herself to be a woman unrestrained by the acceptable standards of feminine behaviour, and conventional gender norms – to be respectful and polite and to speak in a measured way. She failed to 'behave before the men'.

Shebesh's star has faded since this altercation. Shortly after 'the slap', she faced an online smear campaign which sought to link her to the controversial Nairobi political figure, and sitting MP at the time,

Mike Sonko,[68] with crude pastiches of her face superimposed on another woman's body in compromising positions with Sonko. Ultimately, both Shebesh and Kidero rescinded their statements and the prosecutors withdrew the charges.[69] Shebesh publicly 'forgave' Kidero at a Christian outreach event in Kasirani, explaining that it was her faith which had promoted her decision, noting that their feud had affected development programming in Nairobi County and that she was ready to work with him again. In hindsight, it was telling that Shebesh thought to frame her decision not to go ahead with the court case in the context of the wider women's rights struggle in Kenya, 'I know the women who have suffered with me might not understand why I have forgiven Kidero but I want to say that forgiveness frees the heart and allows one to do much more and I hope Kidero shares the same feeling.'[70]

Joining a march organised by the upper/middle-class Nairobi women's collective 'Kilimani Mums' to protest the stripping of women by *matatu* touts the following year, she was prevented from addressing the crowd by other women organisers of the rally. Anecdotally, they were unimpressed with the fact that she settled the court case against Kidero and felt that she was seduced by a financial settlement, rather than fighting for women's rights in court.[71] At the 2017 general elec-

[68] Sonko is *Sheng*, a Kenyan slang, for 'rich man' or 'boss'. Sonko has held positions as Senator and Mayor of Nairobi. He is a populist figure with a criminal history: see Dauti Kahura, 'The Sonkoization of Nairobi – How Mike Sonko is Reshaping City Politics', *The Elephant*, 7 August 2017, www.theelephant.info/features/2017/08/07/the-sonkonization-of-nairobi-how-mike-sonko-is-reshaping-city-politics [accessed 10 November 2020].
[69] Kurian Musa, 'Court Terminates Evans Kidero, Rachel Shebesh Assault Case', 19 March 2014, *Standard Media*, www.standardmedia.co.ke/article/2000107314/court-terminates-evans-kidero-rachael-shebesh-assault-case [accessed 10 August 2021].
[70] Stephene Sangira and Ng'ang'a Thairu, 'Shebesh Forgives Kidero', 3 February 2014, *The Star*, www.the-star.co.ke/news/2014/02/03/shebesh-forgives-kidero_c890852 [accessed 10 August 2021].
[71] Several conversations with journalists covering the protest and Kenyan women's rights advocates, 13–20 November 2014. See also Josephine Mosongo, 'From Online Rhetoric to Street Protests: Rise of Kilimani Mums', *Daily Nation*, 22 November 2014, www.nation.co.ke/lifestyle/lifestyle/Rise-of-Kilimani-Mums/1214-2531682-mr5yojz/index.html [accessed 12 August 2021]; and Lulu Akaki, 'Kilimani Mums to Protest in Solidarity with Woman Who Was Stripped by Touts', *HapaKenya*, 13 November 2014, www.hapakenya.com/2014/11/13/kilimani-mums-host-mydressmychoice-miniskirt-protest [accessed 12 August 2021]; for the settlement (estimated to be KSH 15 million), see 'Rachael Shebesh and Kidero Finally Agree on an Out-of-court Settlement after Kidero Gave Her Roughly 15 Million', *Jobs Kenya*, 2014, www.jobskenyahapa.com/rachael-shebesh-kidero-finally-agree-court-agreement-kidero-gave-roughly-15-million-2 [accessed 12 August 2021].

tion, Shebesh contested her seat of Women's Representative for Nairobi, but lost to businesswoman Esther Passaris.[72]

Women across the country had heard of the slap, and had seen the online press and social media coverage of the incident belittling the violence she endured and casting aspersions on her character and capacity to fulfil her obligations as Women's Representative, as well as the parodies joking about slapping women. Perhaps one of the most egregious of the latter was the remix of the audio of the event, titled 'Slap them like Kidero'; as the gossip and popular news site *Ghafla!* explained, '[c]omplete with the slap sound effect, this track is by far the best done by S.N.L Kenya ... It's only in Kenya where serious matters can be turned into the biggest joke. All bull side, this track is seriously sidesplitting.'[73]

The Nyabende Human Rights Network (NHRN) based outside Ahero town, in Kisumu County, is a mixed-gender human rights collective. In discussion, members felt very strongly about the slap. In the group discussion, we are reminded of the interpersonal and social expectations Kenyans have of physical violence, and the ways gender operates with class and rurality to continue to marginalise Kenyan women:

Interviewer:	What did you think when you heard about that story of [Shebesh and Kidero]?
NHRN (interpreter):	It's very bad, it's like ... Kidero was wrong, even if maybe Shebesh was not doing the right thing in the office, but it was wrong for Kidero to have slapped her. So they were not happy.
Interviewer:	What was she doing that was wrong? Was she doing something wrong?
NHRN (interpreter):	[for a NHRN member] As a local woman, she's thinking there are some other systems that

---

[72] Sara Okuoro, 'Rachel Shebesh Concedes Defeat to Esther Passaris', *Standard Media*, 9 August 2017, www.standardmedia.co.ke/article/2001250815/rachel-shebesh-concedes-defeat-to-esther-passaris [accessed 12 August 2021].

[73] S.N.L. – 'Stunnr' New Limits'. A music clip was produced that parodies the event. It was reported on the popular culture and gossip site, *Ghafla*; see Jeff Omondi, 'Hot New Track: "Slap Them Like Kidero" Featuring Dr Kidero & Shebesh', *Ghafla!* 11 September 2013, www.ghafla.com/hot-new-track-slap-them-like-kidero-featuring-dr-kidero-shebesh [accessed 12 August 2021]; Nwasante Khasiani, 'XYZee Make Fun of Shebesh Getting Slapped. You have to Watch This Song They Did For Her', *Ghafla*, 7 October 2013, www.ghafla.com/xyzee-make-fun-of-shebesh-getting-slapped-you-have-to-watch-this-song-they-did-for-her, [accessed 12 August 2021].

	Shebesh should have used, rather than going physically, so she thinks maybe that was not right, although she is also saying that it was not right that Shebesh was slapped.
NHRN (woman):	Also, in our African culture, it is not right for a woman to shout [at] a man, so Kidero acted like an African man. Typical! When a woman confronts you, what [do] you do? You give a slap!
NHRN (man):	A long time ago, slapping a woman in African culture was not a very bad thing, it was a normal thing. Because there is a story also which says, if you don't slap your woman, she'll run out from you.
NHRN (woman):	She'll think you're not a man.
Interviewer:	What do the women think about that saying?
NHRN (woman):	Its not a good saying, and I feel that I should also be given a right to also slap somebody, if they do something wrong, because even me as a woman, I am human, just the same way that my husband is a human. So most of the time, many times men are wrong, and nobody slaps them, so why should I be slapped for something I have done wrong?

The comparatively little serious local commentary on the incident addressed the obvious gender violence but focused almost entirely on the criminal prosecution of Kidero, a campaign which ultimately failed – a failure seen to be aided by Shebesh, herself, when she withdrew her statement. Analysis of Shebesh as a target for gendered public violence was mostly absent. But as Caren Omanga, the leader of the NHRN makes clear, the slap threw into sharp relief the intersections of class and rurality on one hand, and the promises transnational rights discourse makes to these rural women on the other:

NHRN (Caren Omanga):	What I'm thinking about Kidero and Shebesh, as a person I really felt very bad, I felt pained, I felt like I'm the one who is being slapped. Because Shebesh is a product of affirmative action. Shebesh is one of the women we have moulded from grassroot, to wherever she is now. She's not like any other parliamentarian you see in parliament, she was a woman who was like us, a grassroot woman, until now she has come up

there, she is a woman who speaks for the grassroot women, so, when you see her acting the way she is acting, she acting like a grassroot woman, she is speaking like a grassroot woman would want to be done, she would not just sit back in her office and wait for things to go by, because I think something wrong was happening ... they were protesting for the hawkers. More hawkers are single women in town, women who come to sell things at night, and go and pay school fees, and go and eat with their children.

So she had a reason to go and protest, maybe no one was listening ... despite him being an African, and was acting as an African man, he has no respect for women, and for grassroot women, for that matter. I really had very high hopes [for] him, and since that time, since that slap, I think I can never, never, never, ever in my life, think of voting him in for anything.

And given this lady, Shebesh, is our product ... after that slap, a lot of things happened, for Shebesh, they started exposing her, in media, to show ... and many men do worse things than her ... Why wasn't Sonko being scrutinised the way Shebesh was!? ... And if we have women parliamentarians they should be given respect, and especially women that we have moulded ... It's not only Shebesh, we have others who are there, but Shebesh is part of us. We really feel bad. Like grassroot women, we have never forgiven Kidero. Even if [Shebesh and Kidero] met and compromised, we have never forgiven him.

Omanga's protective relationship and affinity with Shebesh, and the symbolic act of slapping the inaugural Women's Representative, is central to Omanga's gender politics and activism. She was sold the promise of the new Constitution, and the benefits of women's representation, only to be brutally reminded of the way women 'like [her], a grassroot woman', are treated by the political elite – she 'felt pained ... like [she] was the one who is being slapped'. The body of Shebesh is imbricated with multiple identities, but those which were the most important to her election – her grassroots origins and commitment to women's issues, her gendered, public identity – were the identities which created the cultural space for a politician to slap another politician across the face and be congratulated for it. Omanga feels this lack of respect – not only in the slap itself, but also in the subsequent treatment of Shebesh and smearing of her in the press as a loud, loose woman with questionable morals – is central to the marginalisation of all Kenyan women, but particularly women like her at the grassroots. Omanga's recognition of Shebesh's behaviour, as the forthright actions of a grassroots activist – 'when you see her acting the way she is acting, she acting like a grassroot woman, she is speaking like a grassroot woman would want to be done, she would not just sit back in her office and wait for things to go by' – speaks to the hazardous nature of the advocacy work of grassroots women. Recognising her own strategies in Shebesh's behaviour, Omanga has also witnessed the treatment of such women by an elite, urban man, and by the online Kenyan community. Stepping into political and other public spaces in the future recalls this violence and the history of violence so many women in Kenya live with in their homes, and speaks to the domination of political and public space by elite, urban men. The disdain Kidero shows for Shebesh in slapping her, and the withdrawal of criminal charges against him in the face of compelling video evidence, perfectly illustrates the gendered and classist barriers to representation and redress.

The Shebesh incident describes a fundamental dissonance; this altercation between the Governor and the inaugural Women's Representative for the most influential and populous county in the country illustrates the gendered power dynamics of public life. It also emphasises the centrality of bodies as sites, and origins, of authority. Examining their appointments as Women's Representative and Governor in terms of the ritual efficacy of their appointment exposes the reliance on gendered bodies to organise and regulate public space.

A woman human rights defender in Ahero town told me the story of Jonny, the toddler of friends of hers. As his parents had felt that the anatomically correct names for body parts were too indecorous, Jonny had always been taught that this penis was called his *heshima*, a word which directly translated from KiSwahili means 'respect'. When his parents received visitors one afternoon, Jonny was ill-behaved, jumping over the furniture and preventing the adults from enjoying their afternoon. Exasperated, his mother reproached: '*Wewe* [you]! Show the visitors some respect!' At which point, the little boy pulled down his pants and proudly showed the room his *heshima*, explaining '*Hii ni heshima yangu, hii ni heshima yangu!*' ('This is my respect, this is my respect!').[74]

Considering the reception of the Gender Principle and the women's rights provisions of the Constitution, women were hopeful that the Constitution *alone* would provide some material changes to their experience of their rights – that it would assist them to *know* their

---

[74] Nyando HuRiNet, Ahero, 3 October 2012, focus group with Christina Kenny and four women living in or around Ahero town.

rights a little more intimately. As we have seen in earlier chapters, constitutional reform itself has attained a kind of ritual efficacy in popular imagination – the fact of its existence is meaning-making. The Constitution is transformative of the nation. But the Constitution, and the associated processes of democracy it ushered in, was subject to the underlying and, so far, barely challenged gendered cultural politics which have characterised Kenya's history. The misconception that only women can vote for Women's Representative seats echoes the gender separation of communal rites of passage which *are* efficacious – women initiate girls and men initiate boys. If we understand the process of being elected to office as a ritual transformation – from citizen to Governor, citizen to Women's Representative – women face particular barriers to this transubstantive process of contesting public office. Corinne Kratz explains that:

> each performance of a ceremony transforms (or tries to transform) some aspect of a shared cultural definition of the world – this child is now an adult, that person is now the king ... the transformation works through the communicative forms with which that definition is created, in a form agreed to have the authority and ability to effect that change.[75]

While men can rely on the cultural assumption that they are natural leaders, Kenyan women do not have rituals which permit them entry to and occupancy of public space. Tabitha Kanogo asserts that women use different methods each time they transgress or step outside their cultural strictures, arguing that,

> more often than not, travel and modernity were deemed responsible for women's unacceptable abandonment of traditional obligations, roles and spaces ... in some respects, the lives of African girls and women attained the substance of public spectacle, performative existences that were subject to public surveillance and sanction.[76]

This creates such a diffusion of strategies and outcomes that no new rituals replace the old ones – only the continual rejection of traditional roles and responsibilities, which are still opportunistically called on to contain and control women in public spaces.[77] No strong, new identities are present for women to access; instead, women continue to have to insist, from first principles, that they have are *doli capax* – they are still fighting to be legal persons, and legally responsible citizens.[78]

---

[75] Corinne Kratz, *Affecting Performance: Meaning, Movement and Experience in Okiek Women's Initiation* (Washington: Smithsonian Institution Press, 1994), 16.
[76] Tabitha Kanogo, *African Womanhood in Colonial Kenya 1900–1950* (Oxford: James Currey, 2005), 23.
[77] *Ibid*.
[78] See, for instance, 'A native woman is "capax doli" according to the rules which apply to women of other races, or to persons of the other sex': Attorney

But even before the ritual takes place, candidates must be eligible to undergo the transformation. As we have seen, a primary condition for leadership in Kenya is to be sexed male. Shebesh is emblematic of the reality that although women can theoretically pass through the same ritual as men, women are not accorded the same respect and have not been able to accrue the tangible and intangible trappings of office. These transgressive women are, therefore, able to be disciplined in ways which recall, and often drive them back to, private spaces. As a woman in Bar Ober explained to me, when I asked the group about how the Shebesh incident affected them: 'that's why we are saying we don't have power. ... That picture shows that women in Africa don't have power.'[79] Luce Irigaray has argued that:

> in the system of production that we know, including that of sexual production, men are distanced from their bodies. They have relied upon their sex, their language, and their technology to go on and on building a world further and further removed from their relation to the corporeal. But they are corporeal.[80]

These technologies were evident in Kidero's case – his suit, masculinity, stature and position, and the way he physically controlled the space around his person, speak to the sanctity of his corporeal body: 'men, of course use speech as a screen. They speak through a rationality quite external to their bodies.'[81] The slap exists in that liminal space – a private sanctioning of public behaviour. Shebesh's grabbing Kidero's crotch (assuming it as a fact for the moment) draws him from the rarefied position of Governor, back into his physical body, back into the corporeal world. To some, Kidero responded intemperately, perhaps even irrationally. To others, he behaved as they would have expected an African man to behave; after all, it was not so long ago that slapping a woman was not that bad, or was interpreted as a sign of affection or, at least, an affectionate rebuke.

The reception of the slap by popular media reinforced the social fact that Kenyan women do not hold an inherent dignity – this 'respect'. Their dignity can be tarnished, questioned and mobilised in reproach. Passing through the ritual of nomination and popular election does not transform women into politicians or leaders. Women are not capable of being leaders, for reasons more fundamental than a lack of qualifi-

---

General [AG] to CNC, KNA: AG 4/2791 Status of Native Women, Legal Status of Native Girls, 7 September 1931, as reprinted in Kanogo, *African Womanhood in Colonial Kenya*, 15.
[79] Bar Ober, Church at Bar Ober, focus group meeting, 10 September 2014, translator and facilitator Joan Ouma.
[80] Luce Irigaray, *The Irigaray Reader*, ed. Margaret Whitford (Massachusetts: Blackwell Publishers, 1995), 49.
[81] *Ibid.*, 50–51.

cations or their leadership style. Women do not naturally embody the qualities of leadership – a key component of which is an acceptable performance of masculinity, the possession of (a) *heshima*. Men can be similarly excluded or failing to perform and embody appropriate masculinities, for instance, a Gĩkũyũ community criticism of Raila Odinga, veteran opposition leader (who is uncircumcised due to his Luo ethnicity), is 'we will not be led by a child'.[82]

Rather than promoting equal gender representation as a panacea for the lack of women's voices, programming and protection, we need to focus much more fully on the content and implications of particular gendered identities, and the ways in which gender identity and expression affects the ability of anyone to take up new, risky identities including those offered by the transnational rights project.

---

[82] Beth M. Ahlberg *et al.*, '"We Cannot Be Led by a Child": Forced Male Circumcision during the Post-election Violence in Kenya' (Uppsala: Department of Women's and Children's Health, Uppsala University and Karaborg Institute for Research and Development, 2011).

Conclusion

'So I will tell you a story, Maitu, Wanjiku is dead. Wanjiku was one of those strong African women you see around Nairobi with a huge load of Sukuma Wiki, onions, potatoes and lots of other food, which they sell from place to place. You could call her a hawker, I prefer Wanjiku.'[1]

Through this account of the sociopolitical rights of African women in Kenya, from the late colony through to the contemporary period, we have witnessed the establishment and entrenchment of colonial ethno-patriarchal politics and its insidious reproduction in the postcolonial republic. Violence against women – especially violence adjacent to and during elections – has drawn the world's attention but, as we have seen, rather than an extraordinary deviation from an otherwise peaceful life, electoral violence is symptomatic of a wider sphere of pervasive institutional and everyday violence.

With the embodied trauma of the 2007 elections still hanging in the air, for Kenyans the 2013 elections served as a painful reminder. Friends in low voices explained to me the burnt-out shopfronts as we passed – 'that one was a Kikuyu business', 'that was a Luo shop' – or why the markets outside Valley Arcade were so makeshift – the structures of a more established market were destroyed in the 2007 violence and never rebuilt. Talk of voting in 2013 prompted stories of terror from 2007 – 'this is how I fled', 'these are who were chasing me'. As much as the 2010 Constitution and the success of the 2013 elections signalled important and long overdue reform, the key power structures, cultural biases and modes of endemic corruption remained untouched. Although far from perfect, a kind of collective relief took hold in the aftermath of the 2013 elections. The fact that they were relatively peaceful, and comparatively transparent, was combined with a profound exhaustion across Kenya – the stress of remembered trauma, the skyrocketing price of necessities including cabbage, clean water, cooking oil, kerosene, charcoal and transport, and lost days of work as everyone sheltered in place until the threat of violence had passed.

---

[1] *Maitu* (Sw.), a respectful title for an older woman; *sukuma wiki* (literally 'stretch the week') is a kale, a staple and one of the most affordable vegetables for poor Kenyans. Mwendwa Kivuva, 'Can We Escape Snare of Corruption?' *Mwendwa Kivuva's Blog: The Round Peg In The Square Hole*, May 2012, archived at https://web.archive.org/web/20151029020504/http://lord.me.ke/2012/05/ [accessed 20 August 2021].

The good example set by the 2013 elections was not repeated in 2017. At an estimated cost of almost US$500 million to administer, the 2017 General Elections in Kenya were the most expensive elections per capita ever to have taken place on the African continent, and the second-most expensive in the world.[2] Even this unprecedented investment in monitoring, security, training and equipment did not achieve an uncontested result. In fact, the poll was so corrupted that the results were annulled by the Supreme Court – the first time a court had done so in Africa.[3] The opposition leader, Raila Odinga, withdrew from the new poll and, claiming there was no hope of a credible election, refused to acknowledge Kenyatta's subsequent landslide win. Informally installed by supporters as the 'People's President' in protest, Odinga had no access to state power or coffers. Not only were the elections profoundly and deliberately flawed but, as is always the case in Kenya, the 2017 polls were fatally violent – characterised by state-sponsored violence and extrajudicial killings as well as inter-ethnic clashes. At least ninety-two people were killed[4] and police brutality was unbridled – shooting live bullets into crowds of protestors 'armed' with stones, and viciously pursuing and beating people as they fled. The violence was concentrated across opposition stronghold areas, including Dandora, Kariobangi, Mathare and Kibera slums in Nairobi; across Kisumu and Siaya counties in western Kenya; and in Coast Province.[5]

Only a month after Odinga was nominated People's President, he and Kenyatta performed a choreographed 'handshake' designed to dissipate the incredible tension which had resulted from the aborted election and the accompanying violence. The handshake agreement produced the Building Bridges Initiative (BBI), an ambitious and destructive programme of constitutional change which, the instigators claimed, would 'fix' parts of the 2010 Constitution that they felt

[2] A calculation based on the cost per voter to count each vote (it cost Kenya US$25.40 per registered voter, beaten only by Papua New Guinea at US$63 per voter). See George Tubei, 'Kenya's General Election the Most Expensive in Africa and 2nd Most Expensive in the World', *Business Insider Africa*, 18 July 2017, https://africa.businessinsider.com/politics/politics-kenyas-general-election-the-most-expensive-in-africa-and-2nd-most-expensive/ceeb56g [accessed 20 August 2021]; Nanjala Nyabola, 'What Kenyan Voters Got for the $500m Spent on Elections', *Al Jazeera*, 18 August 2017, www.aljazeera.com/opinions/2017/8/18/what-kenyan-voters-got-for-the-500m-spent-on-elections [accessed 19 August 2021].
[3] Rodney Muhumuza, 'Kenya Watchdog Says 92 People Killed in Election Violence', *AP News*, 21 December 2017, https://apnews.com/article/6c686219242c48c1b9a2653a4972a3c3 [accessed 20 August, 2021].
[4] *Ibid.*
[5] 'Kenya: Post-Election Killings, Abuse', *Human Rights Watch*, 27 August 2017, www.hrw.org/news/2017/08/27/kenya-post-election-killings-abuse [accessed 30 August, 2021].

constrained the Government of Kenya. The BBI, framed within the seventy-four amendment articles of the Constitution Amendment Bill, included some interesting and important ideas, such as distributing a constitutionally guaranteed portion of funding to counties and a recommitment to implementing the Two-Thirds Gender Principle.[6] Fundamentally, though, the initiative was the latest attempt by Kenyan ethnic elites to align their interests in preparation for the August 2022 election.

Proponents of the BBI embarked on an incredibly expensive campaign, 'educating' Kenyans on why the changes to the Constitution were necessary and encouraging them to support the initiative. Even as the COVID-19 pandemic closed down Nairobi and locked millions of people into rural areas with poor health information, little work and rising food prices, and as the health sector in Kenya ground to a standstill – unable to pay the doctors who were so often succumbing to COVID-19 in the very hospitals in which they worked – the BBI campaign continued to enjoy substantial government and financial support and a great deal of media coverage.

In striking down the Constitution Amendment Bill, the High Court noted that the 2010 Constitution was designed to respond to 'two sets of pathologies that had plagued Kenyan constitutionalism' in its previous iterations – a 'culture of hyper amendment' and 'a two decade emphasis on a citizen-led [constitutional reform] process'.[7] Significantly, the court held that 'a grasp of Kenyan constitutional history was essential to considering the matter before it', noting that the 1963 Constitution had been so thoroughly amended it was 'stripped of most of its initial democratic and social justice protections' so that the country 'had effectively become an authoritarian state'.[8]

At the time of writing in July 2022, the case has been twice, unsuccessfully appealed by the Government – to the Court of Appeal (judgement handed down 20 August 2021), and finally to the seven justice bench of the Supreme Court (the 1089 page judgement was handed

---

[6] Makau Mutua, 'BBI Realignments May Spring Surprises on Kenyans', interview by John Githongo, *The Elephant* (blog), 18 November 2020, www.theelephant.info/videos/2020/11/18/makau-mutua-bbi-realignments-may-spring-surprises-on-kenyans [accessed 20 August 2021].

[7] Gautam Bhatia, 'Notes From a Foreign Field: An Instant Classic – The Kenyan High Court's BBI Judgment', *Indian Constitutional Law and Philosophy* (blog), 14 May 2021, https://indconlawphil.wordpress.com/2021/05/14/notes-from-a-foreign-field-an-instant-classic-the-kenyan-high-courts-bbi-judgment [accessed 30 August 2021].

[8] Yaniv Roznai, 'Basic Structure Doctrine: Winds of Change for Constitutionalism in Africa?' *The Elephant*, 24 May 2021, www.theelephant.info/features/2021/05/24/basic-structure-doctrine-winds-of-change-for-constitutionalism-in-africa [accessed 27 May 2021].

down 5 April 2022). Legal scholar, Gautam Bhatia has offered perhaps the most comprehensive analysis of the judgements at the time of writing noting that the scope and novelty of the issues addressed will generate a great deal of commentary. Most hearteningly, albeit cautiously, Bhatia argues the Supreme Court has now

> firmly established that the purpose of Chapter XVI – and, specifically Article 257 – is to constrain the imperial Presidency, check abusive amendments, and safeguard against hyper-amendments. But as history shows, the imperial Presidency is not so easy to contain: its 'taming' will need more than one set of judgments, but rather, it is a constitutional commitment that will need to be renewed and renewed again.[9]

This new constitutional case law has 'signalled the winds of change for constitutionalism in Africa'.[10] We can hope that this case may help to spare Kenyans from the, hitherto familiar and regular, attempts at hyper-amendment of the Constitution.

In spite of the ever-increasing cost of living, the inaccessibility of safe and high-quality primary and secondary education for the majority of Kenyan children, the precarity of employment even for university graduates, and a health system in constant crisis, an inordinate amount of international donor and scholarly attention, as well as local advocacy and popular energy, continues to be directed towards Kenya's elections. Such myopia comes at a cost. Rather than the doctors' and nurses' strikes, the catastrophic flooding of urban areas of Nairobi, the brutal droughts in northern Kenya that destroy lives and livelihoods, or the extravagant increase in extrajudicial killings perpetrated in broad daylight, most scholarly attention, international policy and monitoring, and local and social media commentary, will again be drawn to the 2022 elections. But the impact of the 2010 Constitution extends beyond the election cycle. Part of the work of this project has been to demonstrate that formal democratic processes and systems, while important, are only a small part of the lives of most Kenyans, who are much more affected by interactions with local police officers, their relationships with their spouses and families, and local access to essential services and education.

---

[9] Gautam Bhatia, '2022. The Kenyan Supreme Court's BBI Judgment – III: On Referendum Questions, Other Implications and Untidy Endnotes', *Indian Constitutional Law and Philosophy* (blog), 6 April 2022, https://indconlawphil.wordpress.com/2022/04/06/the-kenyan-supreme-courts-bbi-judgment-iii-on-referendum-questions-and-other-implications [accessed 4 July 2022].
[10] Gautam Bhatia, 'Notes From a Foreign Field'. See also Ambreena Manji, 'The BBI Judgment and the Invention of Kenya', *Verfassungsblog* (blog), 22 May 2021, https://verfassungsblog.de/the-bbi-judgment-and-the-invention-of-kenya [accessed 30 August 2021].

Gendered citizenship and the public lives of Kenyan women

The death of Wanjiku has been announced by several commentators in recent years. She has variously died from injuries sustained by being attacked and robbed by local security guards, or police; or of a broken heart, 'lying in bed, caressing the scars that had formed when she had used thorns to hold her flesh together' after devoting her life to supporting her ultimately thankless local community.[11] Her death, like her life, is an object lesson meant to shock Kenyans into taking seriously the effect of endemic state corruption, nepotism and state-sponsored violence on the nation's most vulnerable citizens. Unmoved by her suffering in life, perhaps Kenyans might be spurred into action by her death.

Within Kenyan popular discourse, Wanjiku has lost any personal sense of identity, representing more a collection of problems to be solved than an embodied citizen of the republic. This lack of identity is a direct result of her disembodiment. As Wangechi Mwangi argues:

> Wanjiku's emergence in the male-dominated Kenyan public sphere didn't necessarily imply more equitable gender relations, or even awareness to gendered issues ... Wanjiku seems to lack any awareness of her body's processes – such as menstruation, pregnancy, or the need to eat – and she also has strangely male-inflected concerns. The Kenyan universalism she portrays is coded male. Not having a body, Wanjiku is unable to experience or mediate the lived politics of a body's situation and concerns.[12]

Disembodied, here Eunice Karanja has stripped Wanjiku of her remaining, defining characteristics – her ethnicity, her gender, her level of education and her class:

> Wanjiku is you and I and every woman on earth, be they black or white, tall or short, she refers to every woman ... At another level, Wanjiku refers to the poor, weak and marginalized, whether they are male or female, white or black, educated or not, Christian or not. At this level there is neither male or female. The powerful, be they male or female do things in the name of Wanjiku with little regard for Wanjiku's needs or aspirations.[13]

---

[11] 'Wanjiku Is Dead but Who Will Mourn Her When Everyone Wants to Move On?' *The Nation*, 4 July 2020, www.nation.co.ke/oped/opinion/Wanjiku-is-dead-but-who-will-mourn-her/440808-1735496-uvrat4/index.html [accessed 20 August 2021].

[12] Mwangi, Wambui, 'Silence is a Woman', *The New Inquiry*, 4 June 2013, http://thenewinquiry.com/essays/silence-is-a-woman [accessed 16 August 2021].

[13] Eunice Karanja in conversation with Naomi Shitemi as quoted in Naomi L. Shitemi, 'Identities, Diversities and Inferences: A Discourse Analysis on the

This denial of Wanjiku's personhood by her fellow Kenyans led the late Kenyan scholar Naomi Shitemi to argue that 'Wanjiku was never a woman, she was just this convenient though fluid sociopolitical category'.[14] But disadvantage and discrimination are by their nature embodied.

Godfrey Mwampembwa, better known by his pseudonym 'Gado', the cartoonist whose illustrations of Wanjiku have made her famous, explains that Moi's Wanjiku was:

> a no body sort of woman ... some sort of lumpenproletariat – somebody who does not really understand issues, somebody who (leaders/politicians) others should decide for. Very much in line with how we dismiss the village *mama mboga*[15] ... with time, I fashioned my Wanjiku as somebody who is articulate, smart, funny, and aware of her rights, and knows what she wants.[16]

Unconsciously, Mwampembwa owns Wanjiku too: 'with time, *I fashioned my* Wanjiku'. Such is the need for Wanjiku, she has been claimed by anyone who needs her – to invoke her as the lone figure standing against all kinds of unfettered power, her essence stripped away, an amorphous entity deployed to demonstrate the corrosive effects of the voracious contest for power on vulnerable populations.

In seeking to improve the lives of Kenyan women, the international and Kenyan national human rights policy environment has also created a broad 'sociopolitical category' of person. This nondescript recipient of training and services, and the subject of multitudinous reports on the rights violations she has suffered, has similarly lost her embodied, gendered self. I have addressed these limitations by offering case studies which trouble these assumptions: of women as victims and objects of cultural violence; of women and myths of the sorority of African women; women as victims of political and state violence; and women as actors in national political processes. In the four cases, we have seen that the assumptions and demands of contemporary human rights discourse are built on unstable historical and methodological foundations. Cursory engagements with Kenyan colonial history, and failures to seriously engage with the role of the colonial encounter in forming the postcolonial masculine citizen, have led to gender programming which is blind to the deep and insidious cultural and logistical barriers to women's access to social services, justice and positions of authority.

Wanjiku Phenomenon', in Naomi Shitemi and Eunice Kamaara (eds), *Wanjiku: A Kenyan Sociopolitical Discourse* (Nairobi: Contact Zones, Kindle Edition, 2012).
[14] Shitemi, 'Identities, Diversities and Inferences'.
[15] *Mboga* is the KiSwahili word for vegetables; a *mama mboga* is a local woman who sells vegetables at the market.
[16] Godfrey Mwampembwa, 'Who Is Wanjiku? A Popular Analyst's View', in Shitemi and Kamaara, *Wanjiku: A Kenyan Sociopolitical Discourse*.

Similarly, reading Kenyan women's agency only in terms of its feminist liberatory potential is also a limiting project. Difficult questions need to be asked of human rights discourse regarding whether the expression of agency in non-liberal environments, or towards non-liberal goals, should itself be understood as a feminist endeavour. The postcolonial African academy would also benefit from this critical complexity: the valorisation of motherhood needs to be recognised as only one of a series of potential gendered subjectivities open to African women. Currently, the totalising effect of the emphasis on motherhood entrenches heteronormative subjectivities and limits the political and cultural lives of all those who identity as African women. In spite of these limitations, the centrality of bodies for African womanism and the power to be found in cultural practice – remembering the dynamic and mutable nature of culture – must be taken more seriously by the international human rights policy community as deep sources of authority and strength, rather than dismissed by Western feminism as static and too essentialising of women's identities.

In searching for those 'slumbering embers' of agency among marginalised populations, human rights programming often seeks actions and motivations which promote particular goals, preferring those goals which seek to move women towards *equality* rather than *complementarity* with men. Mahmood offers the possibility of conceiving of self-realisation outside of liberal modes of autonomous subjectivities, and of decoupling self-fulfilment from individual autonomy.[17] As I have argued here, the specificity of Kenyan women's needs, aspirations and identities – grounded in temporal, cultural and geographic locations – is 'constitutive at times of very different forms of personhood, knowledge and experience'.[18] The campaign for the inclusion of the Two-Thirds Gender Principle in the 2010 Constitution was hailed as a victory among Kenyan and international women's rights advocates. But the repeated failures to implement its provisions, and the unabated escalation of violence and intimidation women aspirants and leaders face within their communities, in public life and within their own parties, are evidence of the shallow achievement of legal protection that does not take account of culture.

Mukabi Kabira, an academic and women's rights advocate explains that during the years of the constitutional reform process, for many 'women leaders, our focus had been ensuring [that] women's interests were taken on board [in] the process and in the body and soul of

---

[17] Saba Mahmood, 'Feminist Theory, Embodiment and the Docile Agent: Some Reflections on the Egyptian Islamic Revival', *Cultural Anthropology*, 16:2 (2001), 207.
[18] Ibid.

the new constitution'.[19] This is a noble and important aspiration, but in the years following the triumphant promulgation of the 2010 Constitution, the victories which were expected to flow for women have remained largely abstract. The overwhelming preoccupation of elite women with the enlivening of the Two-Thirds Gender Principle demonstrates the disconnect between the goals and aspirations of the middle/upper class – who comprise the great majority of advocates, civil society leaders and employees – and the women 'down there at the grassroots'. As Harri Eglund explains, for urban civil society advocates, 'the starting point is not the actual concerns and aspirations of the people, their particular situations in life and experiences of abuse, but freedom, democracy and human rights as universal and abstract values'.[20]

The problem is that there remains a 'gnawing gender gap' among government appointees and elected members of parliament at all levels. But this failure is repeated each time a new call for the implementation of the Gender Principle is thwarted. The institutional women's rights movement persistently fails to mobilise women around the principle: as Nanjala Nyabola laments, there 'has been little coalition building outside formal institutions' and 'no attempt to translate the provisions into KiSwahili and other local languages so that people could understand why this principle was so important'.[21] We can contrast Nyabola's analysis of the failures of the women's movement in Kenya with the conviction and determination Kabira explains was at the heart of women's advocacy for the Gender Principle:

> It became clear as the implementation process got under way in 2011 that the provisions on the two-thirds rule in representation in appointive and elective bodies was threatened. Women did not rest – they returned to the battle field to safe guard their gains in the new constitution.[22]

These disparate positions illustrate a deep disagreement, emblematic of the fundamental disconnect between different generations of feminists and women's rights organisers in Kenya, and between urban and rural women. Writing on her experience advocating for women's rights to be enshrined in a new constitutional dispensation, Mukabi Kabira explained the journey in the genre of the daily struggles of grassroots Kenyan women:

[19] Mukabi Kabira, *Time for Harvest: Women and Constitution Making in Kenya* (Nairobi: University of Nairobi Press, 2012), 1.
[20] Harri Eglund, *Prisoners of Freedom: Human Rights and the African Poor* (Berkeley: University of California Press, 2006), 9.
[21] Nanjala Nyabola, 'Kenyan Feminisms in the Digital Age', *Women's Studies Quarterly*, 46:3&4 (2018), 270.
[22] Kabira, *Time for Harvest: Women and Constitution Making in Kenya*, 2.

> It was like walking a very long distance to fetch water, as many women of Africa do, fetch water in a big pot, walk the long journey home, and as you get into the house ready to quench the thirst of your family, you drop the pot and the water spills. It doesn't matter whether the pot dropped accidentally or you dropped it – the spilt water cannot be collected. So, you sit down to get over the shock, but you cannot sit there for long or forever; you have to gather your strength and start the water fetching journey all over again. The constitution making process has had various miscarriages for women. Every time the issue of review was picked up, women got up again and walked the journey.[23]

The distance between the metaphor of fetching water, and the embodied reality of a gruelling daily routine is the distance between 'rights' or 'democracy' as a universal abstract ideal, and the reality of grinding poverty and exclusion from systems of capital, knowledge and power that are mobilised against every move you make.

Haki hizi si zetu (These rights are not ours)

In 2022, the Kenyan writer, Carey Baraka, wrote an article titled 'Hii Nai si yetu' ('This Nairobi is Not Ours')[24]. Here, Baraka explains:

> Nairobi wasn't built for walking. Outer Ring Road in the morning is a nightmare, all the construction – good luck not falling into a ditch at six in the morning. Jogoo Road is a rhapsody of vehicles, and people – people walking and running and shouting and crying and yelling and driving and steering and hooting and vehicling and nuisancing ... and people moving, always moving, except when they're not, but sitting and staring and complaining and cursing and grinding teeth and being still because Jogoo Road was not built for all these different peoples, fat and thin and tall and short and moribund and oblique and round and obtuse and oval and black, always black, black ants scurrying forward, or *not* scurrying forward, seated in their vehicles, vehicling.
>
> There [also] exist Nairobi walkers. Homo Nairobi Mobilae. At six, seven, eight, nine in the morning, walking up Jogoo Road, always up, never down, and this because we suppose the CBD to be *up,* not *down*. We think Nairobi spreads outwards from its center. We've been told to think Nairobi spreads outwards from its center, its headquarters and government offices and important roads, where the trees of colonialism still exist, jacarandas blooming in beautiful violence every October, where

---

[23] *Ibid.*, 1–2.
[24] Carey Baraka, 'Hii Nai Si Yetu', *Down River Road* (blog), 30 December 2021, https://downriverroad.org/2021/12/30/carey-baraka-hii-nai-si-yetu [accessed 22 February 2022].

the money is, where people venture to hustle, where if you ask what they are doing in the CBD, they say that, you know, it's just hustle ...
Nairobi isn't built for Homo Nairobi Mobilae ... Lakini the walkers, Homo Nairobi Mobilae, how do they survive??

Throughout this project, we have walked *up* to town, and *down* to Kibera, as well as *out* to Kisumu County. Although Nairobi was not built *for* Homo Nairobi Mobilae, the city certainly relies on their labour as maids, mechanics, stall holders, cleaners and *askaris* (Sw. watchmen). Homo Nairobi Mobilae also belongs to rural communities across Kenya, continuing the colonial migration to the city in search of opportunities and work to send remittances home. Women, 'down there at the grassroots' have, throughout Kenya's history, contributed critical political and cultural interventions, through leading and supporting resistance movements, grassroots human rights networks and political parties, and it is here with these women, and these movements, that the most vibrant and urgent calls to action continue to be made. Of course, women's experience is only one lens through which human rights goals can be understood, and the women working in rural areas – like Caren Omanga and the Nyabende Human Rights Network – join networks of grassroots urban organisations including the Mathare Social Justice Centre and the Kibera Joy Initiative in Nairobi in tackling a range of urgent issues including endemic domestic and family violence, extrajudicial killings, food insecurity and land justice.

The work of this volume has centred Kenyan and African authors, scholars, activists and grassroots women in an effort to oblige formal international rights systems and scholarship to take African histories seriously, to understand the effect of the long reach of British coloniality into modern day Kenyan popular culture and politics, and to appreciate the serious limitations of international rights programmes hampered by an uncritical dismissal of local cultures and politics; essentially, to engage actively with African perspectives on gender and rights on their own terms.

It is also important to note that, while this book has dealt with the gender binary created by the colonial encounter and reinforced by the modern project of gender and women's rights, there are African movements energetically engaged in complicating the frameworks around gender and sexuality in Kenya, and across the African continent. These movements, which are built on African philosophies, including radical African lesbian feminism, have taken on the biological essentialism of African womanism and provided a rich and growing body of scholarship, advocacy, policy interventions, performance, and art that responds to the othering of non-heteronormative sexualities and gender identities. These scholars, activists, NGOs and collectives seek to excavate African histories of diverse gender and sexuality, silenced and erased by the colonial archive and missionary interventions, while also building innovative strategies for rights advocacy and support of queer communities living in hostile cultural and political environments.[25] It is in rich and diverse movements like these across Kenya that a future which holds the aspirations of Kenya's 45 million people, spread over 117+ ethnic groups and migrant, rural and urban communities, can be found.

In asking, 'What can a human rights regime offer? And to whom?' we must challenge ourselves to think expansively – linguistically, culturally and geographically. To reach people where they are – not everyone can drive into Nairobi. To realise the potential of human rights, rather than promoting a mono-narrative that creates similarly mono-dimensional subjects based on bureaucratic constructions of gender and women, and regressive 'African' gendered identities, the frameworks and interventions must acknowledge the multiple subjectivities and identities that women inhabit and find the strength in these complexities.

[25] Keguro Macharia, 'Wanjiku?' *Gukira* (blog), 26 December 2012, https://gukira.wordpress.com/2012/12/26/wanjiku [accessed 2 February 2021].

Appendix:
Field Work, Focus Groups and Interviews

The Kenya Human Rights Commission

The KHRC is a non-government organisation working on several key areas of human rights advocacy, including civil and political rights, and gender and the rights of people of diverse sexual orientation, gender identity and/or expression (SOGIE). The KHRC is actively engaged with twenty-one community-based human rights networks (HuRiNets) in five key regions of Kenya, and prioritises timely human rights monitoring, documentation and reporting.

The KHRC was established in 1991 and registered in Washington, USA, named the 'Kenya Human Rights Commission'[1] to draw attention to the fact that the Moi government had no care for the human rights of Kenyans, and had not established a national commission (the statutory body, the Kenya National Commission on Human Rights (KNCHR) was established by Moi's successor Mwai Kibaki in 2002). Since its establishment the KHRC has increasingly focused on strategies aimed at enhancing community driven human rights advocacy, through building the capacity of citizens to deal with their immediate human rights concerns as well as engaging in strategic actions to transform structures responsible for human rights violations.

The Commission's focus on human rights monitoring and reporting and commitment to community engagement and human rights education continue to build their strong community connections across Kenya. Working with the Commission for several months allowed me to build relationships of trust within the human rights sector in Nairobi and to become known to and establish trust in local communities in Nairobi.

---

[1] Kenya Human Rights Commission, 2016, www.khrc.or.ke/about-us/history.html.

Focus groups

Over the two trips I conducted semi-structured focus groups and interviews in the following locations. I visited those locations in **bold** type on both trips:

1. Central County	Nairobi (**Kibera slum**, and **Kangemi**, low-income areas)
2. Kisumu and Siaya Counties	Bumala, **Bar Ober**, Butere, Ugunja, **Ahero**, **Aweyo Canteen**, and Nyando villages in the province of Nyanza, around Lake Victoria
3. Taita-Taveta County	Taveta town

I conducted semi-structured focus group interviews, with between five and twenty participants at each focus group, about 120 women in total. The women I interviewed in these focus groups were women from two particular groups – those who were peer-to-peer human rights educators or otherwise volunteered with local right promotion groups and/or who belonged to grassroots, voluntary women's advocacy organisations (for instance, the KHRC's HuRiNet partners). I also interviewed women who were not involved with civil society in any way and who did not have significant contact with institutional services, sourced via snowball sampling through facilitators' invitations to local women to join the focus groups.

Groups and locations were similarly chosen through a snowball methodology where facilitators I had met and worked with in Nairobi also recommended new sites to conduct interviews outside the city. This strategy provided some measure of safety in planning field trips outside Nairobi. Women in these new locations also trusted the facilitator as they were often from their home community, or had worked on human rights issues in the area for an extended period.

The locations I visited twice provided richer material for two key reasons. Firstly, because I came to know these groups a little better at the second meeting and could follow up on issues we had discussed eighteen months earlier. I had also maintained and continued to build relationships with the facilitators in the intervening period, so we had good working relationships. I had also introduced the facilitators to each other and we held face-to-face meetings to discuss the election, and share ideas for building women's financial resilience and training opportunities.

I also benefited immensely from informal discussions with my colleagues at the Kenya Human Rights Commission, local facilitators and friends.

Kangemi Women's Health Support Group, Nairobi

The group was formed in 2009 by people living with HIV and was originally called 'Keep the Promise'. This group formed with the aim of maintaining participants' health and prolonging their lives to take care of their children. They also wanted to fight the stigma of HIV diagnosis and to fight against discrimination in the community. Since inception, the group has grown to include strategies both for income generation and to 'empower each other, and to gain skills that we can use to get income to start our own small businesses'. The group meets once a week and the participants educate each other about drug adherence, fighting stigma and discrimination, as well as teaching women to make beaded necklaces, earrings and baskets for sale. Camilla Mwenda, community health worker attached to Kangemi Health Centre is the organiser of the women's group.

Nyabende Human Rights Network, Aweyo Canteen, Kisumu County

The Nyabende Women's Network was formed in January 2008 and is affiliated with six other self-help groups in East Kano and Wawidhi, Kenya. The group brings together women and men who are affected by social and economic challenges and who are interested in exploring solutions to their common problems. It aims to improve the standards of living in their community through financial education and microfinance programmes, as well as running income-generating activities. The network reaches over 150 members ranging from 20 to 80 years old.

The group organises activities in two key areas: microfinance and financial education; and promoting and protecting rights of girl children and those affected by HIV/AIDS. Caren Omanga facilitates this group.

Bibliography

Books

Ahlberg, Beth Maina, *Women, Sexuality and the Changing Social Order: The Impact of Government Policies on Reproductive Behaviour in Kenya* (Philadelphia: Gordon and Breach, 1991).

Ahlberg, Beth M., Kezia Njoroge and Pia Olsson, '"We Cannot Be Led by a Child": Forced Male Circumcision during the Post-election Violence in Kenya' (Uppsala: Department of Women's and Children's Health, Uppsala University and Karaborg Institute for Research and Development, 2011).

Ahluwalia, D. Pal, *Post-Colonialism and the Politics of Kenya* (New York: Nova Science, 1996).

Amadiume, Ifi, *Reinventing Africa* (London: Zed Books, 1997).

Anderson, Benedict, *Imagined Communities: Reflections on the Origin and Spread of Nationalism* (London: Verso, 1983).

—— *Imagined Communities: Reflections on the Origin and Spread of Nationalism*, 2nd edn (London: Verso, 2006).

Andrieu, Kora, 'Political Liberalism after Mass Violence: John Rawls and a "Theory" of Transitional Justice', in Susanne Buckley-Zistel, Teresa Koloma Beck, Christian Braun and Friederike Mieth (eds), *Transitional Justice Theories* (New York: Routledge, 2014), pp. 85–105.

Annan, Kofi, Graça Machel and Benjamin Mkapa, *Back from the Brink: The 2008 Mediation Process and Reforms in Kenya* (Geneva: African Union Commission, 2008).

Atieno-Odhiambo, Eisha Stephen, 'The Invention of Kenya', in B.A. Ogot and W.R. Ochieng' (eds), *Decolonization and Independence in Kenya 1940–93* (London: James Currey, 1995), pp. 1–7.

Berman, Bruce and John Lonsdale, *Unhappy Valley: Conflict in Kenya & Africa, Book Two: Violence and Ethnicity* (Nairobi: Heinemann Kenya, 1992).

Branch, Daniel, *Kenya: Between Hope and Despair, 1963–2012* (London: Yale University Press, 2011).

Brantley, Cynthia, *The Giriama and Colonial Resistance in Kenya, 1800–1920* (London: University of California Press, 1981).

Buel, Raymond Leslie, *The Native Problem in Africa* (New York: Macmillan Company, 1928).
Centre for Rights Education and Awareness (CREAW), *Women Paid the Price!* (Nairobi: CREAW, 2008).
Cock, Jacklyn, *Colonels and Cadres: War and Gender in South Africa* (Cape Town: Oxford University Press, 1991).
Comaroff, John L. and Jean Comaroff, *Ethnicity, Inc.* (Chicago: University of Chicago Press, 2009).
Das, Veena, 'The Act of Witnessing: Violence, Poisonous Knowledge, and Subjectivity', in Veena Das, Arthur Kleinman, Mamphela Ramphele and Pamela Reynolds (eds), *Violence and Subjectivity* (Berkeley: University of California Press, 2000), pp. 205–25.
Das, Veena and Arthur Kleinman, 'Introduction', in Veena Das, Arthur Kleinman, Mamphela Ramphele and Pamela Reynolds (eds), *Violence and Subjectivity* (Berkeley: University of California Press, 2000), pp. 1–18.
Davies, Margaret Jane, *Asking the Law Question* (Sydney: Thomson Law Book Company, 1994).
Davison, Jean, *Voices from Mutira: Changes in the Lives of Rural Gikuyu Women, 1910–1995* (Boulder: Lynne Rienner, 1995).
—— *Voices from Mutira: Change in the Lives of Rural Gikuyu Women, 1910–1995*, 2nd edn (Boulder: Lynne Rienner, 1996).
Dembour, Marie-Benedict, *Who Believes in Human Rights? Reflections on the European Convention* (Cambridge: Cambridge University Press, 2006).
Dialogue Africa Foundation, 'Kriegler and Waki Reports: Summarized Version' (Konrad Adenauer Stiftung, 2009).
Diop, Chiekh Anta, *Precolonial Black Africa: A Comparative Study of the Political and Social Systems of Europe and Black Africa from Antiquity to the Formation of the Modern States* (Westport: Lawrence Hill, 1987).
Eglund, Harri, *Prisoners of Freedom: Human Rights and the African Poor* (Berkeley: University of California Press, 2006).
Elkins, Caroline, *Imperial Reckoning: The Untold Story of Britain's Gulag in Kenya* (New York: Henry Holt and Company, 2005).
Essed, Philomena, Karen Farquharson, Kathryn Pillay and Elisa Joy White (eds), *Relating Worlds of Racism: Dehumanisation, Belonging, and the Normativity of European Whiteness* (Cham: Springer, 2018).
Foran, William R., *The Kenya Police Force 1887–1963* (London: Robert Hale, 1962).
Geiger, Susan, *TANU Women: Gender and Culture in the Making of Tanganyikan Nationalism, 1955–1965* (Portsmouth: Heinemann, 1997).
Ginsburgh, Nicola, *Class, Work and Whiteness: Race and Settler Colonialism in Southern Rhodesia, 1919–79* (Manchester: Manchester University Press, 2020).

Goldsworthy, David, *Tom Mboya: The Man Kenya Wanted to Forget* (London: Heinemann Educational, 1982).
Gregory, Robert, *Sidney Webb and East Africa: Labour's Experiment with the Doctrine of Native Paramountcy* (Berkeley: University of California Press, 1962).
Gulliver, P.H., *Tradition and Transition in East Africa* (London: Routledge, 1969).
Harries, Patrick, 'Exclusion, Classification and Internal Colonialism: The Emergence of Ethnicity among the Tsonga-Speakers of South Africa', in Leroy Vail (ed.), *The Creation of Tribalism in Southern Africa* (London: James Currey, 1989), pp. 82–117.
Hendrickson, Hilda (ed.), *Clothing and Difference: Embodied Identities in Colonial and Post-colonial Africa* (Durham: Duke University Press, 1996).
Heng, Geraldine, '"Great Way to Fly": Nationalism, the State, and the Varieties of Third World Feminism', in M. Jacquie Alexander and Chandra Talpade Mohanty (eds), *Feminist Genealogies, Colonial Legacies, Democratic Futures* (London: Routledge, 1997), pp. 30–45.
Hinderlier, Beth and Noelle Chaddock, 'A Rejection of White Feminist Cisgender Allyship', in Noelle Chaddock and Beth Hinderlier (eds), *Antagonizing White Feminism: Intersectionality's Critique of Women's Studies and the Academy* (London: Lexington Books, Rowman & Littlefield, 2019), pp. 137–46.
Hobsbawm, Eric and Terence Ranger (eds), *The Invention of Tradition* (Cambridge: Cambridge University Press, 1983).
Holtzman, Jon D., *Killing Your Neighbours: Friendship and Violence in Northern Kenya and Beyond* (Berkeley: University of California Press, 2017).
Hornsby, Charles, *Kenya: A History Since Independence* (New York: Palgrave Macmillan, 2013).
Hughes, Anthony J., *East Africa: The Search for Unity* (Baltimore: Penguin Books, 1963).
Human Rights Watch, *Ballots to Bullets* (New York: Human Rights Watch, 2008).
—— *'I Just Sit and Wait to Die': Reparations for Survivors of Kenya's Post-election Sexual Violence*, 15 February 2016, www.hrw.org/report/2016/02/15/i-just-sit-and-wait-die/reparations-survivors-kenyas-2007-2008-post-election [Accessed 10 September 2018].
Ingham, Kenneth, *A History of East Africa*, 2nd edn (London: Longmans, 1963).
International Crisis Group, *Kenya's 2013 Elections*, Africa Report No. 197 (Brussels: International Crisis Group, 2013). www.crisisgroup.org/africa/horn-africa/kenya/kenya-s-2013-elections [accessed 10 September 2018].

―― *Kenya in Crisis*, Africa Report No. 137 (Brussels: International Crisis Group, 2008) www.crisisgroup.org/africa/horn-africa/kenya/kenya-crisis [accessed 10 September 2018].

Irigaray, Luce, *The Irigaray Reader*, ed. Margaret Whitford (Massachusetts: Blackwell Publishers, 1995).

Itote, Waruhiu, *'Mau Mau' General* (Nairobi: East African Publishing House, 1967).

Jensen, Casper Bruun and Brit Ross Winthereik, 'Monitoring Movements', in Casper Bruun Jensen and Brit Ross Winthereik (eds), *Monitoring Movements in Development Aid* (Cambridge: MIT Press, 2013), pp. 147–67.

Jones, Thomas Jesse, *Education in East Africa* (London: Edinburgh House Press, 1925).

Kabira, Mukabi, *Time for Harvest: Women and Constitution Making in Kenya* (Nairobi: University of Nairobi Press, 2012).

Kamaru, Marilyn Muthoni, 'The Missing Piece: The Legislature, Gender Parity and Constitutional Legitimacy in Kenya', in Nanjala Nyabola and Marie-Emmanuelle Pommerolle (eds), *Where Women Are: Tracing Kenyan Women's Involvement in Elections and Political Leadership from 1963–2002* (Nairobi: Africae, 2018), 194–47.

Kanogo, Tabitha, *African Womanhood in Colonial Kenya 1900–1950* (Oxford: James Currey, 2005).

――*Squatters and the Roots of Mau Mau* (London: James Currey, 1987)

Kapur, Ratna, *Erotic Justice: Law and the New Politics of Postcolonialism* (London: GlassHouse, 2005).

Kenyatta, Jomo, *Facing Mount Kenya* (New York: Random House, 1962).

Kihoro, Wanyiri, *The Price of Freedom: The Story of Political Resistance in Kenya* (Nairobi: MvuleAfrica, 2005).

――*Politics and Parliamentarians in Kenya, 1944–2007* (Nairobi: Centre for Multiparty Democracy, 2007).

Kinyanjui, Mary Njeri, *African Markets and the Utu-Ubuntu Business Model: A Perspective on Economic Informality in Nairobi* (Cape Town: African Minds, 2019).

Kolawole, Mary E. Modupe, *Womanism and African Consciousness* (Asmara: Africa World Press, 1997).

Kratz, Corinne, *Affecting Performance: Meaning, Movement and Experience in Okiek Women's Initiation* (Washington: Smithsonian Institution Press, 1994).

Kweheria, Nduta J., *Achieving Gender Equality in Elective Public Office in Kenya by March* 2013, KHRC Internal Briefing Paper (Nairobi: Kenya Human Rights Commission, 2012).

Lamb, Geoff, *Peasant Politics* (London: Julian Friedman Publishers, 1974).

Leakey, L.S.B., *The Southern Kikuyu before 1903* (London: Academic Press, 1977).

Lebeuf, Annie, 'The Role of Women in the Political Organisation of African Societies', in Denise Paulme (ed.), *Women of Tropical Africa* (Berkeley: University of California Press, 1963), pp. 93–121.

Levertov, Denise, New Selected Poems (Bloodaxe Books, 2003).

Likimani, Muthoni, *They Shall Be Chastised* (Nairobi: East African Literature Bureau, 1974).

Lindburg, Staffan (ed.), *Democratisation by Elections: A New Mode of Transition* (Baltimore: Johns Hopkins University Press, 2009).

Lindenmayer, Elizabeth and Josie Lianna Kaye, *A Choice for Peace? The Story of Forty-One Days of Mediation in Kenya* (New York: International Peace Institute, 2009).

Llewelyn-Davies, Melissa, 'Women Warriors, and Patriarchs', in Sherry B. Ortner (ed.), *Sexual Meanings: The Cultural Construction of Gender and Sexuality* (Cambridge: Cambridge University Press, 1981).

López, Alfred J. (ed.), *Postcolonial Whiteness: A Critical Reader on Race and Empire* (Albany: SUNY Press, 2012)

Lorde, Audre. *The Black Unicorn* (New York: W. W. Norton & Company, 1995).

Lutomia, Anne Namatsi, Nyandiko Saya and Dorothy Rombo, 'Examining and Contextualising Kenya's Maendeleo ya Wanawake Organisation (NYWO) through an African Feminist Lens', in Christina Schwabenland, Chris Lange, Jenny Onyx and Sachiko Nakagawa (eds), *Women's Emancipation and Civil Society Organisation: Challenging or Maintaining the Status Quo?* (Bristol: Policy Press, 2016), pp. 321–41.

Maloiy, Lanoi, 'Tracing Kenyan Women's Involvement in Elections and Political Leadership from 1963–2002', in Nanjala Nyabola and Marie-Emmanuelle Pommerolle (eds), *Where Women Are: Gender & the 2017 Kenyan Elections* (Nairobi: Africae, 2018), pp. 24–49.

Mamdani, Mahmood, *Define and Rule: Native as Political Identity* (Cambridge: Harvard University Press, 2012).

Mangua, Charles, *Son of Woman* (Nairobi: East African Publishers, 1971).

Maupeu, Hervé and Rachel Robertson, 'Kenya's Ethnic Somalis and Access to Identity Papers: Citizenship and Nation-Building in North-East Kenya', in Séverine Awenengo Dalberto and Richard Banégas (eds), *Identification and Citizenship in Africa: Biometrics, the Documentary State and Bureaucratic Writings of the Self* (London: Routledge, 2021), pp. 166–85.

Maxon, Robert M., 'The Establishment of Colonial Economy', in W.R. Ochieng' and Robert M. Maxon (eds), *An Economic History of Kenya* (Nairobi: East African Publishers, 1992), pp. 63–74.

—— *Conflict and Accommodation in Western Kenya: The Gusii and the British* (Rutherford: Fairleigh Dickinson University Press, 1989).

McGhie, Meredith Preston and E. Njoki Wamai, *Beyond the Numbers: Women's Participation in the Kenya National Dialogue and Reconciliation* (Geneva: Centre for Humanitarian Dialogue, 2011).

Mehta, Deepak, 'Circumcision, Body, Masculinity: The Ritual Wound and Collective Violence', in Veena Das, Arthur Kleinman, Mamphela Ramphele and Pamela Reynolds (eds), *Violence and Subjectivity* (Berkeley: University of California Press, 2000),

Merry, Sally Engle, *Human Rights and Gender Violence: Translating International Law into Local Justice* (Chicago: Chicago University Press, 2006).

Moore, Henrietta L., *Space, Text and Gender: An Anthropological Study of the Marakwet of Kenya* (New York: Guilford Press, 1996).

Morris, David, B., 'About Suffering: Voice, Genre, and Moral Community', in A. Kleinman, V. Das and M.M. Lock (eds), *Social Suffering* (Berkeley: University of California Press, 1997), pp. 25–47.

Mudimbe, Valentin Y., *The Invention of Africa: Gnosis, Philosophy, and the Order of Knowledge* (Bloomington: Indiana University Press, 1988).

Murray-Brown, Jeremy, *Kenyatta* (London: George Allen and Unwin, 1972).

Murunga, Godwin R., Duncan Okello and Anders Sjögren (eds), *Kenya: The Struggle for a New Constitutional Order* (London: Zed Books, 2014).

Mwampembwa, Godfrey, 'Who is Wanjiku? A Popular Analyst's View' in Godfrey Mwampembwa, Naomi Shitemi and Eunice Kamaara (eds), *Wanjiku a Kenyan Sociopolitical Discourse* (Nairobi: Contact Zones, Kindle Edition, 2012).

Nduta, J. Kweheria and Charles B.G. Ouma, *Achieving Gender Equality in National and Devolved Legislature without Amending Kenya's Constitution (2010)* (Nairobi: Kenya Human Rights Commission, 2012).

Newman, Edward, Roland Paris and Oliver P. Richmond (eds), *New Perspectives on Liberal Peacebuilding* (New York: United Nations University Press, 2009).

Nicholls, Brendon, *Ngugi wa Thiong'o, Gender and the Ethics of Postcolonial Reading* (Farnham: Ashgate, 2010).

Ngugi, Mumbi, *The Women's Rights Movement and Democratization in Kenya: A Preliminary Inquiry into the Green Formations of Civil Society* (Brighton: Eldis, 2000).

Njogu, Kimani, Kabiri Ngeta and Mary Wanjau (eds), *Ethnic Diversity in Eastern Africa: Opportunities and Challenges* (Nairobi: Twaweza Communications, 2010).

Nussbaum, Martha, *Women and Human Development: The Capabilities Approach* (Cambridge: Cambridge University Press, 2000).

Obeler, Regina S., *Women Power and Economic Change: The Nandi of Kenya* (Stanford: Stanford University Press, 1985).

Ochieng', William Robert and Eisha Stephen Atieno-Odhiambo, 'On Decolonization', in B.A. Ogot and W.R. Ochieng' (eds), *Decolonization and Independence in Kenya 1940–93* (London: James Currey, 1995), pp. xiv–xv.

Odhiambo, Eisha Stephen Atieno; T.I. Ouso, and J.F.M. Williams, *A History of East Africa* (Hong Kong: Longman Press, 1977).

Oduol, Wilhemina and Wanjiku Mukabi Kabira, 'The Mother of All Warriors and Her Daughters: The Women's Movement in Kenya', in Amrita Basu (ed.), *The Challenge of Local Feminisms: Women's Movements in Global Perspective* (Boulder: Westview Press, 1995), pp. 187–208.

Ogola, Margaret, *The River and the Source* (Nairobi: Focus Publishers, 1994).

Ogunyemi, Chikwenye Okonjo, *Africa Wo/Man Palava* (Chicago: University of Chicago Press, 1995).

Okeyo, Achola Pala, 'Daughters of the Lakes and Rivers: Colonisation and the Land Rights of Luo Women', in Mona Etienne and Eleanor Leacock (eds), *Women and Colonisation: Anthropological Perspectives* (New York: Praeger Publishers, 1980), pp. 186–213.

Okonjo, Kamene, 'The Dual Sex Political System in Operation: Igbo Women and Community Politics in Midwestern Nigeria', in Nancy J. Hafkin and Edna G. Bay (eds), *Women in Africa: Studies in Social and Economic Change* (Stanford: Stanford University Press, 1976).

Oliver, Roland P. and Gervase Matthew (eds), *History of East Africa*, vol. 1. (Oxford: Clarendon Press, 1963).

Otto, Dianne, *Queering International Law: Possibilities, Alliances, Complicities, Risks* (New York: Routledge, 2018).

Owuor, Yvonne Adhiambo, *Dust* (London: Granta Books, 2015).

Oyěwùmí, Oyèrónkẹ́, *The Invention of Women: Making an African Sense of Western Gender Discourses* (Minneapolis: University of Minnesota Press, 1997).

Parkin, David, *Sacred Void – Spatial Images of Work and Ritual among the Giriama of Kenya* (London: Cambridge University Press, 1991).

Pavin, Melinda, G. Odingo, C. Jeon, V. Frajz and P. Perchal, *Assessing Two Strategies for Expanding Coverage of Adult Male Circumcision in Nyanza Province, Kenya* (New York: EngenderHealth, 2011).

Peterson, Derek R., *Creative Writing: Translation, Bookkeeping and the Work of Imagination in Colonial Kenya* (Portsmouth: Heinemann, 2004).

Presley, Cora Ann, *Kikuyu Women, the Mau Mau Rebellion, and Social Change in Kenya* (Boulder: Westview Press, 1992).

Ranger, Terence, 'Missionaries, Migrants and the Manyika: The Invention of Ethnicity in Zimbabwe', in Leroy Vail (ed.), *The Creation of Tribalism in Southern Africa* (London: James Currey, 1989), pp. 118–50.

—— 'The Invention of Tradition Revisited: The Case of Colonial Africa', in Terence Ranger and Olufemi Vaughan (eds), *Legitimacy and the State in Twentieth Century Africa: Essays in Honour of A.H.M. Kirk-Greene* (London: Macmillan, 1993), pp. 62–111.

Richmond, Oliver P., *Peace in International Relations* (London: Routledge, 2008).

Richmond, Oliver P. and Jason Franks, *Liberal Peace Transitions: Between Statebuilding and Peacebuilding* (Edinburgh: Edinburgh University Press, 2009).

Robertson, Claire, C., 'Putting the Political in Economy: African Women's and Gender History, 1992–2010' in Pamela S. Nadell and Kate Haulman (eds), *Making Women's Histories: Beyond National Perspectives* (New York: New York University Press, 2013), pp. 61–90.

—— *Trouble Showed the Way: Women, Men and Trade in the Nairobi Area, 1890–1990* (Bloomington: Indiana University Press, 1997).

Roland, Matthew Gervase (ed.), *History of East Africa*, Vol. 1 (Oxford: Clarendon Press, 1963).

Rosberg, Carl G. Jnr and John Nottingham, *The Myth of Mau Mau: Nationalism in Kenya* (Nairobi: East African Publishing House, 1966).

Sano, Hans-Otto, 'Social Accountability in the World Bank: How Does It Overlap with Human Rights?' in LaDawn Haglund and Robin Stryker (eds), *Closing the Rights Gap: From Human Rights to Social Transformation* (Berkeley: University of California Press, 2015), pp. 219–39.

Scully, Pamela, *Liberating the Family? Gender and British Slave Emancipation in the Rural Western Cape, South Africa, 1823–1853* (Cape Town: David Philip, 1998).

Sekyiamah, Nana Darkoa, *The Sex Lives of African Women* (London: Random House, 2021).

Shadle, Brett, *Girl Cases: Marriage and Colonialism in Gusiiland, Kenya 1890–1970* (Portsmouth: Heinemann, 2006).

Shaw, Carolyn Martin, *Colonial Inscriptions: Race, Sex and Class in Kenya* (Minneapolis: University of Minnesota Press, 1995).

Shitemi, Naomi L., 'Identities, Diversities and Inferences: A Discourse Analysis on the Wanjiku Phenomenon', in Naomi Shitemi and Eunice Kamaara (eds), *Wanjiku: A Kenyan Sociopolitical Discourse* (Nairobi: Contact Zones, Kindle Edition, 2012), www.amazon.com/Wanjiku-Socialpolitical-Discourse-Contact-Nairobi-ebook/dp/B00PG-V93Y2.

Shitemi, Naomi L. and Eunice Kamaara (eds), *Wanjiku: A Kenyan Sociopolitical Discourse* (Institute of International Education, 2012).

Silberschmidt, Margrethe, *'Women Forget that Men Are the Masters': Gender Antagonism and Socio-economic Change in Kisii District, Kenya* (Stockholm: Elanders Gotab, 1999).

Spronk, Rachel, *Ambiguous Pleasures: Sexuality and Middle Class Self-Perceptions in Nairobi* (Oxford: Berghahn, 2012).

Sweetman, David, *Women Leaders in African History* (London: Heinemann Educational, 1984).
The Carter Center, *Observing the 2002 Kenya Elections* (Atlanta: The Carter Center, 2003), www.cartercenter.org/documents/1355.pdf [accessed 20 August 2021].
Thomas, Lynn M. *Politics of the Womb: Women, Reproduction and the State in Kenya* (Berkeley: University of California Press, 2003).
Thornberry, Patrick, 'Indigenous Peoples and the Discourses of Human Rights: A Reflective Narrative', in *Indigenous Peoples and Human Rights* (Manchester: Manchester University Press, 2002).
Tibbetts, Alexandra, *Mamas Fighting for Freedom in Kenya* (Cambridge: Harvard University Press, 1993).
wa 'Thiong'o, Ngũgĩ, *The River Between* (New York: Penguin Random House, 1965).
——*Weep Not Child* (London: Heinemann, 1964).
Wamai, E. Njoki, 'Mediating Kenya's Post-Election Violence: From Peace-Making to a Constitutional Moment', in Godwin Murunga, Duncan Okello and Anders Sjögren (eds), *Kenya: The Struggle for a New Constitutional Order* (London: Zed Books, 2014), pp. 66–78.
Wanyeki, Muthoni, *Women's Agency and the State: The Kenyan Experience* (African Women's Development Fund, 2006).
White, Luise, *The Comforts of Home: Prostitution in Colonial Nairobi* (Chicago: University of Chicago Press, 1990).
Widner, J.A., *The Rise of a Party-state in Kenya: From 'Harambee' to 'Nyayo'* (Berkeley: University of California Press, 1993).
Wipper, Audrey, 'Riot and Rebellion among African Women: Three Examples of Women's Political Clout', in Jean O'Barr (ed.), *Perspectives on Power: Women in Africa, Asia, and Latin America* (Durham: Duke University Press, 1982).
——*Rural Rebels* (Nairobi: Oxford University Press, 1977).
Yancy, George, *Look, a White! Philosophical Essays on Whiteness* (Philadelphia: Temple University Press, 2012).
Youe, Christopher P., *Robert Thorn Coryndon: Proconsular Imperialism in Southern and Eastern Africa, 1897–1925* (Waterloo: Wilfrid Laurier University Press, 1986).
Wrong, Michela, *It's Our Turn to Eat: The Story of a Kenyan Whistle-Blower* (New York: Harper Perennial, 2010).
Zeleza, Paul Tiyambe, 'The Protracted Transition to the Second Republic in Kenya', in Godwin Murunga, Duncan Okello and Anders Sjogren (eds), *Kenya: The Struggle for a New Constitutional Order* (London: Zed Books, 2014), 17-43.
Zolkos, Magdelena, 'Redressive Politics and the Nexus of Trauma, Transitional Justice and Reconciliation', in Susanne Buckley-Zistel, Teresa Koloma Beck, Christian Braun and Friederike Mieth (eds), *Transitional Justice Theories* (New York: Routledge, 2014), pp. 176–77.

Zorn, Jean G., 'Translating and Internalising International Human Rights Law: The Courts of Melanesia Confront Gendered Violence', in Aletta Biersack, Margaret Jolly and Martha Macintyre (eds), *Gender Justice and Human Rights: Seeking Justice in Fiji, Papua New Guinea and Vanuatu* (Canberra: ANU Press, 2016), pp. 229–69.

Journals

Ajulu, Rok, 'Thinking Through the Crisis of Democratization in Kenya: A Response to Adar and Murunga', *African Sociological Review*, 4:2 (2000), 133–57.

Amadi, Henry, 'Kenya's Grand Coalition Government': Another Obstacle to Urgent Constitutional Reform?' *Africa Spectrum*, 44:3 (2009), 149–64.

Ambani, J. Osogo and Ombiti, H., 'Female Judicial Officers Fry in Their Hot Temper', *The Nairobi Law Monthly*, 4:4 (2014).

Ampofo, Akosua Adomako, Josephine Beoku-Betts, Wairimu Ngaruiya Njambi and Mary Orsirim, 'Women's and Gender Studies in English-speaking Sub-Saharan Africa: A Review of the Research in the Social Sciences', *Gender and Society*, 18:6 (2004), 685–714.

Anangwe, Alfred, 'From Kenyatta to Kenyatta, the Evolution of the Presidency', *The Nairobi Law Monthly*, 4:11 (2013), 72–75.

Arndt, Susan, 'African Gender Trouble and African Womanism: An Interview with Chikwenye Ogunyemi and Wanjira Muthoni', *Signs: Journal of Women in Culture and Society*, 25:3 (2000), 709–26.

—— 'Perspectives on African Feminism: Defining and Classifying African-Feminist Literatures', *Agenda: Empowering Women for Gender Equity*, 17:54 (2002), 33–44.

Askew, Ian, 'Methodological Issues in Measuring the Impact of Interventions against Female Genital Cutting', *Culture, Health and Sexuality*, 7:5 (2005), 463–77.

Balaton-Chrimes, Samantha, 'Who Are Kenya's 42(+) Tribes? The Census and the Political Utility of Magical Uncertainty', *Journal of Eastern African Studies*, 15:1 (2021), 43–62.

Baxi, Upendra, 'From Human Rights to the Right to be Human: Some Heresies', *India International Centre Quarterly*, 13:3/4 (1986), 185–200.

Bennett, G., 'Political Realities in Kenya', *The World Today*, 19:7 (1963), 294–301

Benson, T.G., 'The Jeanes School and the Education of the East African Native', *Journal of the Royal African Society*, 35:141 (October 1936), 418–31.

Berry, Marie. E., Yolande Bouka and Marilyne Muthoni Kamuru, 'Implementing Inclusion: Gender Quotas, Inequality, and Backlash in Kenya', *Politics & Gender*, 17:4 (2020), 1–25.

Bikketi, Edward, Chinwe Ifejika Speranza, Sabin Bieri, Tobias Haller and Urs Wiesmann, 'Gendered Division of Labour and Feminisation of Responsibilities in Kenya: Implications for Development Interventions', *Gender, Place and Culture,* 23:10 (2016), 1432–49.

Branch, Daniel, 'The Enemy Within: Loyalists and the War Against the Mau Mau in Kenya', *The Journal of African History,* 48:2 (2007), 291–20.

Branch, Daniel and Nicholas Cheeseman, 'The Politics of Control in Kenya: Understanding the Bureaucratic-Executive State, 1952–78', *Review of African Political Economy,* 33:107 (2006), 11–31.

Brantley, Cynthia, 'Gerontocratic Government Age Sets in Pre-colonial Giriama', *Journal of the International African Institute,* 48:3 (1978), 248–64.

Bratton Michael and Mwangi S. Kimenyi, 'Voting in Kenya: Putting Ethnicity in Perspective', *Journal of Eastern African Studies,* 2:2 (2008), 272–89.

Bruce-Lockhart, Katherine, 'Unsound Minds and Broken Bodies: The Detention of "Hardcore" Mau Mau Women at Kamiti and Gitamayu Detention Camps in Kenya, 1954–1960', *Journal of Eastern African Studies,* 8:4 (2014), 590–608.

Canning, Kathleen, 'The Body as Method? Reflections on the Place of the Body in Gender History', *Gender and History,* 11:3 (1999), 499–513.

Carotenuto, Matthew and Brett Shadle, 'Introduction: Toward a History of Violence in Colonial Kenya', *International Journal of African Historical Studies,* 45:1 (2012), 1–7.

Carpenter, Laura M. and Heather Kettrey, '(Im)perishable Pleasure, (In) destructible Desire: Sexual Themes in U.S. and English News Coverage of Male Circumcision and Female Genital Cutting', *The Journal of Sex Research,* 52:8 (2015), 841–56.

Castagno, Alphonso A., 'The Somali–Kenyan Controversy: Implications for the Future', *Journal of Modern African Studies,* 2:2 (1964), 165–88.

Cooper, Frank Rudy, 'Against Bipolar Black Masculinity: Intersectionality, Assimilation, Identity Performance, and Hierarchy', *UC Davis Law Review,* 39 (2005), 853–904.

Cooper, Frederick, 'Conflict and Connection: Rethinking Colonial African History', *American Historical Review,* 99:5 (1994), 1516–45.

Cornwall, Andrea and Althea-Maria Rivas, 'From "Gender Equality" and "Women's Empowerment" to Global Justice: Reclaiming a Transformative Agenda for Gender and Development', *Third World Quarterly,* 36:2 (2015), 396–415.

Coulter, Chris, 'Female Fighters in the Sierra Leone War: Challenging the Assumptions?' *Feminist Review,* 88:1 (2008), 54–73.

Das, Veena, 'The Anthropology of Violence and the Speech of Victims', *Anthropology Today,* 3:4 (1987), 11–13.

―― 'Violence, Gender, and Subjectivity', *Annual Review of Anthropology,* 37 (2008), 283–99.

Doezema, Jo, '"Ouch!" Western Feminists' "Wounded Attachment" to the "Third World Prostitute"', *Feminist Review,* 67 (2001), 16–38.

Dove, Nah, 'African Womanism: An Afrocentric Theory', *Journal of Black Studies,* 28:5 (1998), 515–39.

Ejeta, Gebisa and Richard Strage, 'Obituary – Wangari Muta Maathai 1940–2011', *Food Security,* 3:4 (2011), 412.

Elischer, Sebastian, 'Do African Parties Contribute to Democracy? Some Findings from Kenya, Ghana and Nigeria', *Africa Spectrum,* 43:2 (2008), 175–209.

Erulkar, Annabel S., 'The Experience of Sexual Coercion among Young People in Kenya', *International Family Planning Perspectives,* 30:4 (2004), 182–89.

'Fatal Rioting At Nairobi', *The Times* (London, 18 March 1922), 10.

Feichtinger, Moritz, '"A Great Reformatory": Social Planning and Strategic Resettlement in Late Colonial Kenya and Algeria, 1952–63', *Journal of Contemporary History,* 52:1 (2017), 45–72.

Fields, Karen, 'Political Contingencies of Witchcraft in Colonial Central Africa: Culture and the State in Marxist Theory', *Canadian Journal of African Studies,* 16:3 (1982), 567–93.

Francis, Ashkey, Abdalla Nassar and Khanjan Mehta, 'Are We Formal Yet? The Evolving Role of Informal Lending Mechanisms to Support Entrepreneurship and Poverty Alleviation in Central Kenya', *International Journal of Social Entrepreneurship and Innovation,* 2:2 (2013), 109–29.

Jennifer Galbraith, Athanasius Ochieng, Samuel Mwalili, Donath Emusu et al., 'Status of Voluntary Medical Male Circumcision in Kenya: Findings From 2 Nationally Representative Surveys in Kenya, 2007 and 2012', *Journal of Acquired Immune Deficiency Syndrome,* 66, (2014), 37–45.

Galtung, Johann, 'Cultural Violence', *Journal of Peace Research,* 27:3 (1990), 291–305.

Gathogo, Julius, 'Men Battering as the New Form of Domestic Violence? A Pastoral Care Perspective from the Kenyan Context', *Hervormde Teologiese Studies,* 71:3 (2015), 1–9.

Gugerty, Mary Kay, 'You Can't Save Alone: Commitment in Rotating Savings and Credit Associations in Kenya', *Economic Development and Cultural Change,* 55:2 (2007), 251–82.

Hayford, Sarah R., 'Conformity and Change: Community Effects on Female Genital Cutting in Kenya', *Journal of Health and Social Behaviour,* 46 (2005), 120–40.

Hickel, Jason, 'The "Girl Effect": Liberalism, Empowerment and the Contradictions of Development', *Third World Quarterly,* 35:8 (2014), 1355–73.

Holmquist, Frank W., Frederick S. Weaver and Michael D. Ford, 'The Structural Development of Kenya's Political Economy', *African Studies Review,* 37:1 (1994), 69–105.
House-Midamba, Bessie, 'Gender, Democratization, and Associational Life in Kenya', *Africa Today,* 43:3 (1996), 289–306.
Jensen, An-Magritt, 'Poverty, Gender and Fertility in Rural Kenya', *Forum for Development Studies,* 42:2 (2015), 311–32.
John, Neetu, Charlotte Roy, Mary Mwangi, Neha Raval and Terry McGovern, 'COVID-19 and Gender-Based Violence (GBV), Hard-to-Reach Women and Girls, Services, and Programmes in Kenya', *Gender & Development,* 29:1 (2021), 55–71.
Johnson, Kirsten, Jennifer Scott, Treny Sasyniuk, David Ndetei *et al.*, 'A National Population-based Assessment of 2007–2008 Election-related Violence in Kenya', *Conflict and Health,* 8:2 (2014).
Kahora, Billy (ed.), *Kwani?* 05 'Hung'arisha Haswa!' (2008).
Kandiyoti, Deniz, 'Bargaining with Patriarchy', *Gender and Society,* 2:3 (1988), 274–90.
Kenny, Christina, '"She Grows to Be Just a Woman, Not a Leader": Gendered Citizenship and the 2007 General Election in Kenya', *Intersections: Gender and Sexuality in Asia and the Pacific,* 33 (2013),
'Kenya: Garissa University Massacre', *Africa Research Bulletin: Political, Social and Cultural Series,* 52:4 (2015), 20539–41.
Kenya Today, 'Nairobi Governor Evans Kidero Women Representative Rachel Shebesh Charged with Fighting', 9 November 2013.
'Kenyan Women Clubbed at Protest: Police Attack Hunger Strikers, Supporters in Nairobi Park', *Globe and Mail* (Toronto, 4 March 1992, subscription).
Khau, Mathabo, 'Exploring Sexual Customs: Girls and the Politics of Elongating the Inner Labia', *Agenda: Empowering Women for Gender Equity,* 23:79 (2009), 30–37.
Kihato, Caroline Wanjiku, '"Go Back and Tell Them Who the Real Men Are!" Gendering Our Understanding of Kibera's Post-Election Violence', *International Journal of Conflict and Violence,* 9:1 (2015), 13–24.
Kimemia, Douglas, 'Case of Representation of Women in Kenya', *Current Politics and Economics of Africa,* 5:4 (2012), 451–72.
Kirchgasler, Christopher, 'The Limits of "Knowledge for All": Historicizing Transnational School Reforms in Kenya', *Knowledge Cultures,* 4:2 (2016), 75–76.
Kromm, David E., 'Irredentism in Africa: The Somali–Kenya Boundary Dispute', *Transactions of the Kansas Academy of Science,* 70:3 (1967), 359–65.
Krook, Mona Lena, 'Violence against Women in Politics', *Journal of Democracy,* 28:1 (2017), 74–88.

Lalu, Premesh, 'The Grammar of Domination and the Subjection of Agency: Colonial Texts and Modes of Evidence', Theme Issue, *History and Theory,* 39:4 (2000), 45–68.

Lawless, Jennifer and Richard Fox, 'Women Candidates in Kenya', *Women and Politics,* 20:4 (1999), 49–76.

Leonard, Lori, '"We did it for pleasure only": Hearing Alternative Tales of Female Circumcision', *Qualitative Inquiry,* 6:6 (2000), 212–28.

Levitt, Peggy and Sally Engle Merry, 'Vernacularisation on the Ground: Local Uses of Global Women's Rights in Peru, China, India and the United States', *Global Networks,* 9:4 (2009), 441–61.

Lonsdale, John, 'Kikuyu Christianities', *Journal of Religion in Africa,* 29:2 (1999), 206–29.

Lynch, Gabrielle, 'Negotiating Ethnicity: Identity Politics in Contemporary Kenya', *Review of African Political Economy,* 33:107 (2007), 49–65.

Mahmood, Saba, 'Feminist Theory, Embodiment and the Docile Agent: Some Reflections on the Egyptian Islamic Revival', *Cultural Anthropology,* 16:2 (2001), 202–36.

Mamdani, Mahmood, 'Beyond Settler and Native and Political Identities: Overcoming the Political Legacy of Colonialism', *Comparative Studies in Society and History,* 43:4 (2001), 651–64.

Maxon, Robert M., 'Constitution-Making in Contemporary Kenya: Lessons from the Twentieth Century', *Kenya Studies Review,* 1 (2009), 14–15.

Mazama, Ama, 'The Afrocentric Paradigm: Contours and Definitions', *Journal of Black Studies,* 31:4 (2001), 387–405.

Mboya, Tom J., 'The Party System and Democracy in Africa', *Foreign Affairs,* 41:4 (1963), 650–58.

—— 'The Future of Kenya', *African Affairs,* 63:250 (1964), 6–12.

Meiu, George Paul, 'Belonging in Ethno-erotic Economies: Adultery, Alterity, and Ritual in Postcolonial Kenya', *American Ethnologist,* 43:2 (2016), 215–29.

Merry, Sally Engle, 'Constructing a Global Law – Violence against Women and the Human Rights System', *Law and Social Inquiry,* 28:4 (2003), 941–77.

—— 'Measuring the World: Indicators, Human Rights and Global Governance', *Current Anthropology,* 52:S3 (2011), 83–95.

—— 'New Legal Realism and the Ethnography of Transnational Law', *Law and Social Inquiry,* 31:4 (2006), 975–95.

—— 'Rights Talk and the Experience of Law: Implementing Women's Human Rights to Protection from Violence', *Human Rights Quarterly,* 25:2 (2003), 343–81.

—— 'Transnational Human Rights and Local Activism: Mapping the Middle', *American Anthropologist,* 108:1 (2006), 38–51.

Mikell, Gwendolyn, 'African Feminism: Toward a New Politics of Representation', *Feminist Studies,* 21:2 (1995), 411–19.
Muhoma, Catherine, 'Versions of Truth and Collective Memory: The Quest for Forgiveness and Healing in the Context of Kenya's Post-election Violence, 2012', *Research in African Literatures,* 43:1 (2013), 166–73.
Mungeam, Gordon H., 'Masai and Kikuyu Responses to the Establishment of British Administration in the East Africa Protectorate', *The Journal of African History,* 11:1 (1970), 127–43.
Musandu, Phoebe, 'Daughters of Odoro: Luo Women and Power Re-examining Scripted Oral Traditions', *Women's Studies,* 41 (2012), 536–57.
—— 2019, 'Tokenism or Representation? The Political Careers of the First African Women in Kenya's Legislative Council (LEGCO), 1958–1962', *Women's History Review,* 28:4 (2019), 587–606.
Musungu, Johnstone, 'Free Primary Education in Kenya: A Critical Analysis', *International Journal of Humanities Social Sciences and Education,* 2:7 (2015), 65–77.
Mwanri, Lillian and Glory Joy Gatwiri, 'Injured Bodies, Damaged Lives: Experiences and Narratives of Kenyan Women with Obstetric Fistula and Female Genital Mutilation/Cutting', *Reproductive Health,* 14:38 (2017), 1–11.
Nagy, Rosemary, 'Transitional Justice as a Global Project: Critical Reflections', *Third World Quarterly,* 29:2 (2008), 275–89.
Natsoulas, Theodore, 'The Politicization of the Ban on Female Circumcision and the Rise of the Independent Schools Movement in Kenya: The KCA, the Missions and the Government', *Journal of Asian and African Studies,* 33:2 (1998), 137–58.
Njambi, Wairimú Ngarúiya, 'Irua Atumia and Anti-Colonial Struggles Among the Gĩkũyũ of Kenya: A Counter Narrative on "Female Genital Mutilation"', *Critical Sociology,* 33:4 (2007), 689–708.
Nkealah, Naomi, '(West) African Feminisms and their Challenge', *Journal of Literary Studies, 32:*2 (2016), 61–74.
Nugent, Paul, 2010, 'Do Nations Have Stomachs? Food, Drink and Imagined Community in Africa', Continuities, Dislocations and Transformations: 50 Years of Independence in Africa, *Africa Spectrum,* 45:3 (2010), 87–113.
Nussbaum, Martha, 'Women and Equality: The Capabilities Approach', *International Labour Review,* 138:3 (1999), 227–45.
Nyabola, Nanjala, 'Kenyan Feminisms in the Digital Age', *Women's Studies Quarterly,* 46:3&4 (2018), 261–72.
Nzomo, Maria, 'The Status of Women's Human Rights in Kenya and Strategies to Overcome Inequalities', *Issue: A Journal of Opinion,* 22:2 (1994), 17–20.

O'Barr, Jean F., Irene Tinker, Tami Hultman, Rudo Gaidzanwa *et al.*, 'Reflections on Forum '85 in Nairobi, Kenya: Voices from the International Women's Studies Community', *Signs: Journal of Women in Culture and Society,* 11:3 (1986), 584–608.

Ocobock, Paul, 'Spare the Rod, Spoil the Colony: Corporal Punishment, Colonial Violence and Generational Authority in Kenya, 1897–1952', *International Journal for African Historical Studies,* 45:1 (2012), 38–40.

Odhiambo, E.S., J. Kassilly, L.T Maito, K. Onkware, *et al.*, 'The Reprisal Attacks by Al-Shabaab against Kenya', *Journal of Defence Resources Management,* 4:2 (2013), 53–64.

Okoth-Ogendo, H.W.O., 'The Politics of Constitutional Change in Kenya Since Independence', *African Affairs,* 71:282 (1972), 9–34.

Oloka-Onyango, Joe and Sylvia Tamale, '"The Personal is Political" or Why Women's Rights are Indeed Human Rights: An African Perspective on International Feminism', *Human Rights Quarterly,* 17:4 (1995), 691–731.

Oosterveld, Valeri, 'Sexual Violence Directed at Men and Boys in Armed Conflict or Mass Atrocity: Addressing a Gendered Harm in International Criminal Tribunals', *Journal of International Law and International Relations,* 10 (2014), 107–28.

Osborne, Myles, '"The Rooting Out of Mau Mau from the Minds of the Kikuyu is a formidable Task": Propaganda and the Mau Mau War', *The Journal of African History,* 56:1 (2015), 77–97.

Patel, Ian, 'The Role of Testimony and Testimonial Analysis in Human Rights Advocacy and Research', *State Crime: Journal of the International State Crime Initiative,* 1:2 (2012), 235–65.

Patra, Shraboni and Rakesh Kumar Singh, 'Attitudes of Circumcised Women towards Discontinuation of Genital Cutting of their Daughters in Kenya', *Journal of Biosocial Science,* 47:1 (2015), 45–60.

Pedersen, Susan, 'National Bodies, Unspeakable Acts: The Sexual Politics of Colonial Policy-making', *Journal of Modern History,* 63:4 (1991), 647–80.

Peterson, Derek, 'Colonizing Language? Missionaries and Gikuyu Dictionaries: 1904–1914', *History in Africa,* 24 (1997), 257–72.

Pfeiffer, Elizabeth, '"The Post-Election Violence Has Brought Shame on This Place": Narratives, Place and Moral Violence in Western Kenya', *African Studies Review,* 61:2 (2018), 183–209.

Presley, Cora Ann, 'The Mau Mau Rebellion, Kikuyu Women, and Social Change', Special Issue: Current Research on African Women, *Canadian Journal of African Studies,* 22:3 (1988), 502–27.

Renne, Stuart, Adamson S. Muula and Daniel Westreich, 'Male Circumcision and HIV Prevention: Ethical, Medical and Public Health Tradeoffs in Low-Income Countries', *Journal of Medical Ethics,* 33:6 (June 2007), 357–61.

Roberts, Pepe, 'Feminism in Africa: Feminism and Africa', *Review of African Political Economy*, 10:27/28 (1983), 175–84.
Robertson, Claire, 'Grassroots in Kenya: Women, Genital Mutilation and Collective Action 1920–1990', *Signs: Journal of Women in Culture and Society*, 21:3 (1996), 615–42.
Ruether, Kirsten, 'Heated Debates over Crinolines: European Clothing on Nineteenth-century Lutheran Mission Stations in the Transvaal', *Journal of Southern African Studies*, 8:2 (2002), 359–78.
Schaffer, Kay and Sidonie Smith, 'Conjunctions: Life Narratives in the Field of Human Rights', *Biography*, 27:1 (2004), 13–33.
Shadle, Brett, 'Bridewealth and Female Consent: Marriage Disputes in African Courts, Gusiiland, Kenya', *The Journal of African History*, 44:2 (2003), 241–62.
Silberschmidt, Margrethe, 'Disempowerment of Men in Rural and Urban East Africa: Implications for Male Identity and Sexual Behaviour', *World Development*, 29:4 (2001), 657–71.
Smith, Mohga Kamal, 'Enhancing Gender Equity in Health Programmes: Monitoring and Evaluation', *Gender & Development*, 9:2 (2001), 95–105.
Spronk, Rachel, 'Female Sexuality in Nairobi: Flawed or Favoured?' *Culture, Health & Sexuality*, 7:3 (2005), 267–77.
Tamale, Sylvia, 'Eroticism, Sensuality and "Women's Secrets" Among the Baganda', *IDS Bulletin*, 37:5 (2006), 89–97.
—— 'The Right to Culture and the Culture of Rights: A Critical Perspective on Women's Sexual Rights in Africa', *Feminist Legal Studies*, 16 (2008), 47–69.
'The Colony and Protectorate of Kenya', *The Geographical Journal*, 56.5 (1920), 403–11.
Thomas, Samuel S., 'Transforming the Gospel of Domesticity: Luhya Girls and the Friends of the Africa Mission, 1917–1926', *African Studies Review*, 43:2 (2000), 1–27.
Throup, D., 'Elections and Political Legitimacy in Kenya', *Africa: Journal of the International African Institute*, 63:3 (1993), 371–96.
Tibbetts, Alexandra, 'Mamas Fighting for Freedom in Kenya', *Africa Today*, 41:4 (1994), 27–48.
Tripp, Aili Mari, 'Women in Movement: Transformations in African Political Landscapes', *International Feminist Journal of Politics*, 5:2 (2003), 233–55.
Wallis, Joanne, 'Building a Liberal-Local Hybrid Peace and State in Bougainville', *The Pacific Review*, 25:5 (2012), 613–35.
Wanyeki, Lynne Muthoni, 'Lessons from Kenya: Women and the Post-Election Violence', *Feminist Africa*, 10 (2008), 91–97.
Watkins, Susan Cotts, 'Local and Foreign Models of Reproduction in Nyanza Province, Kenya', *Population and Development Review*, 26:4 (2000), 725–59.

White, Aaronette M., 'All the Men Are Fighting for Freedom, All the Women Are Mourning Their Men, But Some of Us Carried Guns: A Raced-gendered Analysis of Fanon's Psychological Perspectives on War', *Signs: Journal of Women in Culture and Society,* 32:4 (2007), 857–84.

Wilson, Kalpana, 'Towards a Radical Re-appropriation: Gender, Development and Neoliberal Feminism', *Development and Change,* 46:4 (2015), 803–32.

Wipper, Audrey, 'Equal Rights for Women in Kenya?' *Journal of Modern African Studies,* 9:3 (1971), 429–42.

—— 'Kikuyu Women and the Harry Thuku Disturbances: Some Uniformities of Female Militancy', *Africa,* 59:3 (1989), 300–337.

Zinsser, Judith P., 'From Mexico to Copenhagen to Nairobi: The United Nations Decade for Women, 1975–1985', *Journal of World History,* 13:1 (2002), 139–68.

Theses and dissertations

Mwiandi, Mary Ciambaka, 'The Jeanes School in Kenya: The Role of the Jeanes Teachers and their Wives in 'Social Transformation' of Rural Colonial Kenya, 1925–1961' (PhD thesis, Michigan State University, 2006).

Raphoto, Thabo David, 'The Jeanes School in Kenya, 1924–1964: A Social Experience to Train Teachers for Rural Education and Community Development' (PhD thesis., unpublished, Syracuse University, 1984).

Unpublished papers/conference papers/working papers

Bujra, Janet, 'Ethnicity and Religion: A Case Study from Pumwani, Nairobi', IAS Discussion Paper 13 (University of Nairobi, Institute of African Studies, 1970).

Cook, Rebecca J., Bernard M. Dickens, O. Andrew F. Wilson and Susan E. Scarrow, *Advancing Safe Motherhood through Human Rights,* Occasional No. 5 (World Health Organization, 2001), http://apps.who.int/iris/bitstream/10665/66810/1/WHO_RHR_01.5.pdf.

Freccero, Julie, Lauren Harris, Melissa Carnay and Cole Taylor, 'Responding to Sexual Violence: Community Approaches', Working Paper (Berkeley: Human Rights Center, University of California, 2011).

Kwesi, Prah, 'The Burden of English in Africa: From Colonialism to Neo-colonialism', Keynote address to the Department of English 5th International Conference on the theme: Mapping Africa in the English-speaking World, University of Botswana, 2–4 June 2009, www.casas.co.za/FileAssets/NewsCast/misc/file/The%20Burden%20of%20English%20in%20Africa%20University%20of%20Botswana%20June09%20Version2.pdf.

Kenny, Christina, '"She is Made of and Coloured by the Earth Itself": Motherhood and Nation in Yvonne Adhiambo Owuor's *Dust*', Proceedings of the 39th African Studies Association of Australasia and the Pacific Annual Conference, University of Western Australia, Perth, 5–7 December 2016.

Oyaro, Kwamboka, 'Kenya: 87 Percent of Female Candidates are Peripheral to Race' (New York: Global Information Network and Inter Press Service, 22/24 December 2007).

Reports

Government of Kenya, *The 7th Periodic Report of the Government of the Republic of Kenya on Implementation of the International Convention on the Elimination of All Forms of Discrimination Against Women (CEDAW), 2004–2009* (Nairobi: Government of Kenya, 2009), www2.ohchr.org/english/bodies/cedaw/docs/AdvanceVersions/CEDAW.C.KEN.7.pdf [accessed 11 June 2022].

—— *Second Voluntary National Review on the Implementation of the Sustainable Development Goals* (Nairobi: National Treasury and Planning, 2020), https://sustainabledevelopment.un.org/content/documents/26359VNR_2020_Kenya_Report.pdf [accessed 20 August 2021]

Imam, Ayesha, 'Fundamentalism and Women's Rights in Africa' (Report of the First African Feminist Forum, 2006), www.ritimo.org/IMG/pdf/Fundamentalism_20and_20women_20rights.pdf [accessed 15 August 2021].

Kenya Human Rights Commission, 'Achieving Gender Equity in National and Devolved Legislature without Amending Kenya's Constitution (2010)' (Nairobi: KHRC, 2012).

—— 'Foreigners at Home – The Dilemma of Citizenship in Northern Kenya' (Nairobi: KHRC, 2008).

—— 'The Democratic Paradox: A Report on Kenya's 2013 General Elections' (Nairobi: KHRC, 2013).

Kenya National Bureau of Statistics, *Kenya Demographic and Health Survey 2014* (Nairobi: Government Printer, 2014). https://dhsprogram.com/pubs/pdf/fr308/fr308.pdf [accessed 16 August 2021].

Kenya National Commission on Human Rights, Kenya National Commission on Human Rights Act, No. 14, 2011' (KNHCR/National Council for Law Reporting, 2011/2012), www.kenyalaw.org/kl/file-

admin/pdfdownloads/Acts/KenyaNationalCommissiononHuman-Rights_Act_No14of2011.pdf [accessed 10 September 2018].
—— *On the Brink of the Precipice: A Human Rights Account of Kenya's Post-2007 Election Violence – Final Report* (Nairobi: KNCHR, 2008), www.knchr.org/Portals/0/Reports/knchr_report_report_on_the_brink_of_the_precipe.pdf.
'Kenya: Post-Election Killings, Abuse', Human Rights Watch, 27 August 2017, www.hrw.org/news/2017/08/27/kenya-post-election-killings-abuse [accessed 30 August, 2021].
Kriegler, Judge Johan, Lady Justice Imani Daudi Aboud, Professor Marangu M'Marete, Catherine Muyeka Mumma *et al.*, 'Report of the Independent Review Commission on the General Elections Held in Kenya on 27th December, 2007' (Nairobi: Government Printer, 2007).
The Colony and Protectorate of Kenya Education Department. 'Education Department Annual Report, 1924', Nairobi, *East African Standard*, AV/10/1 (Kenya National Archives, Nairobi, Kenya, 7 July 2014).
Waki, Philip N., *Report of the Commission of Inquiry into Post-Election Violence (CIPEV)* (Nairobi: Government Printer, 2008), https://reliefweb.int/attachments/d6939d3c-0869-373d-8612-6a38cb-141f16/15A00F569813F4D549257607001F459D-Full_Report.pdf [accessed 25 May 2022].

Other website sources (including online media)

Australian Human Rights Commission, 'Timeline – Major Human Rights Treaties' (n.d.), www.humanrights.gov.au/publications/timeline-major-international-human-rights-treaties [accessed 4 July 2021].
Akaki, Lulu, 'Kilimani Mums to Protest in Solidarity with Woman Who Was Stripped by Touts', *HapaKenya*, 13 November 2014, www.hapakenya.com/2014/11/13/kilimani-mums-host-mydressmychoice-miniskirt-protest [accessed 12 August 2021].
Baraka, Carey, 'Hii Nai Si Yetu', *Down River Road* (blog), 30 December 2021 https://downriverroad.org/2021/12/30/carey-baraka-hii-nai-si-yetu [Accessed 22 February 2022].
BBC, 'Deal to End Kenyan Crisis Agreed', *BBC News*, 12 April 2008, http://news.bbc.co.uk/2/hi/africa/7344816.stm [accessed 10 June 2022].
Bhatia, Gautam, 'Notes From a Foreign Field: An Instant Classic – The Kenyan High Court's BBI Judgment', *Indian Constitutional Law and Philosophy* (blog), 14 May 2021, https://indconlawphil.wordpress.com/2021/05/14/notes-from-a-foreign-field-an-instant-classic-the-kenyan-high-courts-bbi-judgment [accessed 30 August 2021].

Castillejo, Clare, 'Gender, Fragility and the Politics of Statebuilding', Norwegian Peacebuilding Resource Centre, 2012, http://genderandsecurity.org:8080/sites/default/files/Castillejo_-_G_Fragility_Statebuild.pdf [accessed 6 January 2017].

Centre for Rights Education and Awareness (CREAW), 'Mission, Vision and Values', 2014, http://creawkenya.org/ke/mision-vision-values [accessed 28 February 2015]; this is no longer accessible, and Information on the CREAW can now be found at https://home.creaw.org.

Department for International Development, *Elections in Kenya 2007*, www.dfid.gov.uk/Documents/publications1/elections/elections-ke-2007.pdf [accessed 22 February 2013].

'Dr Evans Kidero – Rachel Shebesh Social Media Reaction', *The Standard*, 2013, www.sde.co.ke/article/2000113556/dr-evans-kidero-rachel-shebesh-social-media-reaction [accessed 4 August 2021].

Houreld, Katherine. 'Women Candidates Face Curses and Worse in Kenyan Elections', *Reuters*, 4 August 2017, www.reuters.com.

Human Rights Watch, *Turning Pebbles: Kenya National Dialogue and Reconciliation (KNDR) Monitoring Project: Draft Review Report, 2011*, http://katibainstitute.org/Archives/images/KNDR%20Review%20Report%202011.pdf [accessed 22 April 2022].

International Criminal Court (ICC), *The Prosecutor v. Uhuru Muigai Kenyatta*, ICC-01/09-02/11, www.icc-cpi.int/kenya/kenyatta?ln=en [accessed 10 September 2018].

International Criminal Court (ICC), *The Prosecutor v. William Samoei Ruto and Joshua Arap Sang*, ICC-01/09-01/11, www.icc-cpi.int/kenya/rutosang?ln=en [accessed 10 September 2018].

IRIN News Network, 'Kenya: Displaced Women "Still Facing Threat of Sexual Violence"', *IRIN* 10 March 2008, www.unhcr.org/refworld/docid/47d658ee5.html [accessed 11 January 2012].

—— 'Kenya: Health Workers Grappling with Conflict-related Sexual Violence', *IRIN*, 28 January 2008, www.irinnews.org/report.aspx?ReportId=76247 [accessed 6 January 2012].

—— '"Merry-go-round" Micro-finance Keeps Slum Residents Fed', *IRIN News Network*, 23 April 2010, www.irinnews.org/feature/2010/04/13/merry-go-round-micro-finance-keeps-slum-residents-fed [accessed 23 November 2017]

—— 'Police Under Fire Over Live Rounds', *IRIN*, 17 January 2008, www.irinnews.org/report.aspx?reportid=76297 [accessed 5 January 2012].

Kahura, Dauti, 'The Sonkoization of Nairobi – How Mike Sonko is Reshaping City Politics', *The Elephant*, 7 August 2017, www.theelephant.info/features/2017/08/07/the-sonkonization-of-nairobi-how-mike-sonko-is-reshaping-city-politics [accessed 10 November 2020].

Kanina, Wangui, 'Kenyan Women Bear the Brunt of Election Violence', *Reuters*, 22 December 2007, www.reuters.com/article/

us-kenya-election-women/kenyan-women-bear-brunt-of-election-violence-idUSL2127700220071221 [accessed 20 August 2021].
Karongo, Catherine, '400,000 Kenyan Men Battered Yearly', *CapitalNews*, 16 February 2012, www.capitalfm.co.ke/news/2012/02/400000-kenyan-men-battered-yearly [accessed 18 October 2017].
Kenya National Commission on Human Rights, 'About Us: Establishment', 2015, www.knchr.org/Aboutus/Establishment.aspx [accessed 10 September 2018].
Kenya National Dialogue and Reconciliation, 'Through the Mediation of H.E. Kofi Annan and the Panel of Eminent African Personalities on the Resolution of the Political Crisis – Annotated Agenda and Timetable', https://peacemaker.un.org/sites/peacemaker.un.org/files/KE_080101_Annotated%20Agenda%20for%20the%20Kenya%20Dialogue%20and%20Reconciliation.pdf [accessed 22 November 2016].
Kenya Parliamentary Chamber: National Assembly, 'Elections Held in 1992', http://archive.ipu.org/parline-e/reports/arc/2167_92.htm [accessed 12 October 2017].
Khasiani, Nwasante 'XYZee Make Fun of Shebesh Getting Slapped. You have to Watch This Song They Did For Her', *Ghafla*, 7 October 2013, www.ghafla.com/xyzee-make-fun-of-shebesh-getting-slapped-you-have-to-watch-this-song-they-did-for-her [accessed 12 August 2021].
Kilonzo, Eunice and Ng'ang'a Mbugua, 'One in 10 Men Beaten by Wives', *Daily Nation*, 8 April 2015, www.nation.co.ke/news/1056-2679830-l80dhoz/index.html [accessed 18 October 2017].
Kinoti, Kathambi, 'Kenya's Elections: How Did Women Fare? Interview with Wangari Kinoti', *Association for Women in Development*, 12 February 2008.
Macharia, Keguro, 'Wanjiku?' *Gukira* (blog), 26 December 2012, https://gukira.wordpress.com/2012/12/26/wanjiku [accessed 2 February 2021].
Magna Carta International Public Opinion, 'Research study conducted for Magna Carta 800th Anniversary Committee Ipsos MORI', 2015, http://magnacarta800th.com/projects/international-poll [accessed 26 January 2017].
Manji, Ambreena, 'The BBI Judgment and the Invention of Kenya', *Verfassungsblog* (blog), 22 May 2021, https://verfassungsblog.de/the-bbi-judgment-and-the-invention-of-kenya [accessed 30 August 2021].
Maters, Karen, .The Nairobi World Conference', Supplement No. 24 to Women of Europe (Brussels: Commission of the European Communities, 1986), http://aei.pitt.edu/33993/1/A470.pdf [accessed 10 June 2017].

Meredith, Thomas and Melanie McDonald, 'Kibera Integrated Water Sanitation and Waste Management Project' (UN Habitat, 2014), https://unhabitat.org/sites/default/files/download-manager-files/Kibera%20Evaluation%20Report%20FINAL.pdf [accessed 20 August 2021].

Michira, Moses, 'Governor Evans Kidero Slaps Rachel Shebesh, Then Quickly Forgets', *Standard Digital*, 7 September 2013, www.standardmedia.co.ke/article/2000092952/governor-evans-kidero-slaps-rachel-shebesh-then-quickly-forgets [accessed 13 August, 2021].

Migiro, Katy, 'Kenya Politics: Cash, Violence Limit Women', *Chicago Tribune*, 27 February 2013.

Mohamed, Guled, 'Kenyan Police Fight Protesters, 2 Dead', *ReliefWeb*, 16 January 2008, http://reliefweb.int/node/254523 [accessed 25 September 2011].

Mosongo, Josephine, 'From Online Rhetoric to Street Protests: Rise of Kilimani Mums', *Daily Nation*, 22 November 2014, www.nation.co.ke.lifestyle/lifestyle/Rise-of-Kilimani-Mums/1214-2531682-mr5yojz/index.html [accessed 12 August 2021].

Muhumuza, Rodney, 'Kenya Watchdog Says 92 People Killed in Election Violence', *AP News*, 21 December 2017, https://apnews.com/article/6c686219242c48c1b9a2653a4972a3c3 [accessed 20 August, 2021].

Musa, Kurian, 'Court Terminates Evans Kidero, Rachel Shebesh Assault Case', 19 March 2014, *Standard Media*, www.standardmedia.co.ke/article/2000107314/court-terminates-evans-kidero-rachael-shebesh-assault-case [accessed 10 August 2021].

Mutua, Makau, 'BBI Realignments May Spring Surprises on Kenyans', interview with John Githongo, *The Elephant* (blog), 18 November 2020, www.theelephant.info/videos/2020/11/18/makau-mutua-bbi-realignments-may-spring-surprises-on-kenyans [accessed 20 August 2021].

Mwangi, Wambui, 'Silence is a Woman', *The New Inquiry*, 4 June 2013, http://thenewinquiry.com/essays/silence-is-a-woman [accessed 16 August 2021].

Mwere, David, 'Kenya: Two-Thirds Gender Rule Still Elusive after 10 Attempts', The Nation Newspaper, 22 December 2020, https://allafrica.com/stories/202012220134.html [accessed 19 August 2021].

'Nairobi Governor Evans Kidero and Rachel Shebesh's Slapping Saga', *KTN News Kenya*, 7 September, 2013, www.youtube.com/watch?v=BY287dKPZkQ [accessed 20 August 2021].

Njogu, Ann, 'Alleged Sexual Violence Committed by Tony Mochama upon the Person of Shailja Patel', *Gukira* (blog), 14 September 2014, https://gukira.wordpress.com/2014/09/25/sexual-violence-committed-by-tony-mochama-upon-the-person-of-shailja-patel [accessed 15 July 2021].

Nyabola, Nanjala, 'What Kenyan Voters Got for the $500m Spent on Elections', *Al Jazeera*, 18 August 2017, www.aljazeera.com/opinions/2017/8/18/what-kenyan-voters-got-for-the-500m-spent-on-elections [accessed 19 August 2021].

Office of the High Commissioner for Human Rights, *Principles Relating to the Status of National Institutions (The Paris Principles)*, GA Resolution 48/134, December 1993, www.ohchr.org/EN/ProfessionalInterest/Pages/StatusOfNationalInstitutions.aspx [accessed 30 August 2021].

Office of the United Nations Humanitarian Coordinator in Kenya, 'Humanitarian Update', 21–28 January 2008, www.icc-cpi.int/RelatedRecords/CR2009_08681.PDF [accessed 13 May 2017].

Okuoro, Sara, 'Rachel Shebesh Concedes Defeat to Esther Passaris', *Standard Media*, 9 August 2017, www.standardmedia.co.ke/article/2001250815/rachel-shebesh-concedes-defeat-to-esther-passaris [accessed 12 August 2021].

Omondi, Jeff. 'Hot New Track: "Slap Them Like Kidero" Featuring Dr Kidero & Shebesh', *Ghafla!* 11 September 2013, www.ghafla.com/hot-new-track-slap-them-like-kidero-featuring-dr-kidero-shebesh [accessed 12 August 2021].

Ongiri, Isaac, 'I Acted Under Pressure, Says Kivuitu', *The Standard Newspaper Online*, 2 January 2008, http://allafrica.com/stories/200801010051.html [accessed 5 January 2012].

Owino, Samwel and Ibrahaim Oruko, 'Kenya: Why It's No Walk in the Park for Nominated MPs', *The Nation*, 10 September 2020, https://nation.africa/kenya/news/politics/why-it-s-no-walk-in-the-park-for-nominated-mps-1936494 [accessed 20 August 2021].

Oyaro, Kwamboka, 'A Call to Arm Women Candidates with More Than Speeches', *IPS News*, 21 December 2007, www.ipsnews.net/2007/12/politics-kenya-a-call-to-arm-women-candidates-with-more-than-speeches [accessed 20 August 2021].

Patel, Shailja, 'Three Poems by Shailja Patel', *The Johannesburg Review of Books*, 5 February 2018, https://johannesburgreviewofbooks.com/2018/02/05/three-poems-by-shailja-patel [accessed 21 August 2021].

'Rachael Shebesh and Kidero Finally Agree on an Out-of-court Settlement after Kidero Gave Her Roughly 15 Million', *Jobs Kenya*, 2014, www.jobskenyahapa.com/rachael-shebesh-kidero-finally-agree-court-agreement-kidero-gave-roughly-15-million-2 [accessed 12 August 2021].

Roznai, Yaniv, 'Basic Structure Doctrine: Winds of Change for Constitutionalism in Africa?' *The Elephant* (blog). 24 May 2021, www.theelephant.info/features/2021/05/24/basic-structure-doctrine-winds-of-change-for-constitutionalism-in-africa [accessed 27 May 2021].

Sangira, Stephene and Ng'ang'a Thairu, 'Shebesh Forgives Kidero', *The Star*, 3 February 2014, www.the-star.co.ke/news/2014/02/03/shebesh-forgives-kidero_c890852 [accessed 10 August 2021].

'SHOCK: Shebesh Hit Kidero Under the Belt Before The Alleged SLAP', *Kenya Today*, 7 September 2013, www.kenya-today.com/politics/nairobi-governor-evans-kidero-slaps-rachel-shebesh [accessed 16 August].

Sum, Abigael and Ngari Gichuki, 'Evans Kidero: What Was She Doing around My Lower Abdomen?' *The Standard Digital*, 8 September 2013, www.standardmedia.co.ke/?articleID=2000093029&story_title=evans-kidero-what-was-she-doing-around-my-lower-abdomen&pageNo=1 [accessed 15 August 2021].

Tubei, George, 'Kenya's General Election the Most Expensive in Africa and 2nd Most Expensive in the World', *Business Insider Africa*, 18 July 2017, https://africa.businessinsider.com/politics/politics-kenyas-general-election-the-most-expensive-in-africa-and-2nd-most-expensive/ceeb56g [accessed 20 August 2021].

UNICEF, *Kenya: Statistical Profile on Female Genital Mutilation/Cutting*, February 2016, https://data.unicef.org/wp-content/uploads/country_profiles/Kenya/FGMC_KEN.pdf [accessed 19 October 2017].

United Nations Development Programme (UNDP), 'Kenya MDG Acceleration Framework and Action Plan', 2014, www.ke.undp.org/content/kenya/en/home/library/government-reports/Kenya-MDG-Acceleration-Framework-and-Action-Plan.html [accessed 19 October 2017].

—— 'Improve Maternal Health – Where We Are?' *UNDP Kenya*, www.ke.undp.org/content/kenya/en/home/post-2015/mdgoverview/overview/mdg5.html [accessed 12 June 2022].

United Nations Fund for Population Activities (UNFPA) and United Nations International Children's Emergency Fund (UNICEF), *UNFPA/UNICEF Joint Programme on Female Genital Mutilation (FGM) in Kenya – Accelerating Change 2014–2017*, 2017, www.unicef.org/kenya/JP_on_FGM_-_BRIEF.pdf [accessed 10 August 2021].

United Nations Human Settlements Programme, 'Kenya Overview', https://unhabitat.org/kenya [accessed 24 April 2022].

Wachuka, Rose and Samuel Ngure, 'Advisory Opinion of the Supreme Court in the Matter of the Principle Gender Representation in the National Assembly and the Senate', KLR e-Newsletter, 48 (2012), http://kenyalaw.org/kl/index.php?id=3660 [accessed 19 August 2021].

Wafula, Paul, 'Western, Nairobi Men Frequently Beaten by Their Wives', *Standard Digital Newspaper*, 15 January 2016, www.standardmedia.co.ke/article/2000188171/western-nairobi-men-frequently-beaten-by-their-wives [accessed 19 August 2021].

Wambua, Sammy, 'Argwings Kodhek: A Native Upstart Who Dared Marry a White Woman', *The Standard Newspaper*, 27 January, 2019.

'Wanjiku Is Dead but Who Will Mourn Her When Everyone Wants to Move On?' *The Nation*, 4 July 2020, www.nation.co.ke/oped/opinion/Wanjiku-is-dead-but-who-will-mourn-her/440808-1735496-uvrat4/index.html [accessed 20 August 2021].

Watiri, Sue, 'Kenyan Celebrities React to Shebesh Getting Slapped!' *Ghafla!* 6 September 2013, www.ghafla.com/kenyan-celebrities-react-to-shebesh-getting-slapped-video [accessed 16 August 2021].

World Health Organization (WHO). 'Classification of Female Genital Mutilation', *Sexual and Reproductive Health*, 3 February 2020, www.who.int/news-room/fact-sheets/detail/female-genital-mutilation [accessed 26 August 2021].

——'Voluntary medical male circumcision for HIV prevention in 14 priority countries in eastern and southern Africa', Progress Brief, August 2017, https://apps.who.int/iris/bitstream/handle/10665/179933/WHO_HIV_2015.21_eng.pdf?sequence=1&isAllowed=y [accessed 16 August 2021].

Index

Letters following a page number indicate the following references: n. (note), fig. (figure), m. (map).

Abwao, Priscilla   154, 155–56
accessing support   84, 101, 119–20, 123
Adimora-Ezeigbo, Akachi   14, 43
advocacy, women's rights   13, 14, 42
African troops (forced)   24
African Union   132, 135, 141
African women's rights   13, 14, 42, 43, 74, 81
agency, women's:
   analysis   11, 70–71, 186
   approaches   9, 41, 44–45, 46, 47
   forms   48, 54, 66, 69, 76
   see also Harry Thuku Riot; Nyanjiru, Mary
Ahero:
   field work   xvii m.1, 17, 104, 164, 168, 192
   population   xiv
Ahero town   167, 173, 176
Annan, Kofi   132, 138
archival research:
   narratives   44, 46
   use   9, 69, 70, 72 n.1, 78, 189
assault, physical   23, 116, 131, 146, 168, 170
   normalised violence   108, 129
   see also beatings; rape; security (physical)

Atieno-Odhiambo, Eisha Stephen   37, 38–9
authority, cultural   41, 62, 65, 70, 106
Aweyo Canteen   18, 192, 193
Bar Ober   99, 100–01, 108, 113, 150, 192
   field work   xvii m.1, 17
   language   123–4, 145
   media   178
   population   xiv
   reporting incidents   119–21
   theft   102, 116
beatings   68, 92–93 n.83, 112–25, 181
   accessing support   123
   elders   116
   police corruption   114
Bill of Rights   151, 152, 157
body modification   40, 41 n.3, 69–71
   see also Female Circumcision Controversy (1928–1931)
British colonial government   21, 27, 54, 73
Building Bridges Initiative (BBI)   181–82
Bumala   xvii m.1, 17, 192
Butere   xiv, xvii m.1, 17, 113–15, 192

candidates, women   109, 112, 125, 126, 159
capitalism   14, 42, 102
Carotenuto, Matthew   129, 140
cartoons   5, 6, 7, 171 fig.3, 185
Central Province   xi, 5, 91, 92, 130
Centre for Rights Education and Awareness (CREAW)   138–39, 145–48
circumcision, female   xii, 9, 52, 53, 54, 62–69
   rates   50
   types   49
   see also Female Circumcision Controversy (1928–1931); female genital cutting (FGC); *guturamira ng'ania* ('showing your mother's secrets')
citizenship rights   11, 47, 153, 165, 167
civilising mission   20, 21, 40, 154
colonial rule:
   liberation from   28
   resistance to   22, 42, 52, 53
   threat to   23, 56
colonial violence   xii, 22, 34, 40, 56, 80
colonisation   8, 45, 46, 69, 78, 79
community groups   73, 75, 84, 86–94
Constitution Amendment Bill   182
constitutional reform:
   expectations   38, 39, 110, 162, 177
   process   134, 151–52, 182, 186
   see also Wanjiku
constitutional safeguards   29, 32, 157, 183, 187
   see also Bill of Rights
Convention on Elimination of Discrimination Against Women (CEDAW)   117, 141, 145
Convention on the Rights of the Child (CRC)   141, 145
corrupt(ion):
   and detribalisation   64
   endemic   17, 122, 129, 135, 180, 184
   governance   38, 165, 181
   moral   84
   police   10, 108, 113, 114, 115, 128
cultural identity   29, 40, 48, 65, 69, 76
curses, performing   59, 60, 96

DhoLuo   113, 124, 145, 179, 180
disembodiment   6, 11, 47, 184

East African Association (EAA)   23, 56
education, access to   7 n.24, 18, 155
Eglund, Harri   16, 187
elders   28, 65, 67, 116, 118
   accessing support   84, 119
   reporting incidents   83
elections (1992)   110, 112
elections (2002)   110–12
elections (2007)   108, 112, 125–30, 142, 143, 180
elections (2013)   98, 157, 158, 159, 162, 180–81
   see also Two-Thirds Gender Principle
elections (2017)   159, 172–73, 181
elections (2022)   182, 183
Electoral Commission of Kenya (ECK)   111, 129
electoral fraud   37, 129, 130
Elkins, Caroline   24, 91
embodiment   10–11, 47, 84
Embu   xi, 27, 53, 54
Emergency, the (1953–1955):
   before   66
   during   29, 30, 34, 68, 90–92

after   30
entrepreneurship   10, 103
essentialism   70, 189
Facing Mount Kenya   xii, 35, 55, 64
Female Circumcision Controversy (1928–1931)   52, 55, 62–65, 70, 76
female genital cutting (FGC)   44, 45, 46, 48–52, 55, 76
  centres   54
  classification   49
  rates   50
  regulation   40–41, 71
  see also circumcision, female; *guturamira ng'ania* ('showing your mother's secrets')
feminisation   7, 137–38
feminist agency   41, 44–45, 46
field work locations   xvii m.1, 192
  see also Ahero; Ahero town; Aweyo Canteen; Bar Ober; Bumala; Butere; Kangemi; Kibera
field work (overview)   15–19, 191–93
food:
  selling   180
  shortages   90, 91, 92, 146
  supply   83, 89, 97, 100, 104

Gado *see* Mwampembwa, Godfrey (Gado)
gender binary   8, 189
gender identity   15 n.47, 90, 179, 189, 191
Gĩkũyũ community   23, 27, 35, 52, 55, 179
grassroots:
  activists   176
  groups   73–74, 75, 95, 166, 192
  human rights networks   165, 189

  origins   175, 176
  women   16, 105, 158, 176, 187
  see also Two-Thirds Gender Principle
groups, women's:
  field work   17
  and neoliberal development   74, 100, 102, 107
  purposes   18, 95, 98, 99, 101, 193
  types   xiv, 85, 99
  see also organisations, women's
  guturamira ng'ania ('showing your mother's secrets')   59–60, 96

Harry Thuku Riot   52, 56–62, 69–70
HIV   7, 18, 41 n.3, 85, 148, 193
  rates   51–52
human rights frameworks   9, 139, 140, 148, 149, 150
human rights networks (HuRiNets)   17–18, 160, 163, 191
humanitarian crisis   134, 136, 138, 142, 144

Imperial British East Africa Company (IBEAC)   20
insults, gendered   11, 47, 61, 79, 114
guturamira ng'ania ('showing your mother's secrets')   59–60, 96
internally displaced person (IDP)   131, 141, 144, 146–47
  camps   131, 141, 146–47
International Covenant on Civil and Political Rights (ICCPR)   141, 145
international rights community   3, 11
interventions   189

external 133
human rights-based 3–4, 7, 116–17
policy 116–17, 146, 154, 189–90

Kabira, Wanjiku Mukabi 77, 78, 93–94, 95, 98, 186–87
Kamba communities 21, 110, 111
Kangemi 18, 82–85, 192, 193
Kanogo, Tabitha 49, 177
Kenya African Democratic Union (KADU) 33, 36
Kenya African National Union (KANU) 31–33, 36–37, 93, 111, 155
Kenya African Union (KAU) 28, 31, 53, 64
Kenya Demographic and Health Survey (2014) 50, 51, 121 n.37
Kenya Human Rights Commission (KHRC) 1, 15 n.47, 17, 160, 162, 191
Kenya National Commission on Human Rights (KNCHR) 138–42, 143–44, 191
Kenya National Human Rights Commission Report (*On the Brink of the Precipice*) 138, 140–45
Kenyatta, Jomo (Johnstone), positioning 27–28, 31–33, 35–36, 55
see also *Facing Mount Kenya*; Kenya African National Union (KANU)
Kenyatta, Uhuru 111, 181
Kibaki, Mwai 110–11, 129, 133, 135, 138
announcements 130, 132
Kibera xiv, 16, 17, 82, 161, 162
slum 165, 192
see also Pillars of Kibera Women's Group

Kidero, Evans 152, 169–76, 178
Kikuyu Central Association (KCA) 53, 61, 62–63, 64–65
Kisumu County xvii m.1, 9, 15, 18, 152, 189
see also Ahero; Aweyo Canteen; Luo; Nyando
Kisumu town 15, 18, 164
KiSwahili 98, 176, 187

labour, forced 23–24, 56, 90
labourer registration (*kipande*) 22, 23, 56
Lalu, Premesh 46, 76, 77
Lancaster House Constitution 29, 33, 154
language(s) xii, 11–12, 29, 71, 92, 98
exclusion 98, 123–24, 125, 187
interpreter 113
terms xiii
Legislative Council of Kenya (LegCo) 24, 153–56
Lennox-Boyd Constitution (1957) 25, 154
liberation 27, 32, 41, 91, 94
second 97, 110
literacy 1, 7 n.24, 166
Luhya xiv, 111, 170–71
Luo xiii, 22, 36, 41 n.3, 94, 131
language (DhoLuo) 123–24
populations xi, xiv

Maat 80, 84
Maendeleo ya Wanawake Organisation (MYWO) 67, 90, 92 n.83, 98, 155
Mahmood, Saba 45–46, 54, 68–69, 70, 186
Mamdani, Mahmood 25–26, 29–30
matriarchy 45, 82, 106
Mau Mau movement:
fighters 33
Gĩkũyũ majority xii, xiii, 24, 35

growth 22 n.12, 27–29
recognition 122
supporters 90
suppression 28, 30, 68, 91–92
uprising 30 n.60, 52–53, 65
Mboya, Thomas (Tom) xiii, 31, 32, 33, 36
media:
coverage 173, 175, 178, 182, 183
houses 96
social 169, 170, 173, 183
Merry, Sally Engle 3, 109, 150
minority groups 32, 33, 38, 39, 109, 152
missionary:
education system 63, 64, 89, 154
groups 62, 63
interests xi, 20, 64, 87
interventions 190
mobilisation:
African troops (forced) 24
anticolonial 5, 22, 23, 55, 64, 69
of communities 22, 55, 64, 104, 132
of cultural structures 62, 107
failure 187
and poverty 188
procolonial 69, 93
of votes 94
Moi, Daniel arap 5, 37, 93, 96, 111
Moi era 60 n.92, 95–96, 110, 191
Mombasa xvii m.1, 20, 21
Morris, David 4, 109, 124, 139
motherhood 10, 61, 75, 80–82, 84, 85
curses, performing 60, 96
respect 70, 107, 186
Murray-Brown, Jeremy 27, 28, 30 n.64, 31, 122
Mutunga, William (Willie) 5–6, 152

Mwampembwa, Godfrey (Gado) 6, 171 fig.3, 185
Mwenda, Camilla 18, 193

Nairobi County 169, 172
Nairobi, description of 16–17, 188–89
nation-building 14, 42, 87
National Assembly 6, 94
national human rights 108, 138–45
nationalism xii, 29, 34, 65, 70
Ncheke, Njuri 65, 66, 67, 68
neoliberal development 9, 74–5, 100, 102–03, 107, 161
Ngaitana movement 52, 65–70, 76
normalised violence 108, 118, 124, 129, 174
Nyando xvii m.1, 163, 167, 192
Nyanjiru, Mary 58–62, 70
Nzomo, Maria 1, 93

Ochieng, Joseph 16, 37, 113 nn.23-24
Odinga, Raila 132–33, 135, 138, 179, 181
see also Orange Democratic Movement (ODM)
Oduol, Wilhemina 77, 78, 93–94, 95, 98
Ogunyemi, Chikwenye 14, 43
Omanga, Caren 18, 174–76, 189, 193
On the Brink of the Precipice (Kenya National Human Rights Commission Report) 138, 140–45
oral histories 46, 77, 80, 100, 119
Orange Democratic Movement (ODM) 130, 132, 136
organisations, women's:
colonial period 72 n.1, 77, 86–94
definition 95
modern 73–75, 98, 105, 107

see also groups, women's; Maendeleo ya Wanawake Organisation (MYWO)
Oyěwùmí, Oyèrónkẹ̀ì 8, 14, 15, 79, 80

Panel of Eminent African Personalities (African Union) 132, 134, 136
Party of National Unity (PNU) 129, 132
Pillars of Kibera Women's Group 17, 161, 162, 166
police corruption 10, 108, 113, 114, 115, 128
political violence (postcolonial) *see* violence, political (postcolonial)
poverty 4, 73, 103 n.120, 107, 134, 188
   feminisation 7
   statistics 2
Presley, Cora Ann 52–53, 121 n.37
prison xii, 28, 31, 58, 60 n.92, 127
privilege (people) xii, 5, 10, 26, 45, 67
   see also Legislative Council of Kenya (LegCo)

rape 23, 56, 147, 168
regional:
   centres 138, 141, 145
   concerns 133, 134, 146
   data 121 n.37
   organisations 15 n.47
   political parties 29
   see also Kenya Human Rights Commission (KHRC)
religious affiliation 31, 50–51
reporting incidents:
   mechanisms 10, 83, 109, 148, 150
   to police 114–15, 124, 127, 146–47, 168

representatives, women 136, 157, 159, 164
resistance movements xii, xiii, 26–7, 29, 30
rights, awareness of 1, 145, 146–47, 165, 185
risk 101, 108, 113, 123, 131, 179
   subjectivities 71, 149–50, 153
rituals, oathing 26, 59
Robertson, Claire 60, 61, 78–79

savings 99, 102, 103–06
secrecy 59, 70, 82, 101, 166
   circumcision, female 66, 68, 69
security (physical):
   everyday violence 160
   institutions 109, 138
   police 102–03, 113, 116, 146
   reporting incidents 131
   state security forces 108, 125, 139
Senate 156, 157, 159, 163
sex work 18, 57, 61
Sexual Orientation, Gender Identity and Expression (SOGIE) 15, 191
sexual violence *see* violence, sexual
sexuality 15 n.47, 43, 44, 70, 189
shame 62, 70, 83, 101
Shebesh, Rachel 152, 169–78
slapping 152, 169–78
slogans 22 n.12, 32, 35
Somalia xiii, xvii m.1, 50, 51, 128, 165
songs xii, 59, 63, 173n73
state power 37, 95, 181
statistics 2, 7–8, 145
strikes 22, 57, 60, 96, 169, 183
subjectivities:
   gendered 5–15
   human rights-based 9, 16, 109, 147, 148–50, 153
   layered 4, 71, 186
   limits 148–50, 190

support, accessing 84, 101, 119–20, 123
Supreme Court 111, 152, 158, 181, 182, 183

Taita-Taveta County xvii m.1, 17, 126, 192
Tamale, Sylvia 42, 44, 77
Taveta xvii m.1, 126–8, 163, 168, 169, 192
taxation 23, 56, 65, 73, 89, 90
  labourer registration (*kipande*) 22
theft xii, 11, 102, 115, 118, 128
Thomas, Lynn 53, 66, 67, 68, 70
Thuku, Harry *see* Harry Thuku Riot
trauma 35, 128, 143, 149, 165, 180
  feminization of 137–38
tribal land 22, 28, 65, 135
trust:
  community groups 101
  field work 191, 192
  HIV 18
  oathing rituals 26
  in police 115, 121
  representatives, women 136
Two-Thirds Gender Principle 154, 182, 186
  at grassroots 157–60, 176
  understanding 151, 158, 160, 161, 163, 187

Uganda xvii m.1, 15 n.47, 76 n.6, 140
unity 31, 53, 58, 59, 141
  see also Party of National Unity (PNU)

victimhood 3–4, 10, 12, 43
violence, colonial xii, 22, 34, 40, 56, 80
violence, gendered 85, 117, 124, 131–32 n.63, 132 n.64, 160
  agency, women's 70, 186
  beatings 112, 113, 114, 115, 118, 121
  citizenship rights 11, 167
  elections (2007) 126, 128, 129, 180
  feminisation 137
  groups, women's 99, 107
  insults *see* insults, gendered
  national human rights 108, 145
  police corruption 10, 108, 113, 114, 115, 128
  reporting incidents 10, 83, 114, 127, 146–47, 168
  slapping 173, 174, 176
  subjectivities 16
  victimhood 3–4
  violence, intimate partner *see* violence, intimate partner
  violence, sexual *see* violence, sexual
  Western feminisms 13, 186
violence, intimate partner 2, 115, 117, 124, 146, 165
  victimhood 10, 12
violence, normalised 108, 118, 124, 129, 174
violence, political (postcolonial) 111, 129–38, 139, 143, 173, 176
  candidates, women 112, 125, 126
  corruption 128, 129, 135, 180, 181
  insults, gendered 11, 47, 59–60, 61, 96
  reporting incidents 127
  state power 37, 181
violence, post-election 10, 41 n.3, 61, 109, 129–36, 141
  causes 136, 140, 142
  constitutional reform 134, 151, 152
  feminisation of trauma 137–38

humanitarian crisis   134, 136, 138, 142, 144
police corruption   108
statistics   145
violence, sexual   108, 116 n.26, 117 n.30, 131, 132 n.64, 145–47
   increase   125, 130
   rape   23, 56, 147, 168
   reporting incidents   114
   statistics   2, 145
violence, state   xii, 9, 111, 185
voters, women:
   barriers   154, 160, 162, 163–64, 165, 166
   perception   158, 177
   population   127–28

Waki Report (2008)   138–39
Wanjiku   5–7, 9, 152, 180, 184–85
Western feminisms:
   and African women's rights   13, 14, 42, 43, 81
   critiques   14, 74, 186
   developments   44
Wipper, Audrey   56 n.72, 59, 60, 61, 85, 92 n.83
   see also Maendeleo ya Wanawake Organisation (MYWO)
Women Paid the Price!   138, 145

Young Gĩkũyũ Association   23, 27, 35

Eastern Africa Series

Women's Land Rights & Privatization in Eastern Africa
BIRGIT ENGLERT
& ELIZABETH DALEY (EDS)

War & the Politics of Identity in Ethiopia
KJETIL TRONVOLL

Moving People in Ethiopia
ALULA PANKHURST
& FRANÇOIS PIGUET (EDS)

Living Terraces in Ethiopia
ELIZABETH E. WATSON

Eritrea
GAIM KIBREAB

Borders & Borderlands as Resources in the Horn of Africa
DEREJE FEYISSA
& MARKUS VIRGIL HOEHNE (EDS)

After the Comprehensive Peace Agreement in Sudan
ELKE GRAWERT (ED.)

Land, Governance, Conflict & the Nuba of Sudan
GUMA KUNDA KOMEY

Ethiopia
JOHN MARKAKIS

Resurrecting Cannibals
HEIKE BEHREND

Pastoralism & Politics in Northern Kenya & Southern Ethiopia
GÜNTHER SCHLEE
& ABDULLAHI A. SHONGOLO

Islam & Ethnicity in Northern Kenya & Southern Ethiopia
GÜNTHER SCHLEE
with ABDULLAHI A. SHONGOLO

Foundations of an African Civilisation
DAVID W. PHILLIPSON

Regional Integration, Identity & Citizenship in the Greater Horn of Africa
KIDANE MENGISTEAB
& REDIE BEREKETEAB (EDS)

Dealing with Government in South Sudan
CHERRY LEONARDI

The Quest for Socialist Utopia
BAHRU ZEWDE

Disrupting Territories
JÖRG GERTEL, RICHARD ROTTENBURG
& SANDRA CALKINS (EDS)

The African Garrison State
KJETIL TRONVOLL
& DANIEL R. MEKONNEN

The State of Post-conflict Reconstruction
NASEEM BADIEY

Gender, Home & Identity
KATARZYNA GRABSKA

Women, Land & Justice in Tanzania
HELEN DANCER

Remaking Mutirikwi
JOOST FONTEIN

The Oromo & the Christian Kingdom of Ethiopia
MOHAMMED HASSEN

Lost Nationalism
ELENA VEZZADINI

Darfur
CHRIS VAUGHAN

The Eritrean National Service
GAIM KIBREAB

Ploughing New Ground
GETNET BEKELE

Hawks & Doves in Sudan's Armed Conflict
SUAD M. E. MUSA

Ethiopian Warriorhood
TSEHAI BERHANE-SELASSIE

Land, Migration & Belonging
JOSEPH MUJERE

Land Tenure Security
SVEIN EGE (ED.)

Tanzanian Development
DAVID POTTS (ED.)

Nairobi in the Making
CONSTANCE SMITH

The Mission of Apolo Kivebulaya
EMMA WILD-WOOD

The Crisis of Democratization in the Greater Horn of Africa
KIDANE MENGISTEAB (ED.)

The Struggle for Land & Justice in Kenya
AMBREENA MANJI

Imperialism & Development
NICHOLAS WESTCOTT

Kamba Proverbs from Eastern Kenya
JEREMIAH M. KITUNDA

Sports & Modernity in Late Imperial Ethiopia
KATRIN BROMBER

Contested Sustainability
STEFANO PONTE, CHRISTINE NOE & DAN BROCKINGTON (EDS)

*Decolonising State & Society in Uganda**
KATHERINE BRUCE-LOCKHART, JONATHAN L. EARLE, NAKANYIKE B. MUSISI & EDGAR CHRIS TAYLOR (EDS)

*Kenya and Zambia's Relations with China 1949–2019**
JODIE YUZHOU SUN

* forthcoming

EASTERN AFRICAN STUDIES

These titles published in the United States and Canada by Ohio University Press

Revealing Prophets
Edited by DAVID M. ANDERSON
& DOUGLAS H. JOHNSON

East African Expressions of Christianity
Edited by THOMAS SPEAR &
ISARIA N. KIMAMBO

The Poor Are Not Us
Edited by DAVID M. ANDERSON
& VIGDIS BROCH-DUE

Potent Brews
JUSTIN WILLIS

Swahili Origins
JAMES DE VERE ALLEN

Being Maasai
Edited by THOMAS SPEAR &
RICHARD WALLER

Jua Kali Kenya
KENNETH KING

Control & Crisis in Colonial Kenya
BRUCE BERMAN

*Unhappy Valley
Book One: State & Class
Book Two: Violence & Ethnicity*
BRUCE BERMAN & JOHN
LONSDALE

Mau Mau from Below
GREET KERSHAW

The Mau Mau War in Perspective
FRANK FUREDI

Squatters & the Roots of Mau Mau 1905-63
TABITHA KANOGO

Economic & Social Origins of Mau Mau 1945-53
DAVID W. THROUP

Multi-Party Politics in Kenya
DAVID W. THROUP & CHARLES HORNSBY

Empire State-Building
JOANNA LEWIS

Decolonization & Independence in Kenya 1940-93
Edited by B.A. OGOT &
WILLIAM R. OCHIENG'

Eroding the Commons
DAVID ANDERSON

Penetration & Protest in Tanzania
ISARIA N. KIMAMBO

Custodians of the Land
Edited by GREGORY MADDOX,
JAMES L. GIBLIN & ISARIA N.
KIMAMBO

Education in the Development of Tanzania 1919-1990
LENE BUCHERT

The Second Economy in Tanzania
T.L. MALIYAMKONO
& M.S.D. BAGACHWA

Ecology Control & Economic Development in East African History
HELGE KJEKSHUS

Siaya
DAVID WILLIAM COHEN
& E.S. ATIENO ODHIAMBO

*Uganda Now • Changing Uganda
Developing Uganda • From Chaos to Order • Religion & Politics in East Africa*
Edited by HOLGER BERNT
HANSEN & MICHAEL TWADDLE

Kakungulu & the Creation of Uganda 1868-1928
MICHAEL TWADDLE

Controlling Anger
SUZETTE HEALD

Kampala Women Getting By
SANDRA WALLMAN

Political Power in Pre-Colonial Buganda
RICHARD J. REID

Alice Lakwena & the Holy Spirits
HEIKE BEHREND

Slaves, Spices & Ivory in Zanzibar
ABDUL SHERIFF

Zanzibar Under Colonial Rule
Edited by ABDUL SHERIFF
& ED FERGUSON

The History & Conservation of Zanzibar Stone Town
Edited by ABDUL SHERIFF

Pastimes & Politics
LAURA FAIR

Ethnicity & Conflict in the Horn of Africa
Edited by KATSUYOSHI FUKUI
& JOHN MARKAKIS

Conflict, Age & Power in North East Africa
Edited by EISEI KURIMOTO
& SIMON SIMONSE

Property Rights & Political Development in Ethiopia & Eritrea
SANDRA FULLERTON
JOIREMAN

Revolution & Religion in Ethiopia
ØYVIND M. EIDE

Brothers at War
TEKESTE NEGASH
& KJETIL TRONVOLL

From Guerrillas to Government
DAVID POOL

Mau Mau & Nationhood
Edited by E.S. ATIENO
ODHIAMBO & JOHN LONSDALE

A History of Modern Ethiopia, 1855-1991(2nd edn)
BAHRU ZEWDE

Pioneers of Change in Ethiopia
BAHRU ZEWDE

Remapping Ethiopia
Edited by W. JAMES, D.
DONHAM, E. KURIMOTO
& A. TRIULZI

Southern Marches of Imperial Ethiopia
Edited by DONALD L. DONHAM
& WENDY JAMES

A Modern History of the Somali (4th edn)
I.M. LEWIS

Islands of Intensive Agriculture in East Africa
Edited by MATS WIDGREN
& JOHN E.G. SUTTON

Leaf of Allah
EZEKIEL GEBISSA

Dhows & the Colonial Economy of Zanzibar 1860-1970
ERIK GILBERT

African Womanhood in Colonial Kenya
TABITHA KANOGO

African Underclass
ANDREW BURTON

In Search of a Nation
Edited by GREGORY H.
MADDOX & JAMES L. GIBLIN

A History of the Excluded
JAMES L. GIBLIN

Black Poachers, White Hunters
EDWARD I. STEINHART

Ethnic Federalism
DAVID TURTON

Crisis & Decline in Bunyoro
SHANE DOYLE

Emancipation without Abolition in German East Africa
JAN-GEORG DEUTSCH

Women, Work & Domestic Virtue in Uganda 1900-2003
GRACE BANTEBYA
KYOMUHENDO & MARJORIE
KENISTON McINTOSH

Cultivating Success in Uganda
GRACE CARSWELL

War in Pre-Colonial Eastern Africa
RICHARD REID

Slavery in the Great Lakes Region of East Africa
Edited by HENRI MÉDARD &
SHANE DOYLE

The Benefits of Famine
DAVID KEEN

Lightning Source UK Ltd.
Milton Keynes UK
UKHW020716011022
409725UK00002B/6